Praise for *What You Need to Know about Healing*

I have treated tens of thousands of patients. When seriously ill, almost all of them want to reach out to God and pray for healing, yet many don't know how and even question, "Does God still heal?" With great wisdom, real-life illustrations, and the firm foundation of God's Word, this book answers all the questions the sick and those that love them ask. Everyone should own it. You need to read this book for your sake and for the sake of those you love. When the valleys of serious illness come, you will be prepared with God's perspective on illness and healing. That has more value than any health insurance policy.

David Stevens, MD, MA, Chief Executive Officer,
Christian Medical & Dental Associations

Harold Sala's book *What You Need to Know about Healing* is a reminder of what many have forgotten—that *Jehovah Rapha*, the God who heals, is still healing today. Sala's book provides a strong Scriptural foundation for healing which gives hope and comfort in the time of need. I recommend it.

Dr. George Wood, General Superintendent of the
Assemblies of God

This book is greatly needed in the body of Christ, and Harold Sala is the one who needed to write it for us! Combining the compassionate heart of one who has personally and individually prayed for the healing of thousands around the world with his strengths as a teacher of the Bible, Harold gives us a book that will strengthen all who work and pray for the healing of those we love.

Tom Holladay, Purpose Driven Connection, P.E.A.C.E.
Plan, Saddleback Church, Lake Forest, California

In this book Harold Sala has combined faith and reason in an understandable, believable manner. Addressing both suffering and healing, this book, like the Bible, gives a clear view of reality! I know that one's faith will be increased in the great Physician after reading *What You Need to Know about Healing.*

Dennis W. Cope, MD, FACP, Professor and Chair of
Internal Medicine, Olive View / UCLA Medical Center

Compelling, convincing, and at times convicting, *What You Need to Know about Healing* is a comprehensive compilation and application of biblical truth by one of America's outstanding Christian communicators. Writing in his easy-to-read, inimitable, irenic style with perfect balance, Harold Sala has produced a reference work unparalleled in contemporary Christian literature. Drawing from a lifetime of cross-cultural ministry around the world, scholarly research, careful documentation and sound doctrine, Sala does not shrink from addressing and answering the difficult questions that frequently arise on the subject of healing. This book is destined to become a classic work on the subject and essential reading for every Christian and a vital resource for every pastor and Christian ministry leader.

Dr. John Redman, Past President,
Conservative Baptists of California

Harold Sala's book *What You Need to Know about Healing* is balanced, biblical, and very helpful. As a physician with experience in overseas medical missions as well as academic medicine in the USA, I have not read another book on healing that is as insightful and reasonable. The perspective on healing portrayed in this book would benefit both physician and patients as they wrestle with deeply felt and personal issues surrounding illness.

David E. Van Reken, MD, Professor of Clinical Pediatrics
Indiana School of Medicine and formerly Attending
Pediatrician at ELWA and JFK Hospitals, Monrovia, Liberia

What You Need to Know about Healing affirms that God ultimately does the healing. The reader is the recipient of ever-increasing faith as he/she reads these miraculous Bible stories and the well-researched contemporary testimonies that Dr. Sala gives. By whatever means God chooses to heal, whether by prayer with the anointing oil, the laying on of hands by believers, with the use of medical science and surgery by doctors, with Christian counseling, etc. Dr. Sala clearly, accurately, and scripturally gives God all the glory!

H. Jack Morris, DMin., LCPC, LCMFT, Pastor, Largo
Community Church, Mitchellville, Maryland

What You Need to Know about Healing, written with heart, depth, and spirituality, explains the three major ways Jesus heals. It is both inspirational and educational. I have read profusely on this subject, but none has explained it in such a succinct way as has Harold Sala. This book will be an asset, encouragement, and a learning tool for health-care workers and laypeople alike who are searching for the truth of Jesus' miracles and His healing touch.

Eithne Keegan, RN, Nursing Administrator,
Mission Hospital Mission Viejo, California, International
HIV/AIDS Educator and Dean of The Nzoia College of
Nursing, Kitale Kenya

In *What You Need to Know about Healing*, Dr. Sala provides a thorough and biblical view of divine healing that will challenge your faith and stimulate your appreciation of our Great Physician. Grounded in Scripture and amply illustrated from church history and contemporary life, Sala's approach answers questions and objections in a practical, easy-to-understand manner. This book, with its step-by-step approach and careful documentation, will find a place in the pastor's library and is a must read for anyone wrestling with physical infirmity and in need of healing."

Dr. Gary Benedict, President, The Christian and
Missionary Alliance U.S.

If you have enjoyed the ministry of Dr. Harold Sala, his new book, *What You Need to Know about Healing*, will truly be a blessing to you. As I traveled through this careful examination of biblical healing, I felt like I was sitting down with Dr. Sala himself. His words are both personal and powerful. One of my favorite aspects of this book is that at the end of each chapter Dr. Sala outlines exactly "what you need to know" in a way that every reader can understand. I can truly say that it ministered to me personally. I highly recommend *What You Need to Know about Healing*, and I am sure every reader will walk away with fresh insights regarding the biblical view of healing.

Jeff Johnson, Pastor, Calvary Chapel, Downey, California

Dr. Harold Sala's *What You Need to Know about Healing* is a brilliantly organized presentation of scriptural accounts and inspiriting testimonies. This is a must read.

Tim James, DPM, Foot and Ankle Surgeon

This book is the most comprehensive study on healing I have ever read. Dr. Sala provides a thoroughly biblical, theological, historical, and practical guide to understanding the complexity of supernatural healing; and it's all deeply rooted in the character of God as our heavenly Father and Great Physician. If you have ever wondered how and why God heals today or been confused because of the variety of opinions in regards to the role of healing, then this book is for you. May God awaken us to His miraculous activity today, and may this awareness contribute to a deeper understanding and experience of the grace, mercy, and abiding love of God.

Ken Baugh, Senior Pastor, Coast Hills Community Church,
Aliso Viejo, California

From the opening chapter to the concluding one, Dr. Harold J. Sala completely engages the reader in thinking seriously about *Jehovah Rapha*, the God who heals. This book on integrative healing stands out among all the other books of healing I have read not only because it rigorously examines and comprehensively synthesizes insights from Scripture, Christian tradition, and contemporary human experience; but it creatively puts together all these insights into a balanced theological framework of holistic healing. I was deeply blessed by reading this book. I highly recommend it to pastors, counselors, and practitioners engaged in healing ministries, and all members of the body of Christ.

Adonis Abelard O. Gorospe, PhD, Associate Professor
on Church History, Systematic Theology and Spirituality
Academic Dean, Asian Theological Seminary

This is one of the best books ever written on healing—sound in its biblical exposition, historical context, and examples. I'm blessed especially with the reality that God is sovereign. I highly recommend this book not just to pastors but to all sincere followers of Jesus that we may all become more acquainted with our amazing God—our *Jehovah Rapha*, our God the Healer and Savior Jesus Christ!

Peter Tan-Chi, PhD, Founder and Senior Pastor,
Christ's Commission Fellowship

This wonderful book places things in perspective with regards to the sometimes extreme approaches to healing. This book serves as a guide and really opens our eyes to strike the perfect balance between extremes. Even with modern science and advancements in health care, this book still keeps us grounded on the fact that it is still the Almighty's ultimate will and power that heals.

Lester Mike Chua, MD, General Practitioner

Well-researched, thoroughly thought through, and excellently written, Harold Sala's book *What You Need to Know about Healing* brings to light the reality that God still heals. It will go down in history as the book that not only builds one's faith to believe for one's healing but also the one that clarifies the issues and questions that pertain to it.

Joey Bonifacio, Senior Pastor, Victory Fort Bonifacio

What You Need to Know about Healing points people to knowing who God is. Understanding God as *Jehovah Rapha* gives us the confidence to minister to and pray for the sick and even face illness ourselves. Combining biblical stories on healing with the documented testimonies of the church fathers and inspiring biographies of men and women who experienced God's miracles, Dr. Harold J. Sala was able to present empirical evidence that the God who heals in the past is the same God we have now. Dr. Sala then explained what that means in relation to us and provided us a specific guide on how to respond to this truth. Unless you will never get sick in this life or know anyone who is sick, then this book is for you.

Christopher M. Uy, National Team Leader, Philippine Campus Crusade for Christ

Practical, sane, and engagingly written, Harold Sala's *What You Need to Know about Healing* teaches positive faith in the sovereign and powerful healer. It is a relief to be reminded that God can perform what is best through our sufferings, or heal us, or both, and that we can exercise full confidence in Him in every case. The book was a blessing and an encouragement to my own faith.

Craig Keener, Professor, Asbury Theological Seminary, and author of *Miracles: The Credibility of the New Testament Accounts*

What You Need to Know about Healing

Harold J. Sala

What You Need to Know about Healing

A Physical and Spiritual Guide

Foreword by Joni Eareckson Tada

PUBLISHING GROUP

Nashville, Tennessee

To Darlene
my beloved wife, companion, and partner in ministry

To Sister Freda
whose compassionate and humanitarian ministry in
Kitale, Kenya, first inspired me to write something
for the Nzoia School of Nursing which she founded

and

To the memory of Guy P. Duffield
my late father-in-law,
one of the most godly men I have ever known

Contents

Acknowledgments

With few exceptions every author stands on the shoulders of his teachers, professors, mentors, and encouragers. I am no exception, and I would like to thank my wife, Darlene, for her patience and for the many hours she has devoted to reading and making suggestions on this book. I also wish to thank Drs. Dennis Cope, Timothy James, and Diane Komp for their input from a medical perspective—each of whom is worthy of honor not only for many years of excellence as caring and compassionate physicians but also as fellow sojourners on the pilgrim pathway. I also want to thank the many who, upon hearing that I was writing this book, shared their stories of the remarkable way God brought healing to their lives—far more fascinating stories than I could ever include in this book.

My thanks also goes to Beng Alba for her editorial advice and counsel, as well as Karen Huang who coedited the manuscript. I also want to thank Luisa Ampil, Loana Bergthold, Linda Elam, and Dee Green for their suggestions and help in proofing of the manuscript.

I am also indebted to Dawn Woods, Matt West, and their colleagues at B&H Publishing Group for their assistance and cooperation in making this book a reality.

Now there are also many other things that Jesus did. Were every one of them to be written, I suppose that the world itself could not contain the books that would be written. (John 21:25)

—JOHN, ONE OF THE TWELVE WHO WALKED WITH JESUS

Foreword

When most people learn that I've lived in a wheelchair for more than forty years, deal daily with chronic pain, and have recently battled breast cancer, they ask, "Surely, you've approached God for healing, right?"

I'll smile and reply, "You've got it!"

Through the years I've wrestled with Scripture in a no-holds-barred inspection of a biblical view on miraculous healing. Why does God heal some people and not others? Does God still perform larger-than-life miracles like Jesus did when He walked on earth? What must one *do* in order to be healed?

Back in 1967, when I first became paralyzed, I begged God to heal me. I followed every scriptural injunction, yet my useless hands and feet never seemed to get the message. And so I remain a quadriplegic.

Why didn't the Lord heal me? I soon discovered an insight into Jesus' priorities on healing in Matthew 18:9, "If your eye causes you to sin, gouge it out and throw it away. It is better for you to enter life with one eye than to have two eyes and be thrown into the fire of hell" (NIV). It's a strong metaphor Jesus uses, but it shows where His main concern lies. The most important Prophet to come along in centuries and the One who healed thousands was willing to sacrifice a person's physical well-being any day for his spiritual healing.

It made me think; *What good is physical healing if you still lack peace and contentment? If you have no joy or hope of heaven? What does it profit a person to experience miraculous healing if his soul ultimately ends up in hell?* I decided I want Jesus' priorities to be mine! Peace that's profound . . . a settled soul . . . contentment, full and rich . . . and joy sent straight from heaven. Jesus Christ is ecstasy beyond compare, and it's worth anything to be His friend. And if it takes a wheelchair or cancer to push me further into His arms, then I'll take it.

That's my story, but your story may be very different. You might think, *God worked in Joni's life one way; what about me? Does her example mean that God never heals miraculously today?* Healing is a perplexing and troublesome topic, and Harold Sala in this new book handles the complexities with skill and ease. If you are searching for healing, you will find much to consider in this special book you hold in your hands. I pray you'll read it with an open heart and mind because I want you to know that God says in Exodus 15:26, "I am the Lord, who heals you" (NIV). How He heals, well . . . that's for you to discover in the following pages.

Yours in His care,
Joni Eareckson Tada
Joni and Friends International

Preface

This book deals with the unexpected challenge of sickness and suffering, helping you understand that what you are experiencing is not a matter of indifference to our heavenly Father. What I have written will also bring encouragement to you who are family and friends of the one who suffers, as well as those of you who are professionals—doctors, nurses, and technicians involved in health care.

When pain wracks your body, it is almost inevitable that your heart cries out: "God, are You there? Do You really care about what is happening to me, or are You so busy running the universe that You haven't noticed me?" And, yes, you also want to know if God can heal you. Having spoken in a church on one occasion, I was greeted at the door by a woman who asked, "Do you believe God heals *anymore?*" Surprised, I paused for a moment and replied, "No," watching the expression on the face of the person but quickly adding, "But I believe He heals *just as much!*"

While God wills healing for your life, the manner in which God brings healing is part of His sovereign dealing with you as an individual. On occasion God touches some individuals in a supernatural manner and brings immediate healing. This, of course, is what everyone would like—no hospital stays, no visits to physicians, no hypodermics, no prescriptions, and best of all, no pain or suffering. Rise up and walk, perfectly whole!

There are times, however, when God works through the hands of skilled physicians, and you benefit from medical science. Healing comes through a combination of His grace and skills given by God to doctors and health-care specialists to alleviate suffering. This I call _integrative healing_. Then there are those times when, for reasons we may never understand, God blesses some with suffering, allowing them to taste His presence and goodness, transforming pain into purpose, sometimes through them blessing the lives of thousands. This I call _redemptive healing_. Of course, ultimate healing for all of God's children is death followed by resurrection in a completely whole body with no pain or suffering.

Ruth Graham was once entertained by an official of the Bank of Scotland. Her host was in charge of the counterfeit division, and Ruth remarked that he must spend a great deal of time training his staff to spot counterfeits. "No," he replied. "On the contrary, we teach them how the real article looks. Then they can quickly spot the counterfeit." Today there are some whom I consider to be counterfeits, those who capitalize on the suffering of humanity; however, rather than fill the pages of this book denouncing them, I have chosen to focus on the positive, on _What You Need to Know about Healing_.

Allow me to provide an overview of how God is bringing healing to broken, hurting lives, healing which started almost four millennia ago. I will take you through the Old Testament, the New Testament, the centuries following the end of the apostles' time, and what has happened in the past 150 years.

Before we dig deeper into this subject, please understand that as a person, you are a combination of the emotional, the physical, and the spiritual, and when you take a hit in any of these areas, all three are affected. Your life cannot be divided into three separate entities because you are an indivisible whole. This explains why, when you are hurting physically, you may also start feeling discouraged, dejected, or depressed. God, to you, may seem distant and detached from your need.

God has a will for your life that includes everything that happens—what you consider to be good and what you consider to be bad—when your life becomes broken, challenged by sickness and pain, and you face the risk of losing your health and, perhaps, even your life.

The manner in which God's will is played out in our lives is not a science—something that can be analyzed statistically, easily understood, and uniformly applied to everyone. It is the work of God's Holy Spirit individually and uniquely applied to you as well as all of God's children.

Challenges to your health will never leave you where they find you. One of two things will happen: They will drive you closer to God, into the loving arms of His Son; or they will embitter you, as you blame God for your difficulty. No wonder C. S. Lewis, the Cambridge professor of medieval literature, once described pain as "God's megaphone."

While almost everyone who hurts would like immediate deliverance from sickness and pain, often what we learn in the process of healing is something akin to the language of heaven—often misunderstood by the critics but affirmed with unspeakable words in the hearts of those who find divine comfort as the Shepherd of our souls walks with us through the dark hours.

Researching the subject before us and bringing together the experiences of many with the clear teaching of God's Word has allowed me to see God in a new and beautiful dimension. I have written this book while constantly praying that what I have experienced will also be your portion—a new vision of a compassionate, caring God who wills His highest good for your life—and that a new and clearer image of Him will emerge, indelibly and eternally touching your life.

Two stanzas from an old English hymn written by Ian MacPherson sum it up,

> With faith's warm finger, through the veil,
> I seek to touch Thy hand;
> I feel the imprint of the nail
> And partly understand.

> But, ah, my lonely spirit tires
> Of knowing Thee in part.
> O Jesus, how my soul desires
> To see Thee as Thou art.[1]

Harold J. Sala

CHAPTER 1

Is the Great Physician Still Practicing?

When Larry and Alice Parker visit a nondescript cemetery in Barstow, California, and stand beside the grave of their son, their eyes mist with tears. They undoubtedly think, *If only we had known*. You see, their eleven-year-old son, Wesley, tragically died in their home on the warm morning of August 22, 1973, three days after a traveling evangelist, at a Sunday service, had pronounced him healed. In my file is a yellowing article from *The Los Angeles Times* telling about the family's ordeal.

Having struggled with diabetes for five years, Wesley and his parents had believed that God could heal him. When the evangelist prayed for the boy and asked, "Wes, do you believe you are healed?" he replied, "Yes." "I believe that you are, too," said the evangelist. Then the parents decided to fast and pray for their son and do what proved to be a tragic mistake—no longer give him insulin. They reasoned that if God had indeed healed him, there was no longer any need to continue with the medication.

When Wes died, the world of his parents collapsed. Not only did Larry and Alice deeply grieve the loss of their son, but they were

also deeply confused and heartbroken. Their friends severely criticized and abandoned them. Then the district attorney filed charges
of involuntary manslaughter against them. The police came and took
them to jail. Anticipating this turn of events, the Parkers had arranged
for friends to care for their remaining children. The child protection
authorities, however, came to their home, took the children, and sent
them to juvenile hall with hardened delinquents.

Imprisoned separately in the San Bernardino jail, Larry and Alice
wondered if they would ever see each other again. The guards taunted
them, saying, "There's no way they're going to let you guys out." The
court found them guilty as charged, and they were placed on probation
for five years.

Before you get overly critical, realize that at the time of Wesley's
death, Larry, then age thirty-nine, had already served three years in the
armed forces as an electronics technician. Larry was an electronics engineer with Bendix Field Engineering and was praised by his superiors as
"an excellent employee." The Parkers were a typical middle-class family,
taking their children to church and living the California dream.

Did Larry and Alice realize at that time that Wesley's dependence
on insulin was so severe? No! Would they have withheld insulin had
they known of the consequences? Absolutely not! So what, then, had
truly caused Wesley's death? Unsound theological teaching and misconceptions about God and healing—convictions about biblical teaching that were sincere but misaligned, convictions held and sincerely
believed by many, even today, who teach that because God wants you
healed, you should trust Him exclusively and avoid medicine because
it is of the devil.

The Parkers eventually authored a book entitled *We Let Our Son
Die*, where they admitted that they had made a "tragic error" in with-
holding insulin from their son.

The Parkers are not alone in wreaking unintentional suffering and
even death on minors. John O'Connor, writing for *The New York Times*,
says, "Over the last 15 years, at least 125 children in the United States
have died because their parents belong to Christian Science churches
or fundamentalist sects that believed prayer alone could cure illness."[1]
What Jesus told the religious leaders of His day aptly applies to these

groups: "You are in error because you do not know the Scriptures or the power of God" (Matt. 22:29 NIV).

Where Is the Truth of Scripture?

C. S. Lewis said that when Satan sends errors into the world, he sends them in pairs—extremes. Christians today are confronted with two positions regarding healing that stand in juxtaposition to each other. On the one hand, dispensationalists teach that the miracles of healing wrought by Christ, those we read about in the Gospels, were only temporal displays of His might and power, certifying His divinity, calling attention to His message, but they gradually lessened during the era of the early church. Dispensationalism teaches that after the work of redemption had been completed, after Jesus ascended to heaven and God's Word was recorded in the Bible, to give us a full understanding of His purpose and plan, miracles gradually ceased.

On the other hand, there are segments of Christendom—extreme charismatics and Pentecostals (such as the evangelist who insisted that Wesley Parker had been healed)—who believe that it is God's will that every Christian be healed because healing is part of the atonement. To validate their belief, they point to Isaiah 53:5 that states, "But he was pierced for our transgressions, he was crushed for our iniquities; the punishment that brought us peace was upon him, and by his wounds we are healed" (NIV). These words were affirmed by Peter in 1 Peter 2:24: "He himself bore our sins in his body on the tree, that we might die to sin and live to righteousness. By his wounds you have been healed." Those who hold to this belief assert that, if you as a Christian are not healed, it is because you have unconfessed sin in your life or you simply do not have enough faith.

In her book *A Place of Healing*, Joni Eareckson Tada, a quadriplegic as the result of a diving accident, tells of one incident after a church service when she was wheeling herself across the parking lot toward her van. A young man stopped her and asked, "Are you Joni?" He explained that he was visiting her church and was hoping that he could personally pray for her healing. "I can't tell you how many people I've met over the years who've done the same thing," she told him. Assuring him that she never refused a prayer for healing, she listened as the young man brought up an obviously scripted statement:

> Have you ever considered that it might be sin standing in the way of your healing," he began, quickly adding, "or that you've disobeyed in some way?" Before Joni could answer, he opened his Bible to Mark 2, to the story of the paralytic brought to Jesus by four men. The four companions had broken through the roof and lowered the paralyzed man into the room where Jesus was.
>
> After reading the brief passage, the stranger pointed out that if Joni would only confess her sin and have faith, then she, too, like the paralytic, would be healed. Clearly he was putting the blame on the one who was in need of healing. He said, "Joni, you must have a lack of faith. I mean, look at you. You're still in your wheelchair." Explaining that it was not the faith of the paralyzed man but the faith of the four companions that Jesus honored, Joni bounced the ball back in his court, suggesting that if he had the faith he thought she should have, then God would heal her.
>
> Then Joni writes, "Does He always heal? Does He heal everyone who comes to Him in faith? Does He miraculously intervene in the lives of all who pray for release from migraine headaches . . . multiple sclerosis . . . prostate cancer . . . a bad case of the flu . . . or in my case, chronic pain? And if not, then why not? And why does He heal some and not others?"[2]

These questions echo the heart cries of many people who also ask: "Is the Great Physician still in business? Does He keep office hours? Is Jesus Christ really the same yesterday, today, and tomorrow? If Jesus healed when He walked the earth two thousand years ago, can He not do the same thing today?"

We are confronted with an issue: If the dispensationalists expect too little of God and the charismatics expect too much, where is God in relation to my need, my pain, and my need for healing in my broken life?

Let God Be God

What you believe about God profoundly affects your life, your marriage, your morality, your purpose in life, your worldview, and certainly your view as to whether or not you can count on God to walk with you through the dark valleys of life, take you out of the pit when you fall, and be your Healer in the time of need.

While nature, history, science, or philosophy tell us little about God—who He is, what He does, how much He cares about us—there is a trustworthy source of knowledge about Him: the Bible. In my book *Why You Can Have Confidence in the Bible*,[3] I make the case for its authenticity, credibility, and trustworthiness. I cited the abundance of manuscript evidence, the fulfilled prophecies that defy human explanation, the compelling testimony of archeology, the collation of what the Bible says with the facts of science, and the remarkable manner in which this book changes the lives of people.

I, therefore, accept at face value what the Bible tells us about God, about ourselves, and about Jesus. He walked the shores of Galilee, teaching as no other person has ever done, healing the sick, the lame, the suffering, even raising the dead on three occasions, among many other acts of love and power. I believe the four biographers—Matthew, Mark, Luke, and John—who wrote about how Jesus Christ was crucified at the hands of Roman soldiers, placed in a tomb for three days, but rose again and showed Himself alive beyond reasonable doubt.

Accepting the fact that *God is God* puts Him in a category above humankind, above time and space, and certainly above all the human logic that defines what He can do and what He cannot do. If God is God, then you and I can accept the fact that He is supernatural—period!

I also acknowledge that this book, the Bible, which countless numbers of individuals have died for rather than repudiate, tells us much about God that has been borne out by human experience down through the centuries. If God is God, then you can accept the fact that He is supernatural—period! What He does cannot always be defined in terms that I can either understand or explain; otherwise, God would simply be a reflection of ourselves—not the divine Creator who placed the stars in the firmament, the planets in orbit, and created Earth and those who live on it.

The supernatural, of course, embraces miracles, something many scientists and even a few theologians deny. What is a miracle? If you need a definition, you haven't seen one; if you have seen one, you don't need a definition.

Nonetheless, I like Lewis Smedes's definition. He wrote:

> In the biblical view a miracle is a signal that God is, for a moment and for a special purpose, walking down paths he does not usually walk. A miracle is not a sign that a God who is usually absent is, for the moment, present. It is only a sign that God who is always present in creative power is working here and now in an unfamiliar style.[4]

A miracle is the suspension of the laws of cause and effect—not a denial of them. And, yes, miracles defy human explanation. If, however, God is supernatural, on occasion He may choose to do that which is entirely outside your experience and even history itself. Never forget that the greatest miracle is that God—He who is from everlasting to everlasting—should become human flesh, born of the virgin Mary, should live a sinless life, be crucified and rise from the dead the third day. From the act of creation to the closing chapters of the book of Revelation, the Bible asserts the miraculous simply because God is God, and, furthermore, the writers of Scripture assert that God is sovereign in what He does and chooses not to do.[5]

What Does the Sovereignty of God Mean in the Context of Life in the Twenty-first Century?

Over the centuries theologians have attempted to explain what God is like, defining the attributes of God. Thus we say God is eternal, unchangeable, all-knowing, wholly good, completely and absolutely just, all-powerful, faithful, compassionate, holy, among many. Yet if there is one attribute or observation about God that you need to remember especially when your body needs physical healing, it is that God is sovereign!

The first known use of the English adjective *sovereign* was in the fourteenth century. This Anglo-French word was used in the Vulgate and means "over," "above," or "supreme." The Greek word usually translated as sovereign is *despota*, which gave us the English word *despot*. It was used in the first century to refer to a slave owner or the master of a household. It was found in ancient manuscripts known as *papyri*, referring to someone who owned a ship.

Today some forty-four countries in the world are ruled by monarchs, and in these countries royalty, in various and different capacities, are considered sovereigns. Kings and queens are esteemed and enjoy rights of succession usually based on descendancy. Countries where royalty is acknowledged are considered to be kingdoms as opposed to republics, which are governed by democracy and the votes of citizens.

In order to marry the love of his life, King Edward VII of Britain abdicated the throne to marry a divorced woman, Mrs. Wallis Simpson; but normally kings and queens are there for life, unlike politicians who sometimes think the same but in reality are elected officials who can be voted out of office in the same manner they were initially elected. It is generally understood that while royalty are keenly aware of the political ramifications of what they do, they are not accountable to any save the Almighty in the same way that other government officials are.

But what of God, who has neither beginning nor end, who is the uncreated Creator, the one described as eternal God? To whom is He accountable? Have we any right to blame Him or make any demands when we don't like what He does?

Should you have the privilege of ever being invited to have an audience with Queen Elizabeth of Britain, you would be advised of protocol—how you should approach her majesty, the proper manner in which you should bow or curtsy, the fact that you should not touch even her hand unless she first offers it to you, and how you should make your exit. You wouldn't expect to give her a bear hug like you would a friend or indulge in trivial nonsense as you might with an old classmate you had not seen for some time. You do not sit down and negotiate with someone who is a sovereign, suggesting, "Let's make a deal!" as many people do with God.

In the days of the patriarchs—Abraham, Isaac, and Jacob—there were two kinds of covenants, or legal contracts as we would think of them today. One kind reflected an agreement between two equals—say, neighbors resolving a dispute over property boundaries, or merchants agreeing on the terms of doing business together—stipulations and consequences of failure. The other kind of covenant was that of a sovereign who blesses his subjects, giving them what they neither deserve nor could purchase. This latter kind comprises the covenants God made with Israel.

There is, however, one significant difference between your relationship with the Triune God, who sent His Son to Earth, and how you would approach a king or queen who is sovereign of an earthly kingdom. If you have been adopted into the family of God, you are God's child. You are a new person. Your sins have been forgiven. Your past is covered with the blood of Christ; and, according to Hebrews 4, you can come boldly, unannounced, and enter into His presence anytime, anywhere. In his book *Miraculous Healings*, Henry Frost writes, "There are two words which would bring to me the assurance that God, from time to time, will give healing to His children, even if there was not another word in the Bible concerning the matter. I refer to the Lord's Prayer and the words, 'Our Father' (Matt. 6:9)."[6]

An incident I watched on TV in 1962 well illustrates the privilege of God's children in relation to our Father. The United States was then engrossed in a ferocious struggle with the USSR over the issue of Russian missiles being planted in Cuba, within easy reach of cities on the eastern seaboard. President John F. Kennedy was in the Oval Office meeting with key advisors when a side door opened and four-year-old John-John, the president's son, came in. The president, seeing the little boy, walked over and picked him up. He sat him on his knee for a few minutes, then put the lad down, who exited as he came in, and the discussion of the serious affairs of the state continued. So, too, can we who are His children have access at any time to our Father's presence.

But even going beyond the warmth of the term "father," the apostle Paul uses an expression for God as Father, the Aramaic word *Abba*. Aramaic was the Hebrew dialect spoken in Jesus' day. With no direct English equivalent of the word *Abba*, the closest term for *Abba* is what little children often use for their father—Daddy or Papa.

If God is your heavenly Father, then you can come into His presence as Jesus taught, praying, "Our Father in heaven." However, does this mean you can demand of the Sovereign God, ordering Him to do your will, holding Him accountable when you ask for something— perhaps healing—and you don't get what you want? Do you hold Him accountable for all sickness, suffering, and injustice in the world? Are you then entitled to think of Him as being indifferent, impotent, or far removed from your need?

Benefits of Acknowledging that God Is Sovereign

"Dear Teacher," read the message on a get-well-soon card a teacher received from her class. "We wish you a speedy recovery by a vote of 14 to 13." Yes, indeed. That's a democracy, where the majority decides what happens. But with God no votes are taken. Public opinion doesn't cause Him to change His mind or thinking. His kingdom has no elected officials. Because God is sovereign, what He wills is absolute.

Since God is sovereign and I am His child, what are the benefits of believing that He—not fate or chance—rules the day? Allow me to focus on several benefits for you:

Benefit 1: The burden of bearing the responsibility for running the world—even the circumstances of your own personal life—has been lifted from your shoulders. A pundit once said if you want to get along with the king, stay off his throne. The day you resign from being the CEO of the universe will be the best day of your life. That good news is exactly what Paul was driving at when he wrote, "And we know that in all things God works for the good of those who love him, who have been called according to his purpose" (Rom. 8:28 NIV). Underline the words "we know." Notice that the verse does not say "we hope," not "we think," or even "we believe." Also underline the phrase, "God works." The outcome isn't dependent on your clever manipulation of the circumstances. You are not the one who has to make it happen; God is! And you can trust the Father.

This also means that the circumstances that confront you are a matter of God's sovereign will—not His failure, weakness, or indifference—and they have been allowed in order to accomplish what may never be fully understood. The British-born evangelist and Bible teacher Allan Redpath knew both illness and deep depression. Understanding that nothing happens to us apart from the Father's hand, he wrote, "There is no circumstance, no trouble, no testing, that can ever touch me until, first of all, it has gone past God and past Christ, right through to me. If it has come that far, it has come with a great purpose."

Benefit 2: You will receive a sense of wholeness and peace as your inheritance. You may not understand everything God does. Whether or not you understand everything isn't important because God has not given you the burden of understanding but the yoke of simple obedience. When we think, as we sometimes do, that nothing is happening, something of which you may be totally unaware is happening as God is quietly working in ways you cannot see. Knowing that He's sovereign and in charge allows you to rest in the confidence that because He is in control, you can turn off the light at night and say, "God, You take over the night shift. I'm going to sleep." I take great heart in the phrase that God neither slumbers nor sleeps (see Ps. 121:4).

The daughter of an engineer, who works in a power plant in one of Norway's fjords, used to ride an open cable car up the steep incline of the face of the fjord to get to school. One day a visiting stranger, having been to the power plant on business, rode up with the little girl. He clutched his seat tightly. The little girl, on the other hand, appeared nonchalant. "Aren't you afraid?" he asked her. "Oh, not at all," she replied, adding, "Father is at the controls; and when he's in charge, I know that everything will be all right."

Accepting the truth that God is sovereign gives you confidence that our world is not under the control of mad men, no matter what the media tell us.

Benefit 3: A sense of security both spiritually and emotionally. Jesus told His disciples that they did not choose Him; rather, He chose them. How does that translate? If you are a believer, this means drawing from Ephesians 1—God chose you before the foundation of the world. You are no chance of fate, no accident of your parents. You are a unique person made in the image of God, and He chose you to be His son or daughter.

Benefit 4: You will have confidence that God listens to you when you pray. Because you are God's child, you can come boldly into the presence of the Father. He sorts out the foolish things you and I ask for and gives us what we really need. He does this because of His great love for us as His children. Take time to read Romans 8, especially the last portion where Paul so beautifully says that nothing can separate us from the love of this sovereign, caring God, neither now nor for all eternity.

Benefit 5: You will have the potential of becoming the person God intended you to be. As His child you are a unique individual who can discover that your weakness can become God's strength. Consider George Washington Carver (1864–1943), the son of slave parents, and an American botanist who became famous for discovering more than three hundred uses for the lowly peanut. The story goes that Carver once asked God, "Lord, what is the universe?" God said, "George, that's too big for your little head. Suppose you let Me take care of the universe." Greatly humbled, the scientist asked, "Then, Lord, if the universe is too big for me to understand, please tell me, what is a peanut?" And then the Lord answered, "Now George, you've got something your own size. A peanut can understand a peanut; go to work on the peanut while I run the universe."[7]

Carver was a gifted and unique individual who overcame tremendous obstacles—race, prejudice, and environmental and physical challenges. Like him each of us is confronted with different challenges, yet knowing that you are God's child and nothing is beyond His power—no person, no situation, no disease, no evil—allows you then to concentrate on fulfilling His purpose for your life.

Carver discovered that if farmers would grow peanuts on the soil that had been depleted of nutrients by years and years of growing cotton, indispensable nitrogen would be put back into the soil. Then he went to work finding uses for the crop in order to make the growing of peanuts financially rewarding. From peanuts Carver made cheese, milk, butter, flour, ink, dyes, soap, stains, and many other substances.

Ethel Waters was right when she said, "God don't make no junk!" As His child you are a unique individual who can discover that your weakness can become God's strength

Benefit 6: You will have increased faith that God will honor the promises of His Word and bring healing and wholeness to your brokenness. God wills healing and restoration for your broken life—emotionally, spiritually, and physically.

The will of the Father was lived out in the life of the Son of whom John wrote, "In him was life, and the life was the light of men. The light shines in the darkness, and the darkness has not overcome it" (John 1:4–5). Satan, God's archenemy, is described as a destroyer; but God is always associated with life and healing. In John 10:10, Jesus says, "I came that they may have life and have it abundantly." He also tells us, "I am the way, and the truth, and the life. No one comes to the Father except through me" (John 14:6).

It is God's nature to bring healing to our brokenness, whether it is emotional, spiritual, or physical. A crimson thread of healing is woven throughout Scripture, beginning with the skins of animals that were slain by God Himself in the garden to provide a covering for our first parents' nakedness, to the closing chapters of Revelation—all of which reveal that healing is reflective of God's nature and character. He stands in marked contrast to Satan, described throughout Scripture as *apollyon* or the destroyer.[8]

Jesus Christ—God in the Flesh—Is Also Sovereign

In his seminal book *Life in the Trinity*, Don Fairbairn, a Ph.D. from Cambridge, points out that what is true of the Father is true of the Son, and what is true of the Father and the Son is true of the Holy Spirit as the third person of the trinity. We do not worship three gods but one, and the life that was lived by Jesus for some thirty-three years on Earth was a reflection of the Father's heart and character. "Whoever has seen me," Jesus told Philip, "has seen the Father" (John 14:9).

Christ's sovereignty in healing was expressed in various ways, such as the following:

1. *He chose whom He healed.* No, Jesus did not heal everyone who was sick during His brief ministry of thirty-six to forty-two months, yet several times we are told that He healed everyone who came to Him. More about this in subsequent chapters.

2. *He chose the manner in which the healings took place and the conditions attached to them.* "Go, wash in the pool of Siloam," He told the blind man (John 9:7). He healed this man by applying mud on his eyes but healed another by spitting on his eyes and laying His hands on them. Why? Most responses to that question are simply conjectures. Because Jesus did nothing without reasons, what He did not reveal cannot always be explained.

3. *He healed sicknesses physicians of the first century could not cure.* (Yes, there were doctors in Jesus' day, including Luke the physician, the author of the Gospel that bears his name as well as the book of Acts.) There are no records of Jesus healing illnesses such as a cold or the flu, toothaches, bruises, or upset stomachs. It wasn't that He could not, but the writers of Scripture focused on His bringing healing to ailments for which there were no human cures, thus demonstrating that He cured what only God could cure.

4. *He chose a total of eighty-four individuals—twelve disciples and the seventy-two who were empowered to heal the sick and cast out demons.* Then in the book of Acts we find four more who were thus empowered—Stephen, Barnabas, Philip, and Paul.[9] Mark tells us that when Jesus began His ministry, He "called to him those whom he desired" (Mark 3:13). The Greek text is even more emphatic, stating that "he called unto himself those whom he himself wanted." Then again in the Upper Room, immediately before His crucifixion Jesus reiterated, "You did not choose me, but I chose you" (John 15:16).

So Who Is Really In Charge—You or God?

Ask yourself a question: "Which of us, Lord, shall really be sovereign—You or me?" I seriously doubt that you will ever hear someone voice that line in his prayers, yet this issue has confronted almost everyone at some point in his or her spiritual walk. It is the issue of control, the question of who really is in charge—God or you?

Jesus, praying in the Garden of Gethsemane, sweating as it were great drops of blood, struggled with this tremendous issue. Never before had He been separated from the presence of the Father. Seeing the black cloud overshadowing the cross, He prayed, "Let this cup pass from Me; nevertheless, not My will but Yours be done!"

Some contend, mistakenly I believe, that because God is sovereign, He is going to do exactly what He pleases. To pray, therefore, about a situation would be an exercise in futility. They believe that even before the world was created, God had decreed that certain things would happen and those things will happen regardless of my prayers or my human will. This thinking can have a chilling effect on my health and happiness, especially when I am on the receiving end of illness.

Others believe that by pleading and even demanding, they can get their way. Both beliefs are incorrect. Do you want to be like Jesus? Then pray as though everything depends on God, and live as though everything depends on you. Understand that God is a good God and He wills His best for you as His child. Remember that Jesus asked, "What father among you, if his son asks for a fish, will instead of a fish give him a serpent; or if he asks for an egg, will give him a scorpion?" (Luke 11:11–12). When you understand God's nature and His design and plan for your life, the issue of "which of us is going to be in control—You or me?" dissipates in the light of His love and care.

Prayer doesn't change God's mind, but it changes our minds, bringing our stubborn, rebellious, sometimes selfish wills into harmony with the will of a sovereign Father so that we can pray with faith and fervency: "Lord, may Your will be done."

What You Need to Know

• Acknowledge that *God is God*, but along with that an understanding of what His Word says is vital. Sincerity is not the issue—truth is! Today Larry and Alice Parker, the couple described at the beginning of this chapter, would surely acknowledge that if they had not been influenced by erroneous teaching, they would have handled their son's physical need differently.

• Accepting the fact that God is sovereign is not implying that He is disinterested, impotent, or out of touch with the needs of your life. The compassion of the Father was lived out in the life of the Son who touched the untouchables, who lifted up the fallen, who treated the down-and-out with dignity and respect. The fact that He is sovereign means He is greater than any need you shall ever experience.

• Because God is sovereign, you do not order Him to do your will; rather you yield your will to His, understanding that doing the will of God is the highest form of faith.

• Keep in mind that supernatural miracles, while they may be rare, reflect the consistency of an all-knowing, loving, and compassionate God. Supernatural miracles go far beyond the lame walking or the deaf hearing but also extend to the orderly process by which our world and our bodies function.

CHAPTER 2

Beneficiaries and Victims

On the morning of Sunday, January 14, 1990, Pastor Duane Miller awakened feeling that he was coming down with flu. His schedule of counseling, speaking four times a week, conducting committee meetings, and coping with family responsibilities was taking its toll. His body ached. His head was stuffy, and he wanted to stay in bed more than anything. Yet he couldn't because he was the senior pastor of First Baptist Church in Brenham, Texas, and he was to preach twice that morning. In his book *Out of the Silence* Miller tells how his voice became more and more raspy as the morning wore on. Forced to cut his second message short, he felt that he had cheated the congregation. One of his deacons, however, tried to make him feel better by saying, "Well, hallelujah, Pastor, this is the first Sunday we've gotten out of church on time in four years."

Miller, however, was not amused. Speaking felt like there was sandpaper rubbing on his throat. After five days with flu and a raw throat, he saw a physician friend who said: "Duane, your body is saying, 'Shut down and rest.' Don't even think about preaching on Sunday." Miller didn't preach that Sunday, or the one following, or the one after. Eventually Duane was sent to the Baylor College of

Medicine where a team of thirteen doctors tried to figure out what the real problem was. He was advised to take a six-month leave of absence and to observe absolute silence. By this time he had been away from his church for five months already.

Feeling that it was unfair to the church to continue supporting him when he was unable to serve the congregation effectively, Pastor Miller resigned amid hugs, tears, and the good wishes of parishioners saying, "We'll be praying for you, Pastor." Returning to Houston where the Millers had been prior to his appointment in Brenham, Duane Miller spent the next eighteen months seeing no less than sixty-three doctors, including specialists who had treated world-renowned singers such as Luciano Pavorotti, Frank Sinatra, Larry Gatlin, and Bruce Springsteen. Eventually scar tissue was observed—a death knell to the vocal cords.

One of his doctors took a videotape of his throat to a symposium of specialists in Switzerland. After a handful of doctors watched the videotape, they eventually showed it to the entire assembly of doctors. The consensus: There was no hope—zero! Within a short period of time, Duane would be completely mute. *Spasmodic dysphonia* was the term used to describe his problem.

"This can't be. God won't let it happen," consoled a friend. "I put my hand over his," wrote Miller, adding, "God has already let it happen!" By this time the Millers were broke and resigned to facing a bleak future. Nothing is more difficult for a man who has fire in his bones and wants to preach than to sit in a pew and listen to someone else, but that's what Pastor Miller did. He did his best to keep his spirits up while wondering where and when his misery would end.

Prior to their taking the church in Brenham, Pastor Miller had taught an adult class at First Baptist Church in Houston. Two years after he lost his voice, the person who had taught the class resigned and gave up the position as teacher. At this time Miller's voice had been reduced to a raspy whisper. Someone suggested that if they could find a microphone sensitive enough to pick up his voice and drown out the ambient noise, he might be able to teach this class of friends and well-wishers. A sound engineer found the right mic—the kind singers often use. Pressing the sensitive mic to his lips, Miller could be heard.

But who would want to listen to me? he thought. With some reluctance he agreed to teach again.

After a year of teaching, on January 17, 1993, something extraordinary happened. Miller was teaching on Psalm 103:1–4 where David wrote:

> Bless the LORD, O my soul, and all that is within me,
> bless his holy name!
> Bless the LORD, O my soul, and forget not all his
> benefits,
> who forgives all your iniquity, who heals all your
> diseases,
> who redeems your life from the pit.

Miller read the first two verses, and following the phrase "who forgives all your iniquity, who heals all your diseases," he told the group that on one side of the issue of healing are some who say it never happens, which puts God in a box, adding, "and He won't be put in a box." He went on to tell the class that on the other side are those who believe God always heals miraculously.

In an interview with the *Baptist Standard*, Miller said,

> I told them that what you have to do with divine
> healing is to just stand back and say, "I know God
> does that from time to time and I can't tell you why;
> I don't understand why some are healed and some
> aren't,' and leave it there and say that is in the Lord's
> wisdom; so be it."[1]

Looking back on that January day, Miller wrote in his book:

> My throat hurt very badly at this point. I had
> been teaching for over twenty minutes, and I had to
> strain especially hard to make even the raspy sound
> come out. I wondered if I'd be able to finish the class.
> After reading verse four, I began saying, "I have had
> and you have had in times past *pit* experiences."

> As soon as the word *pit* escaped from my mouth,
> the hands that had been choking my throat for
> over three years suddenly let go. I was stunned. Just
> seconds before, I felt like I was suffocating under the
> pressure of those unrelenting hands. Now, for the
> first time in three years, I could breathe.[2]

With every phrase that came from his lips, Duane's voice became stronger. Because the lesson he was teaching was being recorded, hundreds of thousands have heard the actual transition of his voice within a period of a few seconds. The tape, later released around the world through Focus on the Family radio, left absolutely no doubt that something wonderful, something inexplicable, something—yes—miraculous had taken place. What David had written three thousand years ago—that God heals all our diseases—was demonstrated one more time before some two hundred people who witnessed that Jesus Christ is, indeed, the same yesterday, today, and tomorrow.

How can what happened be explained? When Miller's physician once again ran the camera probe down his throat and compared the videos—the one shot previously with scar tissue causing the raspy, broken voice and the other that showed the condition of his throat after the healing—he said, "Even if I could explain how you got your voice back by coincidence—which I can't—I could never explain what happened to the scar tissue. . . . Scar tissue never disappears. It just never happens."[3] And that was the testimony of a physician who as a non-Christian didn't believe in the miraculous!

Why Do Some People Find It So Difficult to Believe in God's Intervention in Doing the Miraculous?

Reason 1: Many scientists deny the existence of God, thus refusing to label the unexplainable as miraculous. While some physicians and scientists acknowledge that God is sovereign and that He, on occasion, chooses to set aside the natural laws that govern humankind and do the miraculous, they are a minority. Because they fear criticism, ridicule, and isolation, these men of science are often silent, preferring to separate their faith from the everyday working world where their careers are lived out. The fear of being marginalized or considered "nonscientific" is an ever-present threat to the advancement of their careers.

Most Christians in every nation of the world believe in God and the miraculous. This belief is embodied in the teaching of the churches and groups to which they belong. Timothy Keller, in his book _The Reason for God_, explains why.

> Christians annually celebrate the miracles of the incarnation, the birth of Jesus, each Christmas, and the miracle of the bodily resurrection of Jesus from the dead each Easter. The New Testament is filled with accounts of miracles that Jesus performed during the course of his ministry. Scientific mistrust of the Bible began with the Enlightenment belief that miracles cannot be reconciled to a modern, rational view of the world. Armed with this presupposition, scholars turned to the Bible and said, "The biblical accounts can't be reliable because they contain descriptions of miracles." The premise behind such a claim is "Science has proved that there is no such thing as miracles."[4]

Striving to explain everything in naturalistic terms, excluding any reason or evidence demanding an acknowledgment of or belief in a Supreme Being, most scientists _a priori_ cling to the tenuous, unprovable premise that miracles are "irreconcilable with our understanding of both science and history," as John Macquarrie put it.[5]

In his book _The Language of God_, Francis Collins, the director of the Human Genome Project, an international scientific project involving twenty-four hundred scientists who mapped the twenty to twenty-five thousand genes of the human body, involving the three billion biochemical letters of our genetic blueprint, says that in 1916 researchers asked biologists, physicists, and mathematicians whether they believed in a God who actively communicates with humankind and to whom one may pray in expectation of receiving an answer. "About 40 percent answered in the affirmative. In 1997," he says, the same survey was repeated verbatim—and to the surprise of the researchers, the percentage remained nearly the same.[6]

In the first decade of this century, a new breed of atheists have emerged, strongly asserting that faith in a divine Creator has no place in the laboratory or in education. One of the most vocal, Richard Dawkins, believes that evolution leaves no room for God. This was ferociously rebutted by Collins, who considers God to be the force behind evolution. One of Dawkins' position statements is that "faith is the great cop-out, the great excuse to evade the need to think and evaluate evidence. Faith is belief in spite of, even perhaps because of, the lack of evidence. . . . Faith, being belief that isn't based on evidence, is the principal vice of any religion."[7]

More recently Stephen Hawkins, who in his 1998 book *A Brief History of Time* referred to the "mind of God" (thereby acknowledging God's existence), has come to believe that God is unnecessary. In his 2010 book *The Grand Design*, he writes, "Because there is a law such as gravity, the universe can and will create itself from nothing." In another passage he asserts, "Spontaneous creation is the reason there is something rather than nothing, why the universe exists, why we exist." He concludes, "It is not necessary to invoke God to light the blue touch paper and set the universe going."[8]

No wonder many freshmen in colleges and universities around the world are intimidated by the scientific bias of our day. Many of them leave behind their faith upon entering the laboratory or classroom. It isn't that scientists who are atheists are not brilliant; it is simply that they hold tenaciously to common beliefs in the scientific community that have no actual scientific basis, excluding the possibility that God does exist and, on occasion, chooses to do the miraculous.

A generation ago theologian Cornelius Van Till told a story about a young man who was hiking in the mountains, who slipped and fell into the valley of the blind. When he spoke of red and yellow roses, green grass, and blue sky filled with white puffy clouds, the people with no sight knew something was wrong with him. While they tolerated his ranting and raving with descriptions of landscapes and the beauty of the world, they considered him to be mentally disturbed.

Then one day the young man met a beautiful woman and fell in love with her. He wanted to marry her, but the elders would not allow her union with someone who spoke of things that none of them knew of, and, therefore, believed existed. As the man pressed his plea to marry the young woman, the elders agreed on one condition: the surgeons would sew his eyelids closed, thus making him just as blind as they were. The point is obvious.

Reason 2: We are skeptical when it comes to God's doing the miraculous because of the force of our culture, including the teaching of sincere but less than biblical teaching. "Perception of the truth is more powerful than truth itself," said Imelda Marcos, the wife of an ex-president of the Philippines. If someone is told something repeatedly, though at first the individual may reject what is said, when heard often enough, the lie becomes palatable and accepted as factual.

The church today is influenced by attitudes and mores of a world that grows more secular with every passing decade. The number of young adults who attend church grows slightly fewer with almost every poll while the attitudes and beliefs of a secular society shape our views of morality—what is acceptable and unacceptable, and what God does or cannot do. The bottom line is that the influence of institutional Christianity seems to be weakened with every generation.

It is little wonder that in spite of the fact a large percentage of the population believes God can—should He so choose to—do the miraculous, few, especially those under the age of forty, have ever had a personal encounter with God's miraculous power, and neither do most personally know anyone who can relate firsthand to that which is legitimately known as the miraculous.

Our attitude of "God could . . . but" receives little challenge from many of our churches where even pastors are uncertain if God is that interested in bringing healing. On the other hand, some pastors who believe that God can heal feel intimidated and incompetent when they pray for individuals, and their prayers go unanswered.

The sense of inadequacy these pastors feel is often the result of theological training they received. How so? In 1887, Benjamin Warfield was appointed to the Charles Hodge Chair at Princeton Theological Seminary, where he served until his death in 1921. While

Warfield stood firm for the inerrancy of Scripture and became one of the most respected Evangelicals of his day, he also taught that miracles were a first-century phenomenon. In his book *Miracles: Yesterday and Today, Real and Counterfeit*,[9] published in 1918, he concludes that "the power of working miracles was not extended beyond the disciples upon whom the Apostles conferred it by imposition of their hands." His belief became a doctrinal plank in the teaching of many leading Bible schools and seminaries of the twentieth century. Individuals who later embraced Warfield's views became known as cessationists.[10]

Why did Warfield say that miracles of healing "ceased entirely at the death of the last individual on whom the hands of the Apostles had been laid"?[11] Many believe his was a strong reaction to the excesses of Pentecostal believers whose sparse formal education and theological training were in marked contrast to his educational background. Says Peter Wagner, "Pentecostals were then ranked with Christian Scientists and Mormons." And what Warfield wrote quickly became proof texts for Bible schools and seminaries.

At the time Warfield was writing his denunciation of the miraculous, the writings of church fathers that I quote in chapter 5 were readily available. Based upon both Warfield's integrity and character as well as his commitment to truth, I am convinced that if he had been familiar with the testimonies I quote, his book would not have had the same acerbic tone.[12]

Warfield's position closely followed the teaching of Bible teacher John Nelson Darby (1800–1882), who had developed a theological framework known as dispensationalism. It was based on the belief that God dealt with different people in different ages in different ways. One of the tenets of dispensational teaching is that miracles ceased to be part of the fabric of the church after the days of the early church. For men who have grown up having been taught this by godly, respected professors and teachers, and in spite of the lack of statements from the New Testament affirming dispensational interpretations, breaking out of this mind-set never comes easy.

Thus J. I. Packer writes:

> All Christians are at once beneficiaries and
> victims of tradition—beneficiaries, who received

> nurturing truth and wisdom from God's faithfulness
> in past generations; victims, who now take for granted
> things that need to be questioned, thus treating as
> divine absolutes patterns of belief and behavior that
> should be seen as human, provisional, and relative.
> We are all beneficiaries of good, wise, and sound
> tradition and victims of poor, unwise, and unsound
> traditions.[13]

Jack Deere, formerly an associate professor of Old Testament at Dallas Theological Seminary, a stronghold of dispensational teaching, tells of his spiritual pilgrimage in his book *Surprised by the Power of the Spirit*. In this book Deere tells about a conversation regarding healing that took place with some of his colleagues at the seminary.

Says Deere:

> They started to enumerate the things they would
> not ask God to heal. Some said they wouldn't ask
> God to heal blindness or deafness. Others said they
> wouldn't ask God to heal a deformity or to cause an
> amputated limb to grow out. When they got through
> listing all the things that they wouldn't ask God to
> heal, there wasn't much left to pray for except colds
> and headaches. Before the discussion was over, all
> the professors in that group had virtually denied the
> possibility of any New Testament miracles occurring
> today.[14]

Some say God doesn't heal today. *They are right.*

Others say God does heal today. *They are right as well.*

What Jesus told the two blind men at Jericho is still true: "According to your faith be it done to you" (Matt. 9:29).

Reason 3: We push away from the miraculous because of the abuses of "faith healers" and frauds. At the same time that Benjamin Warfield was influencing the growing body of Evangelicals who morphed into mainline churches (both dispensational and reformed in their theology), which includes most Baptist, Presbyterian, and some Methodist churches, another tradition of teaching developed in the spectrum of beliefs. Among those who held to the new position were Christian and Missionary Alliance churches, founded by A. B. Simpson and Adoniram Judson Gordon, who eventually founded the college bearing his name.[15]

Then when the Pentecostal and charismatic churches emerged following the Azusa Street revival in Los Angeles in 1906, the Simpson-Gordon groups, embracing the fact that God does heal people, separated themselves, rejecting the display of glossolalia or speaking in tongues. Eventually mainstream Pentecostal and holiness groups emerged, such as The Foursquare Church, the Assemblies of God, Pentecostal Holiness, and dozens of offshoots of one kind or another.

Then following World War II, the media made it possible for masses of people to hear and see the same thing, and so some individuals who disdained or refused being accountable to denominational leaders became independent evangelists who capitalized on a healing ministry. Included in this group were personalities such as Aimee Semple McPherson, William Branham, Kathryn Kuhlman, Oral Roberts, who was among the first to use television, Jack Coe, A. A. Allen, Ernest Angley, and Benny Hinn, among many. Some who have become "faith healers" were simply frauds and were exposed as such, but in all fairness it is my conviction that most began their ministries believing that God had called them to preach the Word and bring deliverance to those who were suffering and needed healing: but with the passing of time, many became more interested in their own financial successes and lifestyles than they were in building the kingdom of God. Neither would I minimize or detract from the thousands, if not hundreds of thousands, of men and women who have connected with God through their ministries and come away rejoicing because they found healing.

Because people are fascinating to me, especially in striving to find out why God often uses unlikely individuals to do His work and bypasses better qualified, better trained men and women, I have analyzed the lives of some of the individuals I have named, not to criticize them but to see why God used them. I conclude that, in spite of personal failures and weaknesses of the flesh, God has often honored His word and through them, at times, has chosen to heal those who looked to Christ as the Great Physician.

It would be grossly unfair for me or anyone else to paint all of them with the same wide brush because their social backgrounds, lifestyles, and financial policies differ. However, many of the "faith healers," as they are often called, have some things in common.

- A sense of divine calling often coming from an encounter with God, resulting in personal healing in their own lives.
- Humble backgrounds often marked by minimal theological education.
- Access to large audiences of hurting people who desperately want help and deliverance from sickness and suffering.
- A grasp of showmanship and the ability to read and orchestrate an audience. (Those using television often highlight only their successes, not their failures.)[16]
- Extravagant lifestyles, often costing millions of dollars made possible by large offerings.
- A lack of accountability to a spiritual leader, bishop or elder, a board of responsible individuals, and certainly to the evangelical council for financial accountability. Asserting as many have, "I am responsible only to God," is, in essence, saying, "I can do whatever I please, and because of the separation of church and state, what I do with the money is nobody's business but my own."

While the world remembers their own for their greatest accomplishments, they remember God's own for their greatest failures. While some people walk away from healing crusades rejoicing, an equal or greater number of individuals have gone home disillusioned, disappointed, and thinking, *I just don't have enough faith*, or, *I'm just not good enough.*

I do not hesitate to say that many who started out in all sincerity wanting to make a difference in the world have yielded to the temptations of being unaccountable, and their lifestyles and abuses have not only been a disgrace to the cause of Christ but a revulsion to many people who throw the baby out with the bathwater!

Reason 4: We are hesitant to accept the miraculous because our old natures disbelieve that God is strong enough, cares enough, or we are good enough to merit His attention. After the resurrection Jesus showed Himself to the disciples, then appeared to the women and later showed His nail-pierced hands to doubting Thomas. Yet Matthew says the following about the eleven disciples who went to the mountain where Jesus had directed them: "When they saw him, they worshiped him; but some doubted" (Matt. 28:17 NIV). The Living Bible puts it, "But some of them weren't sure it really was Jesus!"

Why are we gripped with uncertainty, and—yes, doubt? Instead of interpreting what happens to us in the light of God's nature and love for us, we filter everything, including our view of God, through our experiences, feelings, and culture. The end result is often a distorted image of God, one that is much less than the one we read about in the Gospels.

As Warren Wiersbe put it: "The presence of suffering and moral evil in the world has given rise to a classic argument against the existence of God, or at least of a God who will do anything about them."[17] A young woman who has carried a baby in her womb for six months only to lose the child, along with the couple whose son has died in battle, and those who have suffered many other losses have difficulty believing in a personal God who cares or is still in the business of healing.

Like the holocaust that rose as a dark, foreboding specter blocking out any thought of a loving God, their personal loss or catastrophe has created a seemingly impenetrable barrier.

There are many variations of the challenge posed by the Greek philosopher Epicurus (341–270 BC) who was born seven years after Plato's death. Here's what he proposed.

> God either wishes to take away evil, and is
> unable; or He is able and unwilling; or He is neither
> willing nor able; or He is both willing and able.
>
> If He is willing but unable, He is feeble, which is
> not in accordance with the character of God. If He is
> able and unwilling, He is envious which is equally at
> variance with God.

If he is neither willing nor able, He is both envi-
ous and feeble, and therefore, not God. If He is both
willing and able, which alone is suitable for God,
from what source then are evils? Or why does He not
remove them?[18]

This produces several misconceptions that are like a cataract that
gradually turns a fuzzy image of God into a dark, impenetrable cloud.

What Some People Mistakenly Think about God

*Many think of God as an angry God who always takes revenge on
wrongdoers.* When difficulty or suffering comes in life, we then tend
to think of it as God's judgment or punishment. Sarah was like that.
As a little girl, her mother would tell her, "If you are bad, God's going
to get you!" So when Sarah's first baby died, she knew it was God's
punishment for her having conceived the baby out of wedlock and for
her having been a rebellious teenager. When a flood destroyed the
basement of the apartment where she lived, she again thought it was
the hand of God raised in retribution. When her second child was
born with five holes in the baby's tiny heart, Sarah tearfully sobbed,
"Why is God punishing my baby for what I did?" Those who live
with this concept of God always hide in a closet of fear, running in
anger or defiance, hoping to avoid the ultimate punishment they fear
is coming.

Others see God as a loving but weak God who wishes He could deliver
us from the harsh blows that bring suffering and sickness to our bodies, tears to our eyes and pain to our hearts, but lacks the power to
change circumstances in our lives. This is the "limited" God that
Rabbi Harold Kushner wrote of a generation ago.

In this chapter I suggested that we often interpret God in terms
of our culture and experience instead of interpreting what happens in
our lives in light of what God says in His Word. Rabbi Kushner may
well have done just that. You see, their three-year-old son, Aaron, was
diagnosed with a rare disease that strikes one person in some seven million people. Doctors describe the condition as progeria, the rapid-aging

disease. For the next ten years, the Kushners saw the dreaded disease progress.

As a rabbi, Kushner overlooked the fact that God also had one son whose life was cut short. When Aaron succumbed to the affliction at age thirteen, Rabbi Kushner and his wife looked bitterly toward heaven and cried out, "God, how could you do this to us and to our innocent child?" Thus began the search that resulted in Kushner's book *When Bad Things Happen to Good People*.

People who believe in a loving but weak God don't expect much from Him. They see God as gracious and kind but impotent. Babies die and death snatches lovers from our arms, so some of us assume that either God can't or else is too disinterested to help. I'm thinking of a young woman who wrote several letters in response to one of my radio commentaries, each of which outlined her prayer request for healing for a child. With each new letter her frustration built, her faith growing dimmer in God's ability to intervene. Focus on your problem and your faith will grow dim; look to Him who healed the sick with a word or touch, and you will see the Father's face reflected in your suffering.

Some think God is a distant Father. Many believe God is too old or too disinterested to be involved in the affairs of seven billion people on Earth. I once talked with a Jewish guide in Israel. He knew Old Testament history but didn't know the God of Abraham, Isaac, or Jacob. "Where was God," he vehemently asked, "when six million Jews died in the concentration camps of World War II?" Not intending to minimize his grief but striving to answer the question, I said, "In the same place He was when His Son died outside the walls of Jerusalem two thousand years ago." God is neither aloof nor disinterested in what happens in our world though issues as the Holocaust form a dark cloud that becomes an obstacle to many who cannot understand how a loving God could be there and not step in and stop such carnage and bloodshed.

Reason 5: We shy away from the miraculous simply because we do not know it is God's nature to heal and have never been confronted with the reality that Jesus Christ, the Great Physician, is the same yesterday, today, and forever. When the highly respected British pastor Martyn Lloyd-Jones, who served Westminster Chapel in London for thirty years, was asked to write a book on healing, he replied that there was no need for a new book on this subject, saying that Henry Frost "had already dealt with this matter in what I regard as a final and conclusive manner."[19] And who was Henry Frost? This godly man was the successor to James Hudson Taylor, the renowned missionary to China and founder of the China Inland Mission. His book *Miraculous Healing*, printed in 1916, is balanced and grounded in Scripture.

While Frost had the conviction that it is not God's will to heal everyone, he also contended that "there are many saints who are not well and many others who are not strong, simply because they have never asked God to be their physical sufficiency. This is a sad plight for a Christian to be in, and it would seem as if such a person must be a great disappointment to the heart of God."[20]

My first trip to China was in 1979, and on numerous occasions we were with small gatherings of believers who gave thrilling firsthand testimonies of simple faith in a God who heals. When someone was sick, they would call for the elders of the fellowship, who would anoint and pray over the sick person, and then God would heal him or her. I would ask, "Why China? What's the difference?" Simple faith is rewarded there, whereas our sophistication and reliance on medical science, intertwined with unbelief, means that while we believe God can heal, we do not expect Him to respond in such a way that healing will really take place. It's still true: We have not because we ask not, forgetting that Jesus said, "Ask, and you will receive, that your joy may be full" (John 16:24).

Is Anything Too Hard for the Lord?

A few paragraphs back I told you about Sarah, the young mother who was convinced that God was punishing her baby for her once having been a rebellious teenager. Having been told that "God will get you when you are bad," Sarah reasoned, "I'll take my chances. I'm going to have my fun!" She did, too, but then one day while walking down the street, she heard music coming through the open windows of a church. Sarah paused, then went inside and sat down.

That morning she heard a message on God's love and forgiveness. "Could God really forgive me?" she asked herself. Sensing the prompting of God's Spirit, Sarah responded to an invitation to receive Christ. She started going to church yet still did not understand the nature of God or forgiveness, so that when something painful happened, she interpreted it as God's punishment.

When I stood beside the bassinet in a children's hospital and heard the sobs of a mother's heart, my own heart was touched as well. Stepping into the hallway where we could talk, the white fluorescent lights, the smell that hospitals have, along with the sterile environment seemed so far from the presence of Him who had held little children in His arms and said, "Of such is the kingdom of heaven" (Matt. 19:14 KJV).

With the exception of when my sister had lupus, never before in my life had I prayed for a miracle of healing as I did that day. I was a young pastor in my early twenties, yet I believed God would honor His Word. I prayed, asking God to heal that tiny infant's heart so that this mother would know God was not punishing her for sins that had already been forgiven, and that she would know beyond any doubt that when God forgives us, He wipes the slate clean as though we had never sinned. While doctors had said the baby could not live beyond age two because the holes in the infant's heart would only enlarge with time, the tiny heart began to mend and heal. My last contact with the family was years later, when the baby who should have died had become a normal teenager!

Jehovah Rapha, the God who heals, is still in the business of healing broken bodies. No wonder Jeremiah, the prophet of old, asked, "Is anything too hard for God?"

What You Need to Know

• We are both victims and beneficiaries of our culture, what we have been taught, and what is commonly believed today. Your belief system should be brought into conformity with what the Word of God clearly says. You must leave behind the guilt of breaking with tradition for the freedom in Christ that comes by accepting and resting firmly on the certainty and authority of God's Word.

- God's Word always trumps what individuals say the Bible says—mine included!

- Nobody counterfeits brown wrapping paper! Profound? Not really. As far back as Moses' day there were frauds who wanted to capitalize on sickness, attempting to duplicate the supernatural or the miraculous. Today some individuals have amassed great personal wealth and notoriety in "healing" the sick. Focus on the authentic—that which is genuine.

CHAPTER 3

Jehovah Rapha (the God Who Heals) in the Old Testament

S hould you get off a plane in Tel Aviv today, you would be greeted with *Shalom*, a word that is centuries old. You, of course, already know that this word means "peace" and that the word *Jerusalem* is a compound meaning "city of peace," which is ironic, given the fact that probably more blood has been shed in either defending Jerusalem or by an opposing army trying to take the city than any other place on Earth. Israelis, though, don't have a headlock on this word in that the root word is common to all Semitic languages and was used long before Joshua and the entourage that followed him crossed the Jordan into Palestine.

Peace! Yes, we like the thought and the pleasant sound of a greeting wishing us peace. Digging deeper, however, we realize its meaning and significance. John Wilkinson of the Senior College of Physicians of Edinburgh, a theologian and biblical scholar who spent most of his life as a missionary in Africa, has written a definitive book on the Bible and healing. In his book *The Bible and Healing*, he writes:

> The meaning of the common Semitic root of
> the verb *salem* from which the word *shalom* and all its
> related words come is that of totality and complete-
> ness. The usage of the word in the Old Testament is
> to denote the presence of wholeness, completeness
> and well-being in all spheres of life whether physi-
> cal, mental and spiritual, or individual, social and
> national.[1]

The upraised hand, palm extended in greeting, not only signifies that you hold no weapon but also that you are expressing wishes to someone for wholeness, health, prosperity, and success. This concept influenced the World Health Organization to develop the widely known definition of health as "a state of complete physical, mental and social well-being and not merely the absence of disease or infirmity."

When Gideon, one of the judges of ancient Israel, had an encounter with an angel, he built an altar to Jehovah Shalom, the God of peace. That God is the "God of peace" is carried throughout the pages of both Testaments. It echoes in the words of Jesus immediately before He was seized in the Garden as He told the disciples, "Peace I leave with you; my peace I give to you. Not as the world gives do I give to you. Let not your hearts be troubled, neither let them be afraid" (John 14:27).

God's desire for wholeness—spiritual, physical, and emotional—for our brokenness is seen throughout the entire Bible, reflected in many passages. In this chapter I will focus on physical healing throughout the Old Testament. An exhaustive study of this subject, however, does not consist of so many proof texts where an author says, "Here it is!" but rather a comprehensive understanding of God's dealings with people reflecting a deeper will and purpose than simply regaining health. God's intent for *shalom* becomes the fabric of His relationship with His people Israel, and that foundation becomes the cradle into which Jesus, the Great Physician, was laid.

We will look at various incidents that make up the landscape covering at least twenty-two centuries, from the days of Job to the close of the Old Testament canon, when we are told that the Sun of Righteousness will rise with healing in His wings.[2] Some of those accounts involving supernatural healing were centuries apart, which does not necessarily mean that no healings took place between those events but that the writers of Scripture, directed to write as the Spirit of God prompted them, focused on what God wanted us in the twenty-first century to know. Let's get started.

The Oldest Question in the Human Heart

I shall never forget my first serious encounter with this issue that still confronts many people today—why God allows suffering. As a young pastor I went to visit an old man well into his eighties. He had been part of what Tom Brokaw called the "Greatest Generation," having served in World War II. Flat on his back in Veteran's Hospital with pain-etched wrinkles in his forehead, he looked up and fastened his eyes on mine and asked: "Why does God allow me to lie here and suffer as I am? Why can't He just let me die?"

I don't think I have ever felt more inadequate to give a satisfying answer other than at the first funeral I conducted when I also asked myself, "What can I say that will bring comfort to this widow who grieves the loss of her husband?" Actually both are part of the same fabric, and now more than a half-century later, I have what John Calvin called "a learned ignorance," still uncertain that the deep questions of the heart will ever find totally satisfying answers this side of heaven.

It is not by chance, I am certain, that the oldest drama recorded in the pages of Scripture focuses on this issue—the book of Job. First, I would like to establish the fact that this book is not simply an allegory or didactic fiction that encourages those who suffer. Job was a historical person whose existence was affirmed by the sixth century BC prophet Ezekiel, who was taken in chains to Babylon, as well as by James, the half brother of Jesus.[3]

The drama took place in the land of Uz, located to the south and east of Israel today. Archaeologists tell us that Job's name was relatively common in his day, giving us references to individuals bearing the same name in numerous ancient documents.

The English Bible teacher J. Sidlow Baxter called the book "a dramatic poem framed in an epic story," which is not to suggest that the events in the book are less than historical. The drama took place on Earth and not a figurative, make-believe world. What was taken from Job's life are the things we treasure today—commodities, resources, his livelihood, his family, and even the love and respect of his wife, who advised, "Curse God and die" (Job 2:9).

The exchange between Job and his friends and the drama that unfolds is written in the style of the wisdom literature during the days of Solomon. Most Bible scholars, however, believe the action took place in the days of the patriarchs—Abraham, Isaac, and Jacob. The author alludes to Psalm 8:4 (Job 7:17–18) and quotes indirectly from other passages of Scripture as well.[4]

The authorship of the book is unknown, although Elihu, Moses, and even Solomon have been considered. The three prominent figures are known—Job, a wealthy entrepreneur and landowner, God, and Satan, who had been allowed to try Job up to the point of taking his life.

The common perception is that the theme of the book is suffering, specifically why God allows the righteous to suffer. A deeper theme, however, points to the real message of the book: Can a sovereign God be trusted? Is God really in control of our lives when it seems that all is lost and He appears to have disengaged Himself from our lives?

Respected Bible scholar F. F. Bruce says that a second problem about suffering is both raised and convincingly answered by the book: "Is there such a thing as the innocent suffering?" He answers his own question by saying, "The fact we no longer doubt the existence of innocent suffering is partly due to the book itself; for the book speaks out clearly against all cut-and-dried theologies of guilt and punishment by its insistence that the Job who was suffering is a righteous man."[5]

It follows, then, that one of the primary reasons the book of Job is so important today is because this book rebuts the centuries-old mentality that suffering is the result of sin in your life and that, if you would only confess and forsake your sin, you would find healing. Another corollary is the belief, simply, that if it's good, it's God, and if it's bad, it's from the devil.

The reality is that the rain falls on the just and the unjust. Because we live in a broken world, cancer is never selective in its target, touching the lives of godly men and women along with infidels and pagans. If God is sovereign, and that is the clear teaching of both Testaments, whether you think of difficulty and suffering as the permissive will of God (God permits certain events that are not His direct will yet are allowed to accomplish His purpose) or simply that God's direct will is to take some of His children through the fire, the flood, and the ravages of suffering (see Isa. 43:1–3), the issue is this: Can this sovereign God be trusted?

Shortly before his death in a tragic automobile accident, Paul Little, a key person in InterVarsity Christian Fellowship, wrote a magazine article asserting that the bottom line of our theology is this: "Is God a good God?" If so, contended Little, everything else that we read about Him in Scripture falls into place.

When I first read Little's article, I said: "Too simple! There's more to it than that." But as I pondered on what he had written, including the fact that his life was cut short, I realized that Little was right. *Can this sovereign God be trusted? Does He manifest Himself in our times of suffering and loss? Does He walk with us through the darkness? Is there an exit out of every valley through which we must walk?* The answer to these questions is something that is not academic. It is often learned through many tears and sleepless nights as we experience the presence of the Almighty during difficult times. When we ultimately come through to the other side of the suffering, then, with David we can say, "Even though I walk through the valley of the shadow of death, I will fear no evil, for you are with me" (Ps. 23:4). Kenneth Lange Harris, in writing the notes for the book of Job in the English Standard Version of the Bible, says that the most important word in the entire book is "comfort." Indeed!

After Job has endured the accusations and charges of his three friends, Eliphaz, Bildad, and Zophar, along with Elihu, God addresses Eliphaz, the apparent leader of the opposition, with these words: "My anger burns against you and against your two friends, for you have not spoken of me what is right, as my servant Job has" (Job 42:7); then He commands him to offer sacrifices, adding, "And my servant Job shall pray for you, and I will accept his prayer not to deal with you according to your folly," repeating again the phrase, "For you have not spoken of me what is right, as my servant Job has" (Job 42:8).

The bottom line is that God in His mercy has not dealt with any of us according to our folly but has touched our lives with His grace, bringing forgiveness, cleansing, and healing.

Abraham and Abimelech

The first recorded healing in Scripture took place some four hundred years prior to the exodus of the Israelites from Egypt. Abraham, wrote Moses, had journeyed toward the territory of the Negev, and there he encountered Abimelech, who was the king of Gerar.

Here's how it happened: After the destruction of Sodom, Abraham took his wife, Sarah, and his flocks and journeyed south into the Negev. When Abraham met the king of Gerar, Abimelech, he was fearful that the king might take Sarah and add her to his harem. Thus Abraham introduced Sarah to him as his sister (a half-truth).[6] This was the second time Abraham has used this deception. He had done the same thing on a previous journey into Egypt, and for the second time the ruse blew up in his face. Abraham was powerless to prevent the king from taking Sarah for himself.

Before a relationship was consummated, however, Abimelech had a scary dream. In the dream God said (my paraphrase): "You're a dead man, Abimelech! The woman you have taken is another man's wife." In the dream Abimelech argues with God: "Did he not himself say to me, 'She is my sister'? And she herself said, 'He is my brother.' In the innocence of my hands I have done this." God then told him that Abraham would pray for him and he would live; however, should he refuse to let Sarah go, he would die along with his household. There was no ambiguity in that one!

Abimelech was convinced—scared stiff! In no uncertain terms he rebuked Abraham, who, accepting the rebuke and trying to appease the king, prayed for both Abimelech and his household; "God healed Abimelech, and also healed his wife and female slaves so that they bore children. For the LORD had closed all the wombs of the house of

Abimelech because of Sarah, Abraham's wife" (Gen. 20:17–18). The king was so relieved that he sent Abraham and Sarah away with a thousand pieces of silver—publicly given to him so that his wife and his entourage would know that he was an innocent man.

We are also reminded that God not only heals, but, on occasion, He afflicts. Moses records the words of God, who says, "See now that I, even I, am he, and there is no god beside me; I kill and I make alive; I wound and I heal; and there is none that can deliver out of my hand" (Deut. 32:39). In relation to God's closing the wombs of those in Abimelech's household, this truth is not to imply that infertility is the judgment of God. A sovereign God simply chose infertility to protect not only Abraham but Abimelech's entire household from further judgment.

Jehovah Rapha (The God Who Heals)

Now segue forward some four hundred years. Abraham, Isaac, and Jacob are all dead. The scene is the far side of the Red Sea; however, in spite of the enormous display of God's power and sovereignty, the two million plus Hebrews are not so sure they like having left Egypt behind.

Visualize Hebrew women going to the spring at Marah to draw water—a place traditionally located about forty-seven miles southeast of the modern town of Suez, a short distance from the Red Sea, in a wilderness known as Shur. The great display of God's power in Egypt only days before as well as their miraculous crossing of the Red Sea has already faded from their memories, and now three weary days later, the women go to a nearby spring to draw water. But tasting the water, their faces contort. "It's bitter!" they cry, using the Hebrew word *marah*. They spew the water out on the dry ground. And the people grumble against Moses, saying, "What shall we drink?"

The American president Abraham Lincoln once said, "I have been driven many times upon my knees by the overwhelming conviction that I had nowhere else to go."[7] So was it with Moses. He responded to the complaints of many by earnestly seeking God. His was the cry of one who had Egypt at his back and two million plus ex-slaves in his care, who feared that he had led them into the wilderness to perish from hunger and thirst. No wonder Moses was burdened for these for whom he was responsible.

God answered his heart cry, instructing Moses to throw a log into the spring, and the water became sweet. Don't strive to explain this in naturalistic terms—you can't come up with a rational explanation apart from the fact that this sovereign God who had sent a strong east wind to blow back the waters of the Red Sea, allowing His people to cross, had miraculously intervened, causing sweet water to flow from the spring to assuage the thirst of the people.

The next day two women, having heard that the water was now pure, make their way toward this spring. After drawing water, they place the large jars on their heads, as women in the Middle East have done for centuries, and start walking back toward their tents. As the women walk they talk among themselves. "Have you heard that Moses says His name is now *YAHWEH RAPHA* (the God who heals)?" "Not Yahweh the living God?" replies the companion. The other answers, "Yes, I know this for a fact. He says '*Jehovah, the God who heals*' is His name."

God had previously revealed Himself to Moses in Exodus 3 as I AM WHO I AM, a name that should forever be remembered. The Hebrews had a much greater understanding of this because the word meant the totality of existence, but now He was revealing to His people a new aspect of His character. The term "Yahweh Rapha" or even "I am who I am" is almost incomprehensible. But to those who heard, it was a powerful and clear claim to be Sovereign God—the one who was responsible for the totality of existence. For several reasons many translations use the term *Jehovah* for *Yahweh*. The word *Yahweh* is a transliteration of the four Hebrew letters YHWH, and God's name was so sacred, so holy, that the Jews would not pronounce it. Taking the vowel pointing for another term for God—a somewhat more generic one that was also used for pagan gods—*Adonai*, and, adding it to the Hebrew characters YHWH, you have the word found in most English Bibles—"Jehovah." Got that?

When I was teaching Greek and a question was asked for which there was no simple or logical explanation, I would reply, "Don't ask why? It's an old Greek custom," so in this case just take my word for it. *It's an old Hebrew custom.*

The point I want to make is that the Old Testament gives compounds of this word using different words to express something of the nature and character of God

Each of these progressively reveals something of God's care for Israel with the truths being revealed more fully in the New Testament.[8]

Of one thing you can be certain: When God pronounces "I AM" anything, you had better take notice. Remember He had previously told His people, "I am the LORD your God, who brought you out of the land of Egypt, out of the house of slavery" (Exod. 20:2). Frederick Gaiser reminds us:

> Perhaps we can understand the significance of the claim that God is Israel's healer by recognizing the general exclusivity of the "I am" statements. No one other than Yahweh brought Israel out of Egypt. No one other than Yahweh is "the first and the last" (Isa. 48:12); indeed, "besides me there is no god" (Isa. 44:6). "I am he. Before me no god was formed, nor shall there be any after me." (Isa. 43:10)[9]

Of all the Old Testament passages of Scripture that refer to healing, the Exodus 15 and Isaiah 53 are foundational in understanding the nature of God's desire to bring healing, to Israel in particular, with an application to God's children of all ages. Swiss theologian Karl Barth called Exodus 15 "the divine Magna Carta" in all matters of health and all related questions. In his translation of the Bible to German, Martin Luther translated *Jehovah Rapha* as "I am the LORD, your physician."[10]

Later Moses wrote these words: "There the LORD made for them a statute and a rule, and there he tested them, saying, 'If you will diligently listen to the voice of the LORD your God and do that which is right in his eyes, and give ear to his commandments and keep all his statutes, I will put none of the diseases on you that I put on the Egyptians, for I am the LORD, your healer'" (Exod. 15:25–26).

Just as you parse a verb, the words of Moses can be broken down into four statements:

1. The statement that God would be their healer is not a carte blanche, one-policy-fits-everyone health policy. It is conditioned upon the Israelites' obedience to God's commands and statutes. If they are willfully disobedient, the deal is off.

2. God's promise is that their obedience specifically spares them from certain diseases, the implication being that disobedience renders them vulnerable. Specifically, they are to be spared the afflictions and diseases that troubled the Egyptians prior to the exodus. Underline the phrase "none of these diseases" in your Bible.

3. The statement God made implies that affliction or suffering may be God's judgment. The psalmist understood this because he wrote, "Before I was afflicted I went astray, but now I keep your word" (Ps. 119:67).

4. In the last statement God asserts that He is their healer, their physician, their protector.

"The statute was to demonstrate, by means of testing, the principle (a rule) that if the people would diligently listen to the voice of the Lord, he would graciously care for them as their healer," explains Kenneth Laing Harris.[11] This was a meaningful and powerful truth—God is not only Healer but Protector as well.

The Bronze Serpent in the Wilderness

The event recorded in Numbers 20 where murmuring and complaining angered God cannot really be considered independently of the statutes and ordinances attached to God's promise of being their Healer because the first five books of the Old Testament, known as the Torah or "the law" to Jews constitute a whole entity or book as we would think of it in the twenty-first century.

We do know, however, that a period of time elapsed between the crossing of the Red Sea and their arrival at Mount Hor, probably north of the Gulf of Aqaba. The path had been marked by a series of acts of stubbornness that grew progressively more noxious in the nostrils of God. Follow the progression of their complaints.

At Marah the complaints of the people resulted in Moses' intercession with God, who instructed him to throw a log into bitter water, thus removing its foul taste. Then pausing to refresh themselves at Elim, an oasis marked by seventy palm trees and twelve springs of sweet water, "They set out from Elim, and all the congregation of the people of Israel came to the wilderness of Sin, which is between Elim and Sinai," according to Exodus 16:1.

There the people grumbled against Moses and Aaron. Why? Remembering the pots of cooked meat and loaves of bread in Egypt, they accused the leaders of taking them into the wilderness to die from starvation. And how does Moses react? He bluntly counters that they are not complaining against God's leaders—him and his brother Aaron—but against God, their Provider (Exod. 16:8).

God responded by sending manna and quail to satisfy their longing for protein and carbohydrates and fresh water from the rock (Exod. 17:1–7). Still dissatisfied, the people continued to complain about their conditions. There God's hand supernaturally certified that Aaron was to stand alongside Moses in leadership. Here's how it happened: Twelve staffs were collected, one for each of the twelve tribes of Israel. Aaron's name was engraved on the staff of Levi, and they were all assembled in the tent of testimony. The following morning Aaron's rod had budded, certifying he was God's man.

Unimpressed, however, the people continued to grumble even more intensely, to the point that God gave them one final warning, saying that "the rebels" would die if they continued this complaining (Num. 17:10).

Did they heed God's sober pronouncement? No—within a few days the old, ingrained negative practice continued. Numbers 21:4–5 states: "From Mount Hor they set out by the way to the Red Sea, to go around the land of Edom. And the people became impatient on the way. And the people spoke against God and against Moses, 'Why have you brought us up out of Egypt to die in the wilderness? For there is no food and no water, and we loathe this worthless food.'"

God is long-suffering, but there is an end to the patience of the Almighty. Judgment fell, as recorded in Numbers 21. Screams of "Snakes!" pierced the air as venomous snakes indiscriminately bit people and killed them. The historical record says, "Then the LORD sent fiery serpents among the people, and they bit the people, so that many people of Israel died" (Num. 21:6). "How could God do this?" undoubtedly some cried. "We deserve better than this! Moses, do something! Pray to the LORD that he take away the serpents from us" and Moses, once again, interceded for the people who had reviled him.

God instructed Moses to erect a pole where he would put a bronze snake, and "everyone who is bitten, when he sees it, shall live" (Num. 21:8–9). Taking away the serpents wasn't God's remedy; it was looking at the bronze serpent that took away the effects of the poisonous bites—something that unquestionably must have reminded them of Satan's masquerading as a serpent in the Garden. And subsequent generations are reminded that looking to the cross upon which was impaled the sinless Son of God is what produces life and forgiveness.

Though God didn't remove the snakes, He provided healing for those who had been bitten, and instead of death came new life. So writes the apostle John in the New Testament, "And as Moses lifted up the serpent in the wilderness, so must the Son of Man be lifted up, that whosoever believes in him may have eternal life" (John 3:14–15).

Individuals Who Were Healed

Hezekiah—the Man Who Wept Bitterly

Hezekiah was a man whose prayer of desperation resulted in his healing. The story of his healing is segmented in three books of the Bible: Kings, Chronicles, and Isaiah.[12] Hezekiah, king of Judah, had much in his life that is commendable.

In 701 BC Sennacherib of Assyria began to attack the cities along the western edge of Judah and then pushed closer and closer toward Jerusalem, striving to strangle Judah, forcing them to pay tribute to his coffers. The Assyrian army was devastatingly cruel, and their appearance struck fear into the best armies of the world. Lenin, Hitler, and Stalin were all disciples of Assyrian military policy. Lord Byron memorialized the march of the Assyrian hordes descending on Judah with his words, "The Assyrians came down like a wolf on the fold; Their cohorts all gleaming in silver and gold."

Rabshakeh, Sennacherib's representative, alternated insults with attempts to negotiate Hezekiah's surrender; but instead of surrendering, Hezekiah urged the prophet Isaiah to intercede for them. The king prostrated himself before God, who sent an angel who decimated the ranks of the Assyrians and sent the army packing to go home, where Sennacherib was eventually executed by his own sons in a pagan temple.

But one crisis simply faded into another—a personal one. "In those days," begins the account in 2 Kings 20, "Hezekiah became sick and was at the point of death." Undoubtedly Hezekiah had been sick on previous occasions but this time was different. The prophet Isaiah, a man whom Hezekiah esteemed and respected, shows up at the palace and says, "Thus says the LORD, 'Set your house in order, for you shall die; you shall not recover.'" Hezekiah knew that Isaiah had a direct line to heaven, and the prophet's pronouncement was the sentence of death.

Having begun his reign at age twenty-five, Hezekiah was then thirty-nine years old—middle-aged, or "in the middle of my day," as he put it. Not ready to die, Hezekiah then did what you probably would have done as well. He rolled over on his bed and, with his face toward the wall, began to weep bitterly. He reminded God of what He already knew—that he had been faithful in serving the Lord, that he had wholeheartedly lived for Him, and that he had done what was good in His sight.

Hezekiah's record was impressive. Early in his reign he had removed the high places where pagan gods were worshipped and torn down their altars. He destroyed Nehustan, the bronze serpent Moses had made in the wilderness because people were worshipping this instead of the living God. "He trusted in the LORD, the God of Israel; so that after him there was none like him among all the kings of Judah, nor among those who were before him. . . . And the LORD was with him; wherever he went he prospered" (2 Kings 18:5, 7 NASB).

Before Hezekiah finished his prayer, Isaiah, in the outer court of the palace, was ready to head for home when the word of the Lord had come to Isaiah, instructing him to deliver the good news to the king—that God had heard his prayers. This time it was good news, as God's pronouncement was fourfold:

1. "I have heard your prayer" (2 Kings 20:5).
2. "I have seen your tears" (v. 5).
3. "I will heal you" (v. 5).
4. "On the third day, you shall go up to the house of the LORD, and I will add fifteen years to your life" (v. 5–6).

That was the best news Hezekiah had ever heard! God then also told him that He would honor the commitment He had made generations before to David, and He would defend Jerusalem for David's sake.

Isaiah then instructed that a cake of figs be placed on Hezekiah's boil, a picture of how integrative healing takes place as God goes beyond what natural means of healing can do. Theologian and medical doctor John Wilkinson, however, thinks that Hezekiah's was no ordinary boil. He writes:

> Hezekiah's boil was not a simple boil or furuncle for it brought him to the point of death. It may have been a carbuncle complicated by a staphylococcal septicaemia. Another suggestion is that it was the bubo of bubonic plague and that infection may have come from the Assyrian army of Sennacherib which had just withdrawn from besieging Jerusalem. On the basis that Hezekiah's boil may have affected his throat and his speech according to Isaiah 38:14 . . . The most probable diagnosis in Hezekiah's case is that it was a carbuncle, which is essentially composed of a cluster of simple boils most commonly occurring on the nape of the neck.[13]

Then instead of simply taking Isaiah's word that he would be healed, Hezekiah asked for a sign: the shadow on the stairway built by Ahaz should advance backward by ten steps.

Here's how this happened: "On a westward facing flight of stairs the declining sun would normally cause a shadow to move upward so when the shadow went the opposite way, it had to be miraculous. As a confirmatory sign to Hezekiah, the shadow went down ten steps."[14] The story was widely circulated throughout Israel and surrounding nations. God, the sovereign God of Abraham, Isaac, and Jacob, honors the heart cries of those who throw themselves on His mercies.

In the psalm that follows his healing, found in Isaiah 38:10–26, Hezekiah acknowledges that God alone has the power of life and death and that He turned his bitterness into joy. He promises to serve and glorify God for the rest of his life. It is sad, though, that Hezekiah soon forgot what God had done for him.

While I have no intent of spiritualizing every recorded healing we discuss, several impressions are applicable to our lives today. First, while God is concerned with the ebb and flow of nations, He is just as concerned with your personal life. Notice that Hezekiah faced impending death very much alone. When you put on a hospital gown that barely covers your backside, your degrees, money in the bank, or status are meaningless. Hezekiah wore no crown as sovereign of Israel as he faced the wall, his body sobbing tears of grief.

It is also worthy to note that God honors simple, meaningful prayers that rise from the heart. No, it was not Isaiah the prophet whose prayers got through to heaven. Isaiah was simply God's messenger. James, writing centuries later, affirmed that the down-to-business prayer of a person who has been justified brings great gain (James 5:16)!

When the crisis is over, how easy it is for us, like Hezekiah, to forget the dark valley that God brought us through. When you vow to serve and honor God for the rest of your life if only He will heal you, don't forget your promise. God doesn't.

The Shunammite Woman Who Lost Her Son but Not Her Faith

When Elisha asked for a double portion of the Spirit of God which had rested upon his mentor, Elijah, little did he realize how God would eventually use him mightily during his lifetime. Elijah agreed to grant his request but only with the provision that Elisha would see him depart into heaven; Elisha vowed not to leave him. Later in the day when chariots and horses of fire separated the two as they walked together, and a whirlwind carried him to heaven, Elisha cried out, "My father, my father! The chariots of Israel and its horsemen!" (2 Kings 2:12).

From that moment on, Elisha was empowered by God to do super-natural feats that defy human explanation—miracles that testified to the world that there is a God in Israel and Jehovah is His name.

Fast-forward perhaps a year in time. The setting was a typical Israelite village known as Shunem, some seven miles east of Megiddo, overlooking the valley of Jezreel where today tourist buses stop and guides explain that the mother of all battles, described as Armageddon, will someday be fought here. A woman lived there whose husband apparently was a successful merchant because from time to time she provided hospitality to Elisha and his servant Gehazi during their travels. The couple had constructed a little walled chamber, a weath-erproof room on top of their flat house, which became known as "a prophet's chamber." Wanting to repay the woman for her kindness, Elisha asks what he can do for her. Gehazi tells the prophet that she has no son, and Elisha promises that next year at this season she will be holding a baby in her arms. "Don't lie to me," the woman cautions Elisha, but in the spring of the following year, she bears a son.

One day when the child had become a youth, he went into the fields with his father and the reapers. Suddenly the lad cried out, "Oh, my head, my head!" Today he would probably be diagnosed as having either a sunstroke or a brain hemorrhage. At any length the boy was taken home, and the following day he died.

Immediately the mother seeks Elisha, and finding him, says, "Did I ask my lord for a son? Did I not say, 'Do not deceive me?'" (2 Kings 4:28). Grasping the anguish of the woman, Elisha instructs his servant to take his staff, making no conversation with anyone, and go to the Shunammite's home, and place the staff on the boy's body. The drama quickens as the woman vows not to leave Elisha's side, so as they walked towards the village of Shunam, Gehazi, the servant, runs ahead and does as he was instructed. Nothing happens! Absolutely nothing hap-pens, so he retraces his steps, telling Elisha and the boy's mother, "The child has not awakened," a soft way of saying, "The lad is still dead."

And then the inexplicable happens, as recorded in 2 Kings 4:32–37:

> When Elisha came into the house, he saw the
> child lying dead on his bed. So he went in and shut
> the door behind the two of them [Elisha and his

servant] and prayed to the LORD. Then he went up
and lay on the child, putting his mouth on his mouth,
his eyes on his eyes, and his hands on his hands. And
as he stretched himself upon him, the flesh of the
child became warm. Then he got up again and walked
once back and forth in the house, and went up and
stretched himself upon him. The child sneezed seven
times, and the child opened his eyes. Then he summoned Gehazi and said, "Call this Shunammite." So
he called her. And when she came to him, he said,
"Pick up your son." She came and fell at his feet, bow-
ing to the ground. Then she picked up her son and
went out.

Is such a story credible in today's world? Only if you believe the
prophets of old recorded events as they happened and the texts of
Scripture have been preserved without their integrity being compro-
mised—only if you believe the God who revealed Himself as *Jehovah
Rapha*, the God who heals, is sovereign and has power and authority
over disease and death!

How do you explain what happened to the boy? What God has
not revealed cannot be explained. Sam and Ida Lacanienta, however,
have no difficulty accepting this account. You see, Ida's heart monitor
flatlined following heart surgery that had not gone well. A "code blue"
was initiated as medical personnel raced to save her life. Ten eternity-
long minutes elapsed as doctors unsuccessfully tried to start her heart.
Sam, who has served for almost fifty years as a pastor and missionary,
desperately prayed, "God, I want my wife; please don't let her die!"
Then he began praying, "Lord, I put her in Your hands. Whatever You
want is what I want." Suddenly the unexpected and inexplicable happened. The heart monitor began to bleep, bleep . . . bleep . . . and then
started recording a heartbeat that was feeble at first but grew stronger
moment by moment.

About ten minutes, so doctors say, is the length of time a heart
can stop without causing damage to the brain or other organs. Even
so, Ida has completely recovered and as of my writing has returned to

the Philippines, the land of her birth, serving along with her husband as a missionary.

John Donne, the seventeenth century British poet put it so well.

> Death, be not proud, though some have called thee
> Mighty and dreadful, for thou art not so;
> For those whom thou think'st thou dost overthrow,
> Die not, poor Death, nor yet canst thou kill me.
> From rest and sleep, which but thy pictures be,
> Much pleasure; then from thee much more must flow,
> And soonest our best men with thee do go,
> Rest of their bones, and soul's delivery.
> Thou art slave to fate, chance, kings, and desperate
>   men,
> And dost with poison, war, and sickness dwell;
> And poppy or charms can make us sleep as well
> And better than thy stroke; why swell'st thou then?
> One short sleep past, we wake eternally,
> And death shall be no more; Death, thou shalt die.[15]

Naaman—the Man Who Came Bearing a "King's Ransom"

Of the many accounts of individuals who sought healing whose stories are told in the Old and New Testaments, none has more dramatic flair that of the Syrian army officer who came to Israel seeking to be healed from the curse of leprosy.

Here's the story: A domestic servant working in the household of a captain in the Syrian military named Naaman, a highly respected officer, told his wife that there was a prophet in Samaria who could cure the master of his leprosy which was growing progressively worse. What he did not fully understand, explained by the writer of the book of Kings, was that it was not simply because Naaman was a warrior and knew no fear that he had achieved success. It was because the sovereign God of Israel, the *Jehovah Rapha*, who centuries before had identified Himself as the God who heals, had given him victory and notoriety. But leprosy that results in mangled and crippled hands and limbs that slowly lose their sensitivity to pain has no respect for military brass, kings and those in authority, or all the wealth in the world.

The phrase "but he was a leper" explains what caused his world to collapse. Hearing that there was hope to the south, across the border between Syria and Israel, Naaman procured a letter of introduction from the Syrian monarch to the king of Israel. He came laden with valuables—enough to have filled an armored truck, had they existed in that day. Included in the trove that was large enough for a king's ransom were ten talents of silver, six thousand shekels of gold, and ten sets of garments.[16]

In Naaman's day an uneasy truce existed between Syria and Israel, so when Captain Naaman, whose reputation as a military hero was probably already known to the king of Israel, arrived at the palace in Samaria with a large entourage and presented the letter from the Syrian king telling of Naaman's search for healing, the king in Israel was aghast. He tears his clothes (expensive ones at that!), a sign of his great displeasure. He's thinking, *He sent this man to me to pick a fight. He's got leprosy! Nobody cures leprosy but God!*

Elisha, the prophet who succeeded Elijah, hears of the king's distress and responds, "Why have you torn your clothes? Let him come now to me, that he may know that there is a prophet in Israel" (2 Kings 5:8). Elisha was not brazen or proud; he simply knew where he stood in relationship to *Jehovah Rapha* and was confident nothing was too difficult for Him.

So Captain Naaman, accompanied by his chariots and horses, leaves a trail of dust and goes to Elisha's humble dwelling. Signaling his arrival, he must have expected the prophet to come sweeping out of the house to welcome him, honored that someone so important had come to him. But not so! Elisha, not even bothering to come to the door, sends a servant to the door with the message: Elisha says to "go and wash in the Jordan seven times, and your flesh shall be restored, and you shall be clean" (2 Kings 5:10).

No sooner is the message delivered than Captain Naaman's face turns red. He feels insulted, furious, and humiliated. While there is no record of what he thought, he certainly must have felt rage. "Doesn't he know who I am? Who does he think he is? Why, I could wipe him off the face of the earth and leave no ashes behind!"

Naaman, revolted at the thought of bathing in the muddy Jordan, flings out the challenge, "Are not Abana and Pharpar, the rivers of Damascus, better than all the waters of Israel?" (v. 12). In this he was right. The two rivers of Syria, the first of which flowed through the capital city of Damascus, were crystal clear. But bathe in the Jordan?

But before Naaman has time to prepare to return to Syria, his own servants intervene. They remind him that Elisha is a great man with spiritual power. They encourage their commander, "Will you not do it? Has he actually said to you, 'Wash and be clean'?" (v. 13). So Naaman swallows his pride and heads for the Jordan.

When I get to heaven, I'd like to ask this man, "What were your thoughts as you waded into the muddy Jordan?" While we may never know what he was thinking, *we do know clearly what happened!* After the seventh dip, "his flesh was restored like the flesh of a little child, and he was clean" (2 Kings 5:14, italics added).

There is an interesting postscript to this drama: Naaman returns to Elisha's cottage, intent on pressing gifts upon him. Elisha refuses his many entreaties, illustrating that God's grace has never been for sale. Elisha's servant, however, like some today intent on marketing the good news, pursues the entourage and says, in effect, "Elisha has changed his mind so I'll take the gifts on his behalf." Upon his return, though, Elisha asks him, "Where have you been, Gehazi?" Lying, he says he had gone nowhere. Elisha retorts, "Was it a time to accept money and garments, olive orchards and vineyards, sheep and oxen, male servants and female servants?" The last recorded line of 2 Kings 5 reads, "So he [the servant] went out from his presence a leper, like snow" (v. 27), but Naaman returns home cleansed and healed.

Hannah—the Childless Woman Who Had a Baby

Infertility is a distressing issue to women the world over and has been for centuries, something most men don't fully understand. In many cultures a woman's self-worth and her identity as a female are wrapped up in her ability to have children. As a young pastor I was baffled at the terrible emotional upheaval I encountered when a mother-to-be lost an infant not fully formed in the womb. *She can have another one,* I remember thinking but had the good sense not to voice.

In some parts of the world, infertility renders a woman as useless, another mouth to feed, with little intrinsic value. In Papua, New Guinea, where to this day brides are purchased in the currency of so many pigs, if a woman is infertile, her husband can take her back to her parents, saying: "Here is your daughter. She can't have children. I want my pigs back."

Is it little wonder that Hannah, the wife of Elkanah, was greatly distraught because she could not conceive? Her situation was further complicated by the fact that Elkanah had enough property and resources that if he had no heir, all he had spent a lifetime acquiring would have been in jeopardy. The solution, he felt, was to take a second wife, one who could bear an heir. Thus Peninnah became his second wife; yet Hannah was the one he dearly loved.

"On the day when Elkanah sacrificed," says 1 Samuel 1:4–5, "he would give portions to Peninnah his wife and to all her sons and daughters. But to Hannah he gave a double portion, because he loved her, though the LORD had closed her womb." Those words "he loved her" became the barrier that separated the two wives. Peninnah, the second wife, provoked Hannah with snide, cutting remarks, and this went on year after year.

So disturbed was Hannah that she would not eat, and tears of pain coursed down her cheeks. "Hannah, why do you weep?" her husband asked, adding, "And why do you not eat? And why is your heart sad? Am I not more to you than ten sons?" (v. 8). He just didn't get it!

Prostrating herself in the temple on their annual pilgrimage, Hannah prayed and wept bitterly, vowing that if God will give her a son, she will give him to the Lord all the days of his life, and no razor will ever touch his head.

When her swollen eyes, red from crying, could shed no more tears, and her lips could move but uttered no sound, Eli the priest, took her to be drunk. "How long will you go on being drunk?" he asked. "Put your wine away from you."

But Hannah replied, "No, my lord, I am a woman troubled in spirit. I have drunk neither wine nor strong drink, but I have been pouring out my soul before the LORD. Do not regard your servant as a worthless woman, for all along I have been speaking of my great anxiety and vexation" (vv. 15–16). Upon hearing this, Eli assured Hannah that God had, indeed, heard her cry!

I thought of that event when on a recent visit to Israel we walked through a tunnel about eight hundred meters in length lined with magnificent, large pieces of stone adjacent to the Western Wall of the temple that stood in Jerusalem in Jesus' day. In this tunnel, known as the Rabbi's Tunnel, are separate areas where men and women can pray because they are said to be the closest place geographically to the holy of holies that Jews are allowed to access. As we passed quietly through the women's prayer area, I shall never forget the anguish of a young woman who looked to be in her early thirties, who with scalding tears was pouring out her heart to Jehovah. I thought of Hannah and her anguish and wondered if this woman was repraying Hannah's prayer that is now three thousand years old.

And God honored the cry of Hannah's heart. "And in due time," says the record, "Hannah conceived and bore a son, and she called his name Samuel, for she said, 'I have asked for him from the LORD'" (1 Sam. 1:20). The child God gave an anguished woman became the prophet destined by the Lord to anoint two future kings and a man of integrity, mightily used of God.

Hannah's story of conception, nothing short of the miraculous, gives hope to millions of women today because *Jehovah Rapha* who answered her prayer still responds to the tears and pleas of an anguished heart.

Affirmations of God's Power and Purpose in Healing

Isaiah 53:4–6—the One Who Was Chastised and Bore Our Sins on the Tree

If Exodus 15, the passage where God reveals that He is *Jehovah Rapha*, the God who heals, is the "magna carta" of biblical healing, Isaiah 53:4–6 is the constitution and bylaws because this passage was linked to Jesus' healing work by Matthew, quoted by Peter, and affirmed by Paul.[17] Here is Isaiah 53:4–6 in full:

> Surely he has borne our griefs and carried our
> sorrows; yet we esteemed him stricken, smitten by
> God, and afflicted. But he was pierced for our trans-
> gressions; he was crushed for our iniquities; upon him
> was the chastisement that brought us peace, and with
> his sounds we are healed. All we like sheep have gone
> astray; we have turned—every one—to his own way;
> and the LORD has laid on him the iniquity of us all.

Peter tells us that holy men of God wrote as they were "carried along by the Holy Spirit" (2 Pet. 1:21). Only by revelation that came by God could Isaiah have so vividly described what took place outside the city of Jerusalem when Jesus was crucified. His description is as graphic as one would have been had it been written by a bystander on that day when God's Son gave His life for the redemption of human-kind.

Many go to great lengths in weakening the "plain sense" meaning of what Isaiah wrote. Why should this passage be taken as a statement of what Christ did and what resulted from His suffering and death on the cross?

Reason 1: Following the healing of Peter's mother-in-law in Capernaum, the people living in the area "brought to him many who were oppressed by demons, and he cast out the spirits with a word and healed all who were sick." Matthew then explains, "This was to ful-fill what was spoken by the prophet Isaiah, "'He took our illness and bore our diseases'" (Matt. 8:14–17), thus drawing a straight line from Isaiah's text across seven centuries to Jesus' ministry.

Reason 2: Peter, the son-in-law of the woman with fever whom Jesus healed, was in the presence of Jesus the day He took her by the hand and healed her. Perhaps reminiscing of that event, he later wrote, "He himself [referring to Christ] bore our sins in his body on the tree, that we might die to sin and live to righteousness. By his wounds you have been healed." Continuing to link Isaiah's words about all of us as sheep who have gone astray with those to whom he wrote, Peter adds, "For you were straying like sheep, but have now returned to the Shepherd and Overseer of your souls" (1 Pet. 2:24–25).

Reason 3: Paul, recognizing the force of what Isaiah wrote, affirms the obvious meaning of the text in his letter to the Romans as he makes reference to the Lord Jesus "who was delivered up for our trespasses and raised for our justification" (Rom. 4:25).

Scrutinizing more carefully what Isaiah wrote, observe the following assertions this passage makes about the Christ who was born seven hundred years later.

1. He bore our griefs and carried our sorrows.
2. He was wounded for our transgressions ("our sins . . . that ripped and tore and crushed him" (Isa. 53:5) explains Eugene Peterson in his paraphrase in *The Message*).
3. He was crushed for our iniquities.
4. He was chastised (scourged with a Roman cat-o'-nine-tails) for our peace.
5. By His stripes we are healed.
6. He atoned for our iniquities or sins.

In telling us the "why" behind Christ's confrontation with the cross, Isaiah mentions two explicit reasons and provides a picture of the third compelling cause. While Hebrew and Greek words can often have several valid meanings depending on the context, there is almost uniform agreement that "transgressions" and "iniquities" accurately depict what Isaiah wanted us to know—that Christ voluntarily took upon Himself all of the vileness of humankind that had long since separated us from the Father's presence. And the picture that further explains is that of sheep without a shepherd who stray far from the fold.

What Isaiah wrote can be compressed into one English word— sin! Peter used this word in reference to the Isaiah passage. Writes Donald Fairbairn:

> When most of us think of sin we probably have
> in mind a few specific actions that are particularly
> horrific. But the Bible's depiction of sin is quite a bit
> more sweeping than our idea. The main concept is
> conveyed by a Hebrew word (*hata*) that is used nearly
> six hundred times in the Old Testament and a Greek
> word (*hamartano*) used nearly three hundred times in

the New Testament. Both of these words originally came from the sphere of archery and meant the same thing: "to miss a mark."[18]

Fairbairn explains that we miss the mark in three ways: First, by falling short of it, as an archer does when he lacks sufficient strength to drive the arrow to the target. Likewise, we fall short of what God demands. Second, we miss the mark by ignoring the target; and third, we miss the mark by going the wrong direction, like sheep that have wandered far from the shepherd.

Another issue, an important one, needs to be addressed briefly. When Jesus died at Calvary, did He, in fact, pay the price not only for our sins but also for our healing—emotionally, spiritually, and, yes, physically? To assert that He died only for sin brings an unwarranted separation that falls short of complete redemption from the curse of sin.

Psalm 6—David's Cry for Healing and God's Answer and Help

David begins this psalm asking God not to rebuke him in His anger or discipline him in His wrath. Turning to God's grace and mercy, David cries out, "Heal me, O Lord, for my bones are troubled" (v. 2). For whatever reason God has allowed, perhaps even punishing him for David's wrongdoing, it is certain that the fear of death looms largely before him. Thus David says, "For in death there is no remembrance of you; in Sheol who will give you praise?" (v. 5). In his day sheol was considered the abode of the dead.

David uses strong language to describe his emotions. He talks about tears that drench his pillow, the grief that troubles his innermost being, and the insults and jeers of his enemies. But then the momentum of his cry turns toward rejoicing. "The Lord has heard my plea; the Lord accepts my prayer" (v. 9). The result is that his enemies will be silenced.

While much could be written about this great man, David, with all of his flaws and failures that stained the pages of his life, was uniquely known as "a man after God's own heart." God saw beyond his flaws and failures and knew his heart.[19] No other person is so recognized in Scripture.

Psalm 38—David's Troubles and God's Mercy

In most English Bibles this psalm is prefaced with the inscription, "A Psalm of David for the Memorial Offering"; it has been so designated as an offering to God along with the grain that was given for the use of priests who served in the temple (see Lev. 2:2). Here David is in dire distress, and he readily identifies his physical and emotional affliction as God's rebuke. "Your hand has come down on me" (v. 2), says David. He says he's literally over his head in iniquity, and like a burden so heavy he cannot carry it, his failures are destroying him. He describes the turbulence of his life in graphic terms—a groaning, sighing, palpitating heart, friends who have deserted him, and enemies who are ready to pounce on him.

David is alone but knows he has not been not abandoned. "But for you, O LORD, do I wait; it is you, O Lord my God, who will answer," he affirms (v. 15). Then understanding that "with you there is forgiveness, that you may be feared" (Ps. 130:4), David confesses his sins. "I am sorry for my sin" (Ps. 38:18), he writes.

This psalm is considered a "penitential psalm." It is the cry of a man who understands his failures, repents of them, and confesses them—all of which are necessary steps to finding God's forgiveness. The point of this psalm is that some of our afflictions, though certainly not all of them, are the direct result of sin; and we will find healing only through confession and forsaking what we know to be wrong. Although it is true that some sickness is the effect of sin in our world (such as tornados, weeds, and sadness), this is entirely different from suggesting that all sickness is the result of sin.

Psalm 103—Forgiveness for Your Sin and Healing for Your Life

A letter from a friend is as follows:

> I have a question about the first verses of Psalm 103, where the writer says "who heals all your diseases," adding "I know that is a strong verse for those who believe in healing through the atonement. My question is about those words [which] are directed to "my soul." Bless the Lord, Oh, my soul. Is he not

asking for healing of the diseases of his soul? Can you tell me to whom the request is made in the original language?

Generally believed to have been written by David, the words are those of a mature individual, one who had drunk deeply from the well of life's experience and tasted sweet as well as bitter water. This is the same person who in the wilderness, cried out, "Oh, that I had a taste of the sweet water from the well at Bethlehem" causing several of his brave men to risk their lives going behind the lines of the Philistines to satisfy their leader's longing.

If David is the writer of Psalm 103, and nothing precludes this authorship, then this psalm should be read along with Psalm 51, where David pours out his soul in contrition and repentance over his adulterous relationship with the wife of Uriah. "He does not deal with us according to our sins, nor repay us according to our iniquities," says David (Ps. 103:10). He might have realized that under the law, the penalty for what he had done was stoning, forfeiting one's life; and there were no exemptions for those whose adultery took place in the palace at Jerusalem.

Healing for the soul includes the restoration of your emotional and spiritual life; but in this context, linked to the phrase "who heals all your diseases" (Ps. 103:3), it is likely that the intent of the writer is to acknowledge that healing is not metaphorical but actual, including all the sins that distress our souls as well as ruin our lives.

David talks about God's love and mercy as He lifts us from the pit of our failures and mistakes (Ps. 103:4). Corrie ten Boom, the woman who along with her sister and aged father saved the lives of countless Jews in World War II, used to say, "There is no pit so deep that God's love is not deeper still."[20] She knew this because of her time in the Ravensbrück concentration camp, a pit that consumed many people.

David concludes Psalm 103 by urging angels, "mighty ones who do his word" and "ministers, who do his will" (vv. 20–21), and his soul as well, to bless and praise the Lord.

An interesting sidebar to the study of healings that took place, as recorded in the Old Testament, is that there are four accounts of individuals who either sought healing or needed healing, and all four died of their afflictions. These four were as follows: Abijah,[21] the son of Jereboam;[22] Ahaziah,the eighth king of Israel; Gehazi (the servant of Elisha whom you met in reading the account of Naaman's healing);[23] and Uzziah, the tenth king of Judah.[24]

In the first two situations, clearly the dynastic or personal sins of the families resulted in their deaths. In the latter two cases, personal sin of the individuals brought about their deaths.

Throughout History, His Compassions Never Fail

Writing a summary of what happened over a period of time that spanned a thousand years is akin to a student attempting to write a ten-page term paper entitled, "A History of God, Man, and the Devil." From Job's expression of why an innocent person suffers to the closing chapter of the Old Testament that says, "The sun of righteousness shall rise with healing in its wings" (Mal. 4:2), there is clearly an underlying expression of God's intention to bring healing and help to troubled and suffering humankind.

While the miracles of healing are sometimes separated by centuries, the fabric of Scripture is that "His compassions fail not," and that *Jehovah Rapha*, the God who heals, responds to the heart cries of needy people like the prayer of Hezekiah, who poured out his heart with tears, the pleas of childless women, and the pleas of mothers who ask God to heal their children.

Reoccurring in many passages of Scripture, in incidents recorded in these thirty-nine books constituting our Old Testament, is the depiction of God as being sovereign, powerful, compassionate, and incomprehensible in the sense that human logic doesn't overlay the mind of the Almighty. As Paul wrote of God's dealings with Israel, "Who has known the mind of the Lord, or who has been His counselor? . . . But we have the mind of Christ" (Rom. 11:34; 1 Cor. 2:16).

Themes that appear concealed become revealed and understood through the life and deeds of God's Son, Jesus Christ. It's time to turn the page and see how God's healing nature was revealed in the ministry of Christ and the early church.

What You Need to Know

• The earliest biblical records (the book of Job as well as the Genesis account) are clear: God wills restoration and healing for humankind—body, soul, and spirit, or put otherwise, the emotional, the physical, and the spiritual. Make it personal: This is God's purpose and will for you.

• The Old Testament covers a broad span of history. From Moses' day to the end of the Old Testament (the book of Malachi), a period of about a thousand years, many accounts of miraculous healings are disclosed; although they were, at times, separated by decades, they were still significant threads woven into the fabric of history.

• God's revelation of Himself as *Jehovah Rapha* is a picture of what His Son, Jesus Christ, did in His ministry on earth; and the declaration of Isaiah that "He was pierced for our transgressions; he was crushed for our iniquities . . . and with his wounds we are healed" (Isa. 53:5) is the manifesto of eternal grace that has never been repealed. Neglected and often ignored, yes! Distorted, yes! But this great truth stands as a Gibraltar that cannot be moved, reflects the heart of the Father, was lived out in the life of the Son, and is enabled by the Holy Spirit.

• God is displeased when we grumble and complain instead of praising and thanking Him for His copious blessings. Thank God for what you have, for the comfort and sustenance you have, instead of griping about what you don't have.

CHAPTER 4

The Great Physician and His Work in the Early Church

This morning as I downloaded e-mail messages, one jumped out at me. It was from Totick Arnaldo, a dear friend who had been diagnosed with cirrhosis of the liver—something medical science is nearly impotent in addressing. Doctors gave him little hope for a normal life; however, the doctors were not Totick's ultimate source of hope. He surrounded himself with friends who know how to pray, and pray they did. I joined them in asking God to do what only He could do. Several months after the initial procedure, doctors checked what had happened in the intervening months. Wrote Totick, "When I woke up [from the anesthesia], the doctor congratulated me. She said my liver has regenerated. What happened to me is a rare case but not to God. As you have said and reminded me—God is still in the business of healing. Deep inside I know that He has already completely healed me."

Jehovah Rapha, the God who heals, sent His Son to manifest His Father's nature, to demonstrate that He was and is God, and that there is nothing too hard for Him. Totick does not have to be convinced that God cares and that God heals. He himself has experienced the powerful touch of the Great Physician.

Malachi, the last of the Old Testament prophets, ends his book with a promise—that the Son of God would come with healing in His wings. He wrote, "But for you who fear my name, the Sun of Righteousness will rise with healing in his wings. And you will go free, leaping with joy like calves let out to pasture" (Mal. 4:2 NLT). This is a promise with joy attached to it. Yet four hundred long years elapsed before "the fullness of time" had come, as Paul explained in Galatians 4:4. During that time Rome had built roads over which the disciples would eventually walk, and then God sent forth His Son—fully human, fully divine, born under the law, to redeem those who were in darkness, and to demonstrate His love and compassion in the flesh! When God chose to change the destiny of mankind, He did not send an army but instead sent a baby! And when the infant grew to maturity, He changed the course of history.

The Great Physician Was Born in Bethlehem

We will never know, this side of heaven, if in the shepherds' fields outside Bethlehem, angels sang, "Oh Mary, did you know that baby Jesus born last night will heal the sick and walk on water? Oh Mary, did you know?" But that's exactly what was to happen, fulfilling prophecies given hundreds of years before.

In His youth Jesus knew that He had come to fulfill God's purpose. As a twelve-year-old He gently chided his mother (when His parents could not find Him on the journey home from the temple), "Did you not know that I must be about My father's business?" (Luke 2:49 NKJV). Following a brief time of ministry in Capernaum, Jesus returned to Nazareth, where He had grown to manhood, and, as was His custom, went to the synagogue on the Sabbath and stood to read (as a visiting rabbi). "And the scroll of the prophet Isaiah was given to him," says Luke 4:17. Jesus, taking the scroll, fast-forwarded the text (unrolling it almost to the end—probably some twenty or more feet) to Isaiah 61. Then He began reading: "The Spirit of the Lord is upon me, because he has anointed me to proclaim good news to the poor. He has sent me to proclaim liberty to the captives and recovering of sight to the blind, to set at liberty those who are oppressed, to proclaim the year of the Lord's favor" (Luke 4:18–19).

Jesus then rolled up the scroll, handed it to the attendant and sat down. Every eye was riveted upon Him. And after a pause, He said, "Today this Scripture has been fulfilled in your hearing" (v. 21). Those who heard were flabbergasted—amazed, puzzled, and somewhat confused. "Is not this Joseph's son?" they asked. Jesus then said, "Doubtless you will quote to me this proverb, 'Physician, heal yourself.' What we have heard you did at Capernaum, do here in your hometown as well" (v. 23).

They were challenging Him to do something miraculous to prove that He was the fulfillment of Isaiah's words. But Jesus' rebuttal incensed them, and they sought to kill Him. From that time on, however, Jesus as the Great Physician began to proclaim the good news to a lost world, to heal the sick, to raise the dead, and to do mighty works of miracles that no one else had ever done.

The Great Physician and His Mission

From the beginning Jesus made it clear that His primary mission was "to seek and to save the lost" (Luke 19:10). His definitive purpose in coming was the ultimate redemption of mankind that came through the shedding of His blood at Calvary. Paul explained that through His death and resurrection, we "have redemption through his blood, the forgiveness of our trespasses, according to the riches of his grace" (Eph. 1:7). Peter amplifies: "He himself bore our sins in his body on the tree, that we might die to sin and live to righteousness. By his wounds you have been healed" (1 Pet. 2:24).

While this may come as a surprise to you, there is no record of Jesus actually being called "the Great Physician" during His ministry, although the Greek word *iaotros* from which the word for *physician* is derived is used of His healing activities many times.[1] The first to call Jesus a physician was Ignatius, the bishop of Antioch, who before his journey in chains to Rome, where he was martyred, said, "There was only one physician, namely Jesus Christ our Lord."[2] Other church fathers wrote, calling Him by the same term, including Clement of

Alexandria, who described Jesus as "the Physician of Humanity," and Origen, who more frequently than anyone known today called Jesus "the Good Physician," and later Eusebius of Caesarea spoke of Jesus as "like some excellent physician."[3]

Now we turn to what He did in the lives of many people, the actual number of which is far more than those whose healings are recorded in Scripture, those healed by the Great Physician. John concludes his Gospel saying, "Now there are also many other things that Jesus did. Were every one of them to be written, I suppose that the world itself could not contain the books that would be written" (John 21:25).

The first thing you need to know about Jesus' healing ministry is that it was not an adjunct to His teaching ministry—not a separate kind of "dog-and-pony" show that attracted large crowds of people. It was totally intertwined with the proclamation of the good news He came to bring humankind. What He did was the answer to everything that not only separates us from God but also adversely affects us— spiritually, emotionally, and physically.

Jesus specialized in impossible situations—healing diseases and illnesses for which there were no human means of alleviating or curing the suffering. He treated nervous disorders (including bipolarity and manic-depressive disorder), blindness, deafness, paralysis, chronic heart disease, gynecological disease, mutism, illnesses resulting from being demonized, leprosy, and the ultimate healing—restoration from the dead. He, after all, cheated the grave of its victim on at least three occasions.

The writers of the Gospels all considered the supernatural healings of Jesus of sufficient importance that in writing the account of Jesus' life, the space given to healing is significant. Forty percent of what both Matthew and Mark wrote consists of healing narratives. Thirty-five percent of Luke's Gospel describes healings with Luke, a Gentile physician, recording details overlooked by the other writers. And John, stressing the fact that Jesus Christ was the unique and only Son of God, gave one-third of his writing to the theme of healing.[4]

The estimated number of miracles Jesus did in relationship to individuals ranges from twenty-six to thirty-six. Why so? Medical doctor and theologian John Wilkinson explains, "If we count the number recorded in each gospel and add them together we obtain a total of forty-eight accounts, but a careful reading of the gospels will reveal that there are four duplicate accounts and nine triplicate accounts of the same incidents. . . . When we subtract these from the total of forty-eight we arrive at the figure of twenty-six."[5]

Jesus Sovereignly Healed the Afflicted

The healings of Jesus cannot be systematized, categorized, or defined in terms of who was healed for what reason. Some were healed because of their faith. Some were healed because of the faith of others, and others were healed when faith was apparently not involved. Some who had been healed immediately followed Christ, while others walked away failing even to say, "Thank you!" At times Jesus touched people.[6] At other times people touched Him.[7] On occasion He spoke words of healing and touched the sick as well.[8] Sometimes He healed simply with a word or a command (see Mark 1:25: Luke 4:35; Mark 2:11; Luke 5:24; Matt. 12:13; Luke 6:10; etc). Usually individuals were in His presence. At other times they were distant.[9] Most healings were instantaneous, but in some cases a certain action was required first, such as the blind man's having to first go wash in the pool of Siloam (See John 9:7).On three occasions healing involved the use of saliva.[10]

Here are the miracles recorded in the Gospels.

	MATTHEW	MARK	LUKE	JOHN
ACCOUNTS OF PHYSICAL HEALING				
In One Gospel Only				
1. Two blind men	9:27–31			
2. The deaf mute		7:31–37		
3. The blind man of Bethsaida		8:22–26		
4. The woman with a spirit of weakness			13:11–17	
5. The man with dropsy			14:1–6	

6. The ten lepers			17:11–19	
7. Malchus's ear			22:50–51	
8. The nobleman's son				4:46–54
9 The Bethesda paralytic				5:1–16
10. The man born blind				9:1–41
In Two Gospels Only				
11. The centurion's servant	8:5–13		7:1–10	
In Three Gospels (Listed in the Markan Order)				
12. Peter's mother-in-law	8:14–15	1:30–31	4:38–39	
13. The man full of leprosy	8:1–4	1:40–45	5:12–15	
14. The paralyzed man	9:1–8	2:1–12	5:18–26	
15 The man with the withered hand	12:10–13	3:1–6	6:6–11	
16. The woman with the flow of blood	9:20–22	5:25–34	8:43–48	
17. Blind Bartimaeus	20:29–34	10:46–52	18:35–43	
ACCOUNTS OF THE EXORCISM OF DEMONS				
In One Gospel Only				
18. The dumb demoniac	9:32–34			
In Two Gospels Only				
19. The blind and dumb demoniac	12:22–23		11:14–16	
20. The synagogue demoniac		1:21–28	4:31–37	

21. The Syrophoenician girl	15:22–28	7:24–30		
In Three Gospels				
22. The two Gadarene demoniacs	8:28–34	5:1–20	8:26–39	
23. The epileptic boy (Matt 17:14–20)	17:14–21	9:14–29	9:37–43	
ACCOUNTS OF RAISING THE DEAD				
In One Gospel Only				
24. The widow's son at Nain			7:11–18	
25. Lazarus				11:1–46
In Three Gospels				
26. Jairus's daughter	9:18–19, 23–26	5:22–24, 35-43	8:41–42, 49–56	

The fact that Jesus performed these miracles in various ways, touching a wide range of people from the destitute to the influential, underscores that none today need feel He may have failed to meet God's requirements for healing. Simply put, no one who believes is excluded! There is, however, one powerful factor that closed the door to the miraculous in Jesus' day, just as it does today: unbelief. There is not a single record of Jesus' healing anyone who disbelieved that He could or would heal. Sometimes the individual had little or nothing to do with healing, but Jesus simply chose to heal that individual.

Jesus demonstrated His total sovereignty in this regard. In spite of the miracles He did, there were times when the public still refused to believe that God had sent Him or that miracles had been done. Jesus strongly rebuked the cities of Chorazin and Bethsaida near Galilee, saying that if the mighty works that had been done in those cities had been performed in Tyre and Sidon (Phoenician cities on the Mediterranean coast), the people would have repented in dust and ashes. In Capernaum, not only was Peter's mother-in-law healed by Jesus, but a vast multitude also pressed upon Him when they heard what had happened. Yet Jesus said that the city would "be brought down to Hades" because of her people's unbelief and hardness of heart (Matt. 11:23). Mark 6:5 tells us that Jesus could do no mighty works of miracles in Nazareth, where He grew up, because of their unbelief. Matthew tells us that when Jesus taught in the synagogue in Nazareth, those who were present were offended, and Jesus replied, "A prophet is not without honor except in his hometown and in his own household." Matthew adds a postscript, saying, "And he did not do many mighty works there, because of their unbelief" (Matt. 13:57–58).

Why Jesus Healed

Vast numbers of people over the centuries have speculated as to why Jesus healed. Among the many reasons (and there is a scriptural basis for each one) are the following:

- He healed people to demonstrate His authority as the Son of God.[11]
- He healed in fulfillment of Old Testament prophecies.[12]
- He healed to show that it was the will of God to bring healing (see Mark 3:1–6).
- He healed in response to faith that He would heal (see Luke 7:50).
- He healed because of His compassion when He encountered suffering people (see Matt. 14:14).
- He healed to demonstrate that He was the Messiah (see John 5:26; 10:37–38; Acts 2:22).
- He healed to bring people into confrontation with their need of God.

Put simply, *Jesus healed people because it was His nature to heal* just as much as it is Satan's nature to destroy that which God has made. A. J. Gordon, a scholar and Bible teacher widely known in the last century, observed: "It is never intimated that He . . . [healed people] to let people know that He could. He never used power simply to let men see He had it."[13] Jesus healed people because He couldn't walk away from their pain and leave them suffering and abandoned. There is not one record of anyone who came to Christ desirous of healing and was turned away. Jesus never said to anyone:

> "You do not have enough faith."
> "You are not morally good enough."
> "You are not deserving enough for Me to do this."
> "Your situation is just too difficult for Me to handle!"
> "It is not My Father's will for you to be healed."

"Everyone who sought healing found healing?" you may ask. There is no record of anyone who came sincerely seeking help who was ever rejected or turned away. Jesus healed both those who believed and even some who were pagans; however, He never healed disbelieving skeptics who simply wanted to see a miracle. Jesus also didn't heal everyone who was sick or suffering, thereby demonstrating that healing, as such, was part of His purpose in coming but not the main reason. Luke tells us that "for the Son of Man came to seek and to save the lost" (Luke 19:10).

Following the healing of Peter's mother-in-law, large crowds pressed upon Christ and "he healed many who were sick with various diseases" (Mark 1:34). Yet the next morning after praying, Jesus told the disciples He must go on to the next towns "for that is why I came out" (v. 38). And when the lame man was healed at the pool of Bethesda, there were many others in need of healing, yet, apparently, Jesus healed only the one man.

Then there were times when many people were healed, apparently at the same time. On at least twelve occasions, say the writers of the Gospels, large groups of individuals were healed. We find inclusive phrases such as, "And as many as touched it [his cloak] were made well" (Mark 6:56). Or, "he laid his hands on every one of them and healed them" (Luke 4:40). Matthew summarizes: "And Jesus went throughout all the cities and villages, teaching in their synagogues and proclaiming the gospel of the kingdom and healing every disease and every affliction" (Matt. 9:35).

Among the healings recorded are six accounts when demonic activity is directly related to physical and/or mental illness. Evangelicals generally hold to the position that the devil's power in relationship to people today is threefold: demonic influence, demonic oppression, or demonic possession. While most Evangelicals do not believe that a Christian can be "possessed" by the devil, there is no question that they are influenced and at times even oppressed by him. The New Testament writers used a Greek word that means *to demonize*, which leaves the door open to spiritual issues that need to be addressed for the demonic hold in a person's life to be broken.

The subject is too broad for me to address; however, based on my ministry in Latin America, Europe, and Asia, including Russia and Siberia, I believe demons are territorial and often found in areas where Christianity has little influence; and believers who open the door to their activities are subject to adverse situations and even sickness.

While modern psychiatry downplays the connection of demonic activity and mental illness in some cases, the ministry of Jesus directly connected some forms of mental illness to the demonizing of the individual. When Jesus or the disciples took authority over evil spirits and commanded one to depart, the individual at hand would be completely released from his or her affliction.

Jesus, at times, intertwined powerful lessons with healing. Such is the case with the man John described as being born blind. "And his disciples asked him, 'Rabbi, who sinned, this man or his parents, that he was born blind?'" (John 9:2). Jesus' reply was that neither had sinned, but he had been born blind "that the works of God might be displayed in him" (v. 3). Of this John Wilkins writes: "What he is saying is, given that the man was born blind, the result will be that God's power and glory will be manifested in his healing. . . . He is saying to them that they should not be concerned with the sinfulness of the blind man, but with his need of healing."[14] In so doing, Jesus is saying that our job is not to argue about why something happened but to make things right and bring healing to brokenness.

Some people today, noting that almost all of Jesus' miracles were instantaneous (there are a few exceptions, however, and the healing of this man seems to be one), contend that any healing that is progressive in nature is not a work of God. Who are we to limit God or disannul His healing power if all healing comes from Him? God is full of surprises, is He not?[15] If the healings which are recorded in the Gospels are assessed fairly, it becomes evident that Jesus Christ, God in the flesh, is sovereign, just as His Father is. What He chooses to do, He does, and nothing can stand in His way.

When the man who had been healed by Christ was brought before the skeptical religious leaders of his day, the Pharisees, he was questioned, released, and brought back for further interrogation. In exasperation he cried, "I was blind, now I see!" (John 9:25)—irrefutable evidence.

Healing in the Ministry of the Twelve Who Walked with Jesus

Jesus first demonstrated His power and authority by exercising it over nature and ordinary laws of cause and effect. He turned water into wine at the wedding in Cana. He took authority over a storm in Galilee. He multiplied a boy's lunch of loaves and fishes, feeding a large gathering of hungry people. Then He began demonstrating His authority over sickness and disease by healing people.

Realizing that His mission on earth would eventually be fulfilled, He willed that what He had begun would be carried on, first by the twelve who walked with Him, then by His followers who would go into all the world with the message of redemption.

Matthew summarizes, "And Jesus went throughout all the cities and villages, teaching in their synagogues and proclaiming the gospel of the kingdom and healing every disease and every affliction" (Matt. 9:35). Mark continues the narration: "And he called the twelve and began to send them out two by two, and gave them authority over the unclean spirits. . . . So they went out and proclaimed that people should repent. And they cast out many demons and anointed with oil many who were sick and healed them" (Mark 6:7, 12–14).

A short while later Jesus expanded the group He had first commissioned. Luke says, "After this the Lord appointed seventy-two others and sent them on ahead of him, two by two, into every town and place where he himself was about to go" (Luke 10:1).[16] These individuals came back excited and rejoicing, saying, "Lord, even the demons are subject to us in your name!" (Luke 10:17).

In the Upper Room Jesus met with the disciples for the last time as a formal group. All twelve men were there, including Judas! In this powerful discourse Jesus said, "whoever believes in me will also do the works that I do; and greater works than these will he do, because I am going to the Father" (John 14:12).To whom was Jesus speaking? The twelve, all of whom had been born in Israel, none of whom at that time had ventured farther north than Tyre and Sidon (located in what we know as Lebanon today).

Obviously, Jesus was not telling them that miracles performed by them would be greater than what He had done! But He did envision their taking the gospel to the farthest corners of the world. He must have looked far beyond the twelve who sat at that table, seeing the day when Johannes Gutenberg would print the first portion of the Bible with movable type, and centuries later, radio, television, and the Internet would literally encompass the earth and empower those who spread the good news.[17]

After the resurrection Jesus walked with the disciples for forty days, demonstrating that He was alive, that death, humankind's old foe, had been defeated, and that it need no longer hold us in bondage. Then Jesus and the disciples crossed the Kidron valley, walking on an old Roman road that today is adjacent to a church known as St. Peter in Gallicantu in Jerusalem. The group proceeded toward the top of the Mount of Olives in the direction of the site now occupied by the Russian Orthodox Church; and as they walked, Jesus talked with them. He told them to stay at Jerusalem until they had been clothed with the power of the Holy Spirit. Then He gave them a charge, one that has become known as the Great Commission. Recorded by all four Gospel writers, as well as Luke writing the Acts of the Apostles, He commanded them to "go therefore and make disciples of all nations, baptizing them in the name of the Father and of the Son and of the Holy Spirit, teaching them to observe all that I have commanded you. And behold, I am with you always, to the end of the age" (Matt. 28:19–20; see also Mark 16:15; Luke 24:47; John 15:16; Acts 1:8). Then He was lifted up from them in a cloud into heaven.

Should you have a commentary Bible, you will probably notice that Mark's version of the Great Commission has a footnote or explanatory comment telling you that the earliest manuscripts of what Mark wrote do not have the inclusion of these words: "They will lay their hands on the sick, and they will recover" (Mark 16:18).[18] So, are we thus to conclude that healing was not part of the continued work of Christ following His return to heaven? Not for a moment, as Luke's account of the church in the book of Acts and the epistles bear out!

Living Out the Mandate Jesus Gave to the Twelve in the Early Church

Ten days after the ascension of Jesus into heaven, the Holy Spirit empowered the 120 who awaited His coming. No longer were the eleven who remained faithful "apostles in training" and the rest of the disciples "apprentice missionaries" Luke describes the excitement that must have warmed their hearts: "And awe came upon every soul, and many wonders and signs were being done through the apostles" (Acts 2:43). Day by day, Luke explained, they were in the temple area and were breaking bread together in their homes.

Then later, surely no more than a few days, Peter and John were on their way to the temple when they encountered a lame man. This man was carried daily to the Gate Beautiful in the temple area, where he had staked out a spot from which to beg. Seeing Peter and John, he made his plea for some alms. Then Peter, looking intently at the man, said, "Look at us" (Acts 3:4). And he did, expecting to receive money, but Peter said, "I have no silver and gold, but what I do have I give to you. In the name of Jesus Christ of Nazareth, rise up and walk!" (v. 6). Acts 3:7–8 tells us, "And he took him by the right hand and raised him up, and immediately the man's feet and ankles were made strong. And leaping up he stood and began to walk, and entered the temple with them, walking and leaping and praising God."

When worshippers saw the lame man walking and praising God, they "were filled with wonder and amazement" (v. 9). So Peter seized the opportunity to make his case for Christ, explaining, "And his name—by faith in his name—has made this man strong whom you see and know, and the faith that is through Jesus has given the man this perfect health in the presence of you all" (v. 16). There is no ambiguity here! The Great Physician was continuing His work of healing through His followers

The book of Acts begins in Jerusalem and ends in Rome. It covers a span of about thirty-three or thirty-four years, and during this time Paul's thirteen letters, along with most of what are described as general letters or epistles, can be shuffled into the time framework of the book, like how someone would take a deck of cards and shuffle separate ones into a whole. Written by Luke, a physician, the book of Acts tells the story of the growth of the early church, including the same kinds of healing that took place in Jesus' ministry—people being delivered from blindness, individuals who returned from the dead, those suffering from dysentery, crippled or paralyzed, including two delivered from demonic-related illnesses. Two accounts that stand out include Paul's recovery from blindness possibly incurred because of the bright light that shone in his face as he encountered Jesus Christ on the road to Damascus and the reviving of Eutychus from the dead (see Acts 9:18 and Acts 20:2–12).

Luke presents a history of the early church, starting with the ascension of Christ and ending rather abruptly with Paul's imprisonment in Rome. His depictions of healing are less prominent, taking less than 5 percent of the total volume of what he wrote; nonetheless, healings took place with regularity.

Consider the following healings that Luke recorded in the book of Acts:

THE NARRATIVES OF HEALING		
THE HEALING OF INDIVIDUALS		
Accounts of Physical Healing		
1. The lame man at the gate of the temple	By Peter	Acts 3:1–10
2. Paul's recovery of sight	By Ananias	Acts 9:17–19
3. Aeneas healed of paralysis	By Peter	Acts 9:32–35
4. Cripple healed at Lystra	By Paul	Acts 14:8–10

5. Cure of father of Publius	By Paul	Acts 28:8
Accounts of Exorcism of Demons		
6. The Philippian slave girl	By Paul	Acts 16:16–18
Accounts of Raising of the Dead		
7. Tabitha (Dorcas) at Joppa	By Peter	Acts 9:36–41
8. Eutychus at Troas	By Paul	Acts 20:9–12
THE HEALING OF GROUPS		
1. The sick in the streets of Jerusalem	By Peter	Acts 5:15–16
2. The sick in Samaria	By Philip	Acts 8:6–7
3 The sick in Ephesus	By Paul	Acts 19:11–12
4. The sick in Malta	By Paul	Acts 28:9
OTHER GENERAL REFERENCES TO HEALING		
1. Wonders and signs in Jerusalem	By apostles	Acts 2:43
2. More wonders and signs in Jerusalem	By all	Acts 5:12
3. More wonders and signs in Jerusalem	By Stephen	Acts 6:8
4. Signs and wonders in Iconium	By Paul and Barnabas	Acts 14:3

Healing in the New Testament Letters

James, the half brother of Christ and the leader of the early church, addresses the issue of healing in the book that bears his name. James's letter, one of the earliest books to become part of the New Testament, gives explicit instructions that the sick are to call for the elders of the church, who are to pray for them.

In Paul's thirteen letters, as well as in another eight books written by others, there are no descriptions of miraculous healings. This should not, however, be interpreted as indicating that there were none. It should be expected that when James's counsel was followed, God would bring healing to the sick. It should also be noted that the content of most of Paul's writings is primarily that of instruction or correction directed to a specific local church, usually either in response to having heard that things were not going well or to address specific problems. Reports of specific healings were not part of the agenda. The single reference to the miraculous found in Paul's letters is a somewhat ambiguous reference found in Galatians 3:5–6: "Does he who supplies the Spirit to you and works miracles among you do so by works of the law, or by hearing with faith—just as Abraham 'believed God, and it was counted to him as righteousness'?" Paul and his traveling companion and fellow-soldier Barnabas had been to Galatia on their first missionary journey (Acts 13–14). Thus Paul may well have been referring to something miraculous that occurred during that time (and several incidents were well-known to both the writer and those who received the letter), not specifically a supernatural healing.

There is no question, though, that God used Paul on many occasions to bring healing to hurting people. For a period of about eighteen months, Paul ministered in the great city of Ephesus in central Asia Minor. Luke explains, "And God was doing extraordinary miracles by the hands of Paul, so that even handkerchiefs or aprons that had touched his skin were carried away to the sick, and their diseases left them and the evil spirits came out of them" (Acts 19:11–12).

Luke's history of the early church found in the book of Acts incorporated accounts of healings that took place in various parts of the world during the same time period as the rest of the New Testament writings. Likewise, Paul has much to say about the human body, so much so that some scholars believe this was the major theme of his writings.[19] The aging tent maker turned rabbi writes of "the tent which is our earthly home" (2 Cor. 5:1) being tattered and worn. He says that "we groan, longing to put on our heavenly dwelling" (v. 2). In fact, four accounts address the reality that the body is subject to disease. Epaphroditus, a leader in the church at Philippi, took a letter back home written by Paul, telling how he had contracted some kind of infection and nearly died. Timothy had a stomach problem, and Trophimus, a Gentile Christian from Ephesus, had to be left behind at Miletus because of sickness. And, of course, Paul struggled with his thorn in the flesh.

In Paul's first letter to the Corinthians, he speaks of how those who eat or drink at the Lord's table (known as Communion in the church today) in an unworthy manner bring God's judgment. Paul said, "That is why many of you are weak and ill, and some have died" (1 Cor. 11:30). Paul, however, introduced an important concept in this letter. Speaking of spiritual gifts that were given for the building up of the body of Christ unto the work of the ministry, he mentions *charismata iamaton* or gifts of healing that were given to individuals within the church. Mentioned twice in the list of spiritual gifts (1 Cor. 12:14, 28), this gift is always in the plural form. Then, having mentioned this gift for the second time, Paul makes it clear that this gift, along with several other gifts, are not given to all believers but only to select individuals chosen by God.

The recipients of Paul's letter fully understood how this gift functioned in the church. We, however, who are two millennia downstream from Paul's time, often wish that he could have given us a few sentences more or a footnote, for explanation, so we could better understand the place of this gift in the body of Christ.

John Wilkinson explains the challenge of understanding:

> Although these gifts are given to one individual
> . . . this is usually interpreted as meaning that there
> is specialization amongst the gifts of healing with
> different gifts for different diseases, and that no one
> person could heal all diseases. It could also mean that
> a gift may be given to a particular disease. In such
> a case the individual concerned might not be called
> upon for an ongoing ministry of healing. The healing
> of Paul's blindness by Ananias in Acts 9:17 could be
> an example of this.[20]

Peter's healing of the lame man could well have been an exercise of this gift. About the beginning of the fourth century, Athanasius (b. ca. 298–373) wrote a biography of Antony who says of him: "It was as if he were a physician given to Egypt by God. . . . He is a healer but his capacity in this area derives not from medical skill or knowledge of medical prescriptions but is a gift from God."[21] Antony made it clear that it was not he who had healed someone but God alone. Based on what Paul wrote to the Corinthians as well as what we see in the first three centuries, gifts of healing should function within the church—it is not to be an independent function of individuals outside the church.

Lessons from the Great Physician and His Followers

The Great Physician Was and Is a Compassionate Healer

Compassion figures largely in healing. Matthew tells us that "Jesus went throughout all the cities and villages, teaching in their synagogues and proclaiming the gospel of the kingdom and healing every disease and every affliction. When he saw the crowds, he had compassion on them, because they were harassed and helpless, like sheep without a shepherd" (Matt. 9:35–36). The Greek word translated to have compassion, splachnizomai, means "to be moved in the inward parts of your being." It means to feel what the other feels and to empathize with the person.

The word *harass* means to be distressed or trampled upon, and the phrase "helpless like sheep without a shepherd" is the description of someone who is hopelessly lost and estranged. Of all the creatures that God ever made, sheep are among the dumbest and most helpless. The size of their brain in proportion to the rest of their body is rather insignificant. A visit to a sheep ranch in Australia drove this truth home to me. The shepherd said that because of the weight of wool, heavy with dew, a sheep that stumbles and falls is unable to regain its footing without a shepherd's help, and it would expire within three days.

Jesus responded with compassion to those who were hungry, to those who were harassed and helpless (downcast and distressed), to those who were in mourning, and to those who were sick. His unchanging nature and character mean that He is just as compassionate to those in need today as He was then, regardless of what the need may be.

Jesus Responded to Those Who Cried Out for His Mercy

On three different occasions people cried out for Jesus' mercy, and He responded by bringing healing. On two other occasions the cry for mercy came from close relatives of the sick person. This cry came with the understanding and recognition that Jesus had divine power to heal.

Each time someone pled for mercy, he or she would address Jesus as Lord, Son of David; Jesus, Son of David; or Master, thereby expressing belief in His authority to bring healing. They knew He had that power and may have seen Him grant mercy and healing. And Jesus responded to their cry and healed.

Faith Brings a Healing Connection

Faith that brought about the response of healing is mentioned in twelve healings by Jesus, and among these are eight accounts wherein Jesus recognized a person's faith. When Jesus was in Capernaum, a centurion came forward with the plea, "Lord, my servant is lying paralyzed at home, suffering terribly" (Matt. 8:6). Jesus responded by volunteering to come and heal him. The centurion, however, said that it wasn't necessary for Him to come. He believed Jesus could speak the word and the man would be healed. Said Jesus, "Truly, I tell you, with no one in Israel have I found such faith"—a sharp rebuke to Jews who thought they had an inside connection with God. "And the servant was healed at that very moment" (v. 13).

- At times it was the faith of the one who needed healing.[22]
- At times it was the faith of others.[23]
- At times it was a combination of both.

At other times, Christ simply healed individuals and faith is not mentioned.

There Is Healing in the Touch of a Hand

"He touched her hand and the fever left her, and she got up and began to wait on him," wrote Matthew of Peter's mother-in-law (Matt. 8:15 NIV). Jesus had also touched Bartimaeus and his companion, as well as the woman who had been bent over with affliction.

Along with many other dictionaries, *The Oxford English Dictionary* gives more space to define the word *touch* than any other word. Its vast gamut of meanings can hardly be compressed into a single dictionary definition.

The famed scientist Maximilian von Frey mapped the nervous system of the human body as thoroughly as Rand McNally mapped the world. He helped us understand the complex nervous system, which makes it possible for you to feel the slightest tickle on the back of your neck or sense the fly that lands on your nose as you strive to go to sleep at night.

Paul Brand, the noted orthopedic surgeon, known for his advancements in treating leprosy, believed that touch was his most precious diagnostic skill. When God designed the human body, He must have given special attention to the surface of our skin. The nervous system attaches its tendrils to the surface of your skin in such a way that portions of your body are supersensitive to touch, while other surfaces are able to withstand a good deal of onslaught without causing you discomfort.

Why did Jesus touch people? Could He not have simply healed them with a word? Of course, but He touched people to connect with them—one on one, to demonstrate His love, compassion, mercy, and tenderness. The good news is that He still touches hurting people, and His healing touch in your life can make all the difference in the world.

What You Need to Know

• The fact that Jesus healed in so many ways and with so much diversity gives us latitude as to what our expectations should be. God chooses to give us His best; and when you earnestly seek God's will, you leave the door open for Him to answer in His way, not yours. Leave the means and manner of healing to God. But keep in mind, however, that unbelief is always a barrier that closes the door of grace in our lives.

• Your response to illness should not be focused on what caused it but rather on how you can find God's healing to fix it. Don't labor on why you are sick or on the diagnosis. Self-defeating questions such as, How quickly will I die? should be replaced with ones such as, How may I find healing in God's way?

CHAPTER 5

Healings after the Close of the New Testament

I n a court of law, a credible witness is one who is competent to give evidence and is worthy of belief. A legal document states, "In deciding upon the credibility of a witness, it is always pertinent to consider whether he is capable of knowing the thing thoroughly about which he testifies."[1] The credibility of the witness, then, is dependent upon several factors. Does the individual have a vested interest in the outcome of the decision? Is there any reason for the witness to distort the testimony?

In affirming the trustworthiness of those who will be quoted in this chapter, I would point out that these witnesses were respected church leaders—pastors, elders, and bishops whose positions were verified by an ordaining group. Paul's letter to Timothy outlined clearly that Christian leaders were to be men of integrity and honesty. Furthermore, those whose testimonies are considered in this chapter had nothing to gain by distorting the truth. The manner in which they describe healings is forthright and declaratory. They were and are credible witnesses to what the Holy Spirit did in the lives of the people who suffered from diseases that medicine in their day could not cure. Consider the lives and testimony of just five of these witnesses.

Witness 1: Justin Martyr (c. 100–c. 165)[2]

Born in Shechem or modern Nabulus in Israel, Justin received a classical secular education in Alexandria and Ephesus. He pursued philosophy but found it unsatisfying. Two things resulted in his conversion. First, he watched how martyrs died in Ephesus—the same city where Paul debated the skeptics in the School of Tyrannus and where Paul's life was threatened by a mob. Justin was impressed that the martyrs died with purpose and deep commitment to the Christ whom they would not deny. The second factor that resulted in his conversion was an unplanned meeting with an old man walking by the seashore, who showed Justin how Christ was revealed through the Old Testament. Little did Justin realize when he was converted that he himself was also destined to become a martyr of the faith.

Proceeding to Rome, Justin established a school where he debated and defended the tenets of Christianity. Unfortunately, after having offended a cynic in debate, he was arrested and convicted of "being a follower of Jesus Christ," whom he refused to renounce. Christendom properly identifies him as a martyr, his having been put to death in AD 164 with six of his students, one of whom was a woman.

The following are Justin Martyr's own words:

> For numberless demoniacs throughout the whole world and in your city, many of our Christian men, exorcising [casting out demons] in the name of Jesus Christ, who was crucified under Pontius Pilate, *have healed and do heal*, rendering helpless and driving the possessing devils out of men, though they could not be healed by all the other exorcists, and those who used incantations and drugs.[3] [italics added]

Witness 2: Irenaeus of France (c. 130–c. 200)

The date of his birth is uncertain. Some say he was born as early as AD 130, and others say much later. But we do know Irenaeus was a disciple of Polycarp who, in turn, was a disciple of John, the writer of the Gospel and the book of Revelation. Born to a Christian family, Irenaeus grew up in the Christian faith. He is best known for being an apologist (defender of the faith) and strongly opposing Gnosticism (the subject of John's first and second letters), the philosophy that claimed to have secret oral traditions coming from Christ Himself. Serving as pastor of the church in Lyons, France, Irenaeus was a prolific writer who wrote in Greek, and his writings were influential within the church for many years.

Irenaeus saw the healings that took place in the Christian faith as evidence of authentic Christianity, something that was lacking in Gnostic or pagan groups. In his apologia against heretics, he observed, "Those who are in truth His disciples, receiving grace from Him, do in His name perform miracles and they do truly cast out devils. Others still heal the sick by laying their hands upon them, and they are made whole. Yea moreover, as I have said, the dead even have been raised up and remained among us for years."[4]

Writes R. J. S. Barrett-Lennard, whose doctoral dissertation focused on the life and writings of Irenaeus, "He does not therefore simply refer in a general way to 'gifts of healings,' but states in positive terms that 'others, still, heal the sick.' His language here is quite unqualified."[5] Although Irenaeus does not describe healings in which he himself was a participant, he often mentions individuals who were healed, speaking "with the kind of conviction that is consistent with close acquaintance with the matter to which he refers."[6]

Circumstances surrounding his death are unknown, but the heritage he left behind influenced generations to come.

Witness 3: Tertullian of Carthage (c. 160–c. 225)

Raised in Carthage in Africa, Tertullian was the son of a Roman centurion who by profession appeared to have had formal training as a lawyer.[7] While it is uncertain that Tertullian was ever a pastor or bishop, it is clear that he was a leader, and his writings widely influenced the church. Called the father of Latin theology, Tertullian was the first on record to use the term "trinity," one of the most widely debated issues of the third century. While the details of his conversion to Christianity are unknown, what is known is that in about 197–198, Tertullian was converted. It was described as "sudden and decisive, transforming at once his own personality." Of himself he wrote that he could not imagine "a truly Christian life without such a conscious breach, a radical act of conversion," adding, "Christians are made, not born."[8]

And what was Tertullian's witness to the fact that healings of a miraculous nature took place as the Word of God was taught in Africa? He describes a clerk "who was liable to be thrown upon the ground by an evil spirit" who "was set free from his affliction, as was also the relative of another, and the little boy of a third." Then clinching his argument as a lawyer would do, he adds, "And how many men of rank, to say nothing of the common people, have been delivered from devils and healed of disease?"[9]

Witness 4: Clement of Alexandria (c. 150–c. 215)

Born in Athens, Clement received a classical Greek education, and his writings are sprinkled with quotations from Grecian poets and philosophers. As the son of a wealthy pagan, Clement enjoyed a life of luxury traveling through his native Greece, then Italy, Palestine, and finally Egypt, where he became the colleague of Pantaenus, the head of a religious school in Alexandria, and who likely converted him to Christianity. Clement succeeded Pantaenus, taking over the school he had founded. Widely criticized for his attempt to wed Greek philosophy with Christian thought, Clement, nonetheless, impacted the lives of many, including his student Origen, who, in turn was to take his place among Christian leaders of the early church.

And how did Clement view miraculous healings in his day? A letter to a friend explains his position: "Let them [young pastors] therefore with fasting and prayer make their intercessions, and not with well-arranged, and fitly ordered words of learning, but as men who have received the gift of healing confidently to the glory of God."[10]

Witness 5: Origen of Alexandria (c. 185–c. 254)

The next witness to the fact that healings continued following the completion of the New Testament books is a somewhat controversial man who wrote little of his own accomplishments; however, Eusibius, the bishop of Caesarea, collected hundreds of his letters, codified them, and saw that they were preserved. Origen was a young man, seventeen years of age, when a fierce persecution of Christians broke out in Alexandria (Egypt), where he lived. When his father was martyred, Origen became the breadwinner for the family.

Aided by a benefactor who saw great potential in this young man, Origen received a classical education that enabled him later in life to meet pagan Greek philosophers on level ground and to defend the faith. As many of the Christian leaders of the third century were, Origen was staunch in defending Christianity against Greek philosophy. In one his polemics against a false teacher, speaking of individuals in the church who had gifts of healing, Origen wrote the following:

> And some give evidence of their having received
> through their faith, a marvelous power by the cures
> which they perform, invoking no other name over
> those who need their help than that of the God of all
> things, and of Jesus. . . . For by these means we too
> have seen many persons freed from grievous calami-
> ties, and from distractions of mind, madness, and
> countless other ills, which could not be cured by men
> or devils.[11]

Driven out of Alexandria in 232, Origen went to Caesarea, a Roman city on the coast of Palestine, which was less hostile to what he was doing, and there he continued his writing and teaching. Eusibius, the man who collected Origen's works, stated that he had written more than six thousand letters or works, leaving behind a vast trove of materials that became a historical treasure.[12]

Says A. J. Gordon in summarizing the early church, "Prove that miracles were wrought, for example in the second century after Christ, and no reason can be thereafter urged why they might not be wrought in the nineteenth century,"[13] and I would extend that period to continue through the ages unto the coming of God's Son to claim His own at the end of the age.

A Few Among Many[14]

I have focused on the testimonies of five Christian leaders (otherwise known as church fathers) of the period following the close of the New Testament and the death of the apostle John, the last surviving person who was an eyewitness to the healing ministry of Jesus Christ, through the time of the conversion of the Roman emperor Constantine and the forming of the institutional church. They are, however, simply representative of a far larger group—unknown faithful men and women who proclaimed the gospel, anointed the sick with oil, and saw disease and impending death release its hold on God's children. Observes Evelyn Frost,

> The literature of the first 300 years of the church's history is full of evidences of healing of various degrees of value . . . some direct and some indirect, showing that the healing work of Christ and the physical union with him were part of the normal life of the members of his body.[15]

Craig Keener's two-volume book *Miracles—the Credibility of the New Testament Accounts*, published in 2011, is the most comprehesive body of historical data ever assembled demonstrating that supernatural healings continued throughout church history. The sixty-six-page chapter entitled "Supernaturalism in Earlier Christian History" has 580 footnotes documenting testimonies of healing.

As time passed, a small number of individuals, often ascetics or hermits who had dedicated their lives to prayer and contemplation, had "gifts of healing," which Paul described in his letter to the Corinthians (chap. 12). And, yes, there have also been accounts of frauds who feigned spiritual powers and were denounced as such by the church—a loose network of congregations scattered throughout the world.

During those years preceding the recognition of Christianity as a valid religion under Constantine in 313 and the landmark Council of Nicea in 325, the church was finding its way and refining its doctrine. It was striving to determine what was valid, recognized, and believed by church leaders throughout the world. It was however, about to go through, a period when lives would no longer be threatened with death by its enemies, and manifestations of the power that said, "Rise up and walk" to the crippled and the sick would become diminished, though never extinct.

Gaining Respectability or Paying a Price?

Author Evelyn Frost contends that the church lost something vital—independence and the touch of God—when it was no longer a reproach to acknowledge that you were a Christian. Others disagree, contending that Emperor Constantine's conversion was genuine; and although he was politically sensitive, his era gave birth to the greatest age of theological writing the church has ever seen. Constantine, explains Peter Leithart in *Defending Constantine: The Twilight of an Empire and the Dawn of Christendom*, has been the "whipping boy of the church" for a long time, and his name has been identified with anti-Semitism, hypocrisy, and manipulating the church for political gain. Leithart refutes the position that this powerful ruler acted as the final authority in ecclesiastical matters.

At any length the conversion of this powerful ruler, who bore the esteemed title *Pontifex Maximus*, became a kind of continental divide of church history as well as the nature of the church itself. Born in the year 274 to Constantius Chlorus and Helena, Constantine followed in his father's footsteps, becoming a powerful military leader himself. After the death of his father in York (England), he was proclaimed emperor by the legions of Gaul. According to oral tradition not supported by history, he was suddenly converted when a cross appeared in the sky along with the inscription, "By this thou shalt conquer."

The emperor used his sword in keeping political factions in balance, says Clemens Peterson in a religious encyclopedia edited by the respected church historian Philip Schaff. He points out, "Constantine may have seen some phenomenon in the skies; he was no doubt convinced of the superior claims of Christianity as the rising religion; but his conversion was a change of policy, rather than of moral character."[16]

Before this Event, Why Had Christians Been So Hated?

For 270 years, from the death of Stephen, who was stoned in Jerusalem, to the conversion of Constantine, Christians were constantly on the receiving end of persecution. Some were hunted down and killed for their beliefs. Some were burned at the stake. Others were burned to death in the imperial gardens. Some were fed to the lions in the arena. The bodies of others were covered with pitch and oil and became human torches to satisfy the perverted whims of dictators. Tacitus, the Roman historian, tells us that Nero inaugurated an era of persecution that continued, in varying degrees, until the conversion of Constantine. Nero, a depraved and corrupted Caesar, had Christians sewn into the skins of wild animals. They were then attacked by his hunting dogs for sport.

Nero's persecution, however, paled in comparison to the vehemence of Emperor Diocletian who issued the first of four decrees targeting followers of Jesus Christ in AD 303. "When the Romans put their mind to it," says Peter Leithert, "their tortures could be exquisite."[17]

Among the practices that were chronicled by Eusibius, a fourth-century bishop and historian, were butchering by the sword, burning in fire, sometimes slowly roasting parts of the body while trying to keep the victims alive, pounding reeds under fingernails, pouring molten lead down the backs of Christians, gouging out eyes, and severing hands, feet, and appendages.[18] Following Jesus Christ in baptism was like putting a target on your back. Being a committed disciple of the Galilean came with a price.

It was open season on Christians. Why? What had Christians done to become the offscouring of the earth to the pagans of Rome? There were reasons, shallow as they may be.

1. The innate goodness of the believers annoyed individuals whose consciences were pricked by their belief system. Christians were monotheistic and worshipped one God. Furthermore, they came home at night to the same husband or wife. They denounced homosexuality, which was common in early Rome, along with infidelity. The fact that many of the Caesars were openly homosexual only made the distaste that Rome had for this sect of Judaism, as it was first viewed, more pronounced.

2. Rome further disliked the fact that Christianity primarily appealed to the working class, for the rich have always resented the poor. Compound that with the prejudice of anti-Semitism because of the Judeo background of Christianity, and you have a strong case for hostility.

3. The dogmatism of Christianity also rankled the sweeping pantheistic climate of Rome that involved the worship of hundreds of deities, all of which were idols or mythological figures. Christians denounced idols and affirmed that Jesus Christ was Lord of lords and God of gods. Smug arrogance was the way Rome viewed it. In Rome there was a structure of groups known as guilds, similar to unions today, and each of these held to a patron god; but Christians would not participate in the rituals or ceremonies that invoked the blessing of the gods. They would wear neither amulets nor charms for good luck. They stood out as being different, and different they were. Eventually rumors surfaced that in the sacrament of Communion Christians actually ate the flesh of people and drank their blood in a strange love feast that was accompanied by orgies. Naturally individuals chose to believe this rather than to discover the truth.

4. Rome resented the fact that Christians were militantly evangelistic and took advantage of every opportunity to proselytize people from all faiths. Unwilling to let Christianity be just another religion, Christians insisted that there is no other way to gain favor with God apart from believing in Jesus Christ.

5. Christians held dogmatically to a belief in the death and resurrection of Jesus Christ, who spoke of a final judgment when all men would give account for their sins.

6. Christians refused to offer blood sacrifices to pagan rulers which was considered an act of defiance and contempt. Those who refused were forced to leave civil or military service, lost their jobs, and became targets of persecution.

Take these six together and you've woven a fabric of hostility that still surrounds believers in some parts of the world today. In all fairness, however, it should be pointed out that persecution did not blanket the Roman Empire apart from specific times such as the period from Diocletian to Constantine's reign (303–313). At times, much like in China and some of the Muslim countries today, persecution was local. In some areas it was intense but relatively short-lived, and in other areas there was a measure of freedom.[19]

Entering the Mainstream

With the conversion of the Emperor Constantine, marked by the Milan Edict in 313 that made it illegal to stone or kill Christians, things began to change rather rapidly. Properties that had been confiscated were returned. Those who had been imprisoned were released. Then the following year, a cross appeared on Roman coins, and Constantine's children were raised as Christians. No longer was it necessary for believers to meet in the catacombs of Rome, behind locked doors, or deep in the heart of a forest to avoid detection and persecution. No longer was it acceptable to accuse Christians of killing their children and drinking their blood at a ritual believers described as "the Lord's Supper."

Whether the conversion of Emperor Constantine was a heartfelt conviction or a political move of expedience is something historians debate, and since we are so far downstream from the actual event itself, it is unlikely that the issue of his sincerity and motives will ever be fully understood. What is certain, however, is that things changed.[20] Pagan temples were converted to houses of worship, and for the first time in history believers had a place they called "a church." The church eventually became thought of as a *place*, not *the body of Christ*, a living organism. Buildings, such as the massive Temple of Bacchus (the god of wine) at Baalbek in Lebanon and the Temple of Aphrodite in Ephesus, became churches. It often followed that pagan priests who had once worshipped Baal, Bacchus, Ashtoreth, Chemosh, Re, Zeus, and a pantheon of other deities were "converted" and became priests celebrating the Eucharist. Religion became politicized without changes of heart.

Large numbers of individuals also converted to Christianity, though many of them were probably motivated by something other than true faith. A cartoon well depicting what took place shows a Christian, sword drawn, with his foot resting on the neck of a pagan lying on the ground, ready to execute him. The pagan looks up and says, "I'm terribly interested in your new religion; tell me more about it."

Some believe that when Christians gained respect and a measure of authority, it was payback time, as those who had been on the receiving end of discrimination, if not persecution, gained not only status but in some cases a measure of political clout that allowed them to take vengeance on their enemies. Did they do this? To their shame and loss, some did. Gradually, persecution that Christians had endured was generally ended, but unfortunately, in the process—gradually, not overnight—the purity of the suffering church was tarnished. The cross of Jesus Christ became a religious symbol rather than a picture of the cost of redemption paid by Him who was impaled upon it to purchase salvation for humankind.

Slowly, over a long period spanning centuries, the church as a dynamic, living organism whose existence was demonstrated by its supernatural character including gifts of healing and the miraculous became an institution that vied for recognition and eventually political power.

By the time Christianity was no longer *religio illicita*[21] (illegal religion), the Christian faith had become firmly entrenched in every major city of the world—Rome in the West, Constantinople in the East, and Alexandria in Africa, as well as in thousands of cities and hundreds of thousands of villages and hamlets.[22] Church fathers, such as those previously quoted, continued to write, minister, celebrate the Eucharist, and baptize and evangelize; yet the dynamics of Christendom were changing.

The Sovereign God Who Heals Still Healed

Testimonies of healing did not entirely disappear in the life of the church. In the year 429, Theodore of Mopsuete (Mopsuestia was a free town on the Pyramus River in what we know as Central Turkey today), the son of a wealthy merchant, had something to say. While Theodore's personal life was complex—he was torn between the love of a woman and a life of celibate monasticism—his keen intellect and inquiring mind produced many codices (books), some of which were readily embraced by his contemporaries and others that were denounced with the same vehemence; but when it comes to his being an accurate witness of what God was doing, there is no debate. He observed, "Many heathen among us are being healed by Christians from whatever sickness they have, so abundant are miracles in our midst."[23]

In the next generation Gregory the Great became a missionary to Britain.[24] There he used his inherited fortune to establish six monasteries. Adopting a simple cowl (a hood worn by many religious orders), Gregory anointed the sick with oil and prayed for them, quoting the words of James 5:14–15. Later he was recalled to Rome, where he served for fourteen years as Pope Gregory I. He was admired by the reformer John Calvin, who in his *Institutes* called him the last "good pope."

Contrived Works of Healing

When the church began to lose its supernatural power, remembering that Jesus wrought miracles that attracted masses of people, some within the church found it easy to encourage belief with miracles that were often overblown or contrived.

With the rise of fraudulent demonstrations of the supernatural, few were willing to apply the New Testament standard of "by their fruits you shall know them" (Matt. 7:16) and denounce what eventually became the show window to masses of people, many of whom were uneducated and certainly lacked a knowledge of God's Word.

Works of healing—authentic, miraculous displays of the power of God—eventually became fewer. Insidiously weakened and marked by carnality, lacking the power of God and the faith that God would heal, churchmen modified their bankrupt theology, saying, "God no longer does that sort of thing." And, indeed, they were partly right, for works of healing were seldom taking place within the institutionalized church.

Over a period of time there was a gradual shift in theology, allowing a "suffering redemption" concept to develop—that suffering is a cross that God wants the righteous to bear, that the cross reminds us not only that Christ suffered, but that you must also suffer—a flagellant mentality that is observed even today in places such as the Philippines, where devotees beat their backs bloody on Good Friday to take away their sins.

During this era written history, usually the prerogative of educational institutions such as monasteries and the church, was sparse. While there were manifestations of God's grace and power, just as there had been in previous centuries, we have few written records affirming this.

The Church Pitted against the Changing World

As time etched a path through the Middle Ages (a period of history generally considered to be between AD 500 and 1400), the divergence between the church and the world of science became more pronounced. Two camps or disciplines gradually emerged. The church viewed disease as the result of sin whereas individuals with inquiring minds began to see natural causes for sickness and disease, causes not connected with moral behavior. And did the church welcome these tiny advances in knowledge and healing? No, they were challenged by them and often refuted not only what fledgling scientists began to discover but also threatened those who challenged the church's view with excommunication or physical punishment.

Gradually the transition from faith in the church, which believed in the supernatural, to faith in science, which could explain why you were sick and what could cure your suffering and pain, began to drive an intellectual wedge that separated the two groups until recent years.

Do we have further documentation for healing during this period of time? It is fragmentary, but neither do we have documentation for much of what transpired during the Middle Ages, when most historical records were kept by monks. Later, the universities of Europe became places of learning where historical events both theological and political were more widely recorded.

In 1177 Peter Waldo began preaching on the streets of Lyon in France, condeming certain practices of the church. As a result, the church authorities excommunicated him and those who followed him, declaring them to be heretics. Going from town to town and meeting secretly with believers, the Waldensians, as they became known, would hold services and confess sin and wrongdoing, and their leaders would anoint the sick with oil and pray for them. The Waldensis Confession of faith read:

> Therefore, concerning this anointing of the sick,
> we hold it as an article of faith, and profess sincerely
> from the heart that sick persons, when they ask it,
> may lawfully be anointed with the anointing oil by
> one who joins with them in praying that it may be
> efficacious to the healing of the body according to the
> design and end and effect mentioned by the apostles;
> and we profess that such an anointing performed
> according to the apostolic design and practice will be
> healing and profitable.[25]

Persecution followed the Waldensians, who left colonies of believers in Italy, South America, the United States, Germany, and elsewhere.

The Reformers: Luther, Calvin, and Their Followers

It is impossible to understand the thinking of the Reformers (most of whom condemned practices in the Roman Catholic Church such as buying forgiveness for sins, known as an indulgence) apart from putting yourself in their position. You must think as they thought, which means that for centuries the supernatural had been replaced with a kind of pseudo-manifestation of the power of God although He has never closed the door on grace and never failed to respond to the humble heart cries of His children.

The reformers, including Martin Luther, John Calvin, John Huss, and Hugh Latimer, had a natural distaste for the contrived healings that had become part of what captured the interest and devotion of the masses. This is not to suggest that on occasion those who made pilgrimages to holy sites did not receive a healing, but it is to advocate clearly that the process of biblical healing that was handed down by the apostles and practiced in the early centuries in churches in Palestine, Europe, Africa, and elsewhere was abandoned and not retained as an ongoing part of the ministry of the church.

Subsequently, "the reformers argued that the primary purpose of New Testament miracles was to authenticate the apostles as trustworthy authors of Holy Scripture."[26] Nonetheless, as you will see in the section that follows, the reformers believed that genuine miracles did happen.

Martin Luther was a man whose position was never ambiguous. He was either totally in favor of something or vehemently opposed to it. While he denounced the fraudulent, he embraced the authentic. Says A. J. Gordon, "The testimony of Luther's prayers for the healing of the body are among the strongest of any on record in modern times."[27] Luther writes, "How often has it happened and still does that devils have been driven out in the name of Christ, also by calling on his name and prayer that the sick have been healed?"[28] In typical Lutheran fashion, the village priest of Wittenberg, turned reformer, visited his friend Philip Melanchthon, who had become ill and even near to death. According to the Lutheran historian Veit Ludwig von Seckendorf, here is what transpired.

Luther arrived and found Philip about to give up the ghost. His eyes were set; his consciousness was almost gone; his speech had failed, and also his hearing; his face had fallen; he knew no one, and had ceased to take either solids or liquids. At this spectacle Luther is filled with the utmost consternation, and turning to his fellow travelers says: "Blessed Lord, how has the devil spoiled me of this instrument!" Then turning away towards the window he calls most devotedly on God.

He beseeches God to forbear, saying that he has struck work in order to urge upon him in supplication, with all the promises he can repeat from Scripture—*that He must hear and answer now if He would ever have the petitioner trust in Him again.*

After this, taking the hand of Philip, and well knowing what was the anxiety of his heart and conscience, he said, "Be of good courage, Philip, thou shalt not die. Though God wanted not good reason to slay thee, yet he willeth not the death of a sinner, but that he may be converted and live. Wherefore, give not place to the spirit of grief, nor become the slayer of thyself, but trust in the Lord who is able to kill and to make alive." While he uttered these things Philip began, as it were, to revive and to breathe, and gradually recovering his strength, was at last restored to health.[29]

Later, writing to a friend, Philip wrote, "I should have been a dead man *had I not been recalled from death itself by the coming of Luther*." And Luther, in a letter to a friend, conveyed the same thought: "Philip is very well after such an illness, for it was greater than I had supposed. *I found him dead, but, by an evident miracle of God, he lives.*" Never let it be said that Martin Luther did not believe in the power of a sovereign God to bring miraculous healing to whom He chooses, in His will, in His time.

From the Reformation to the Twentieth Century

From the time Johannes Gutenberg invented movable type, about 1440, communication began to expand, and with better communication came greater knowledge of what God was doing in different parts of the world.

Groups such as the Waldensians, Moravians (United Brethren), Huguenots, Covenanters, Friends, Baptists and Methodists all saw healings that were inexplicable apart from the fact that God sovereignly chose to heal individuals. In his book *The Ministry of Healing*, A. J. Gordon cites numerous examples of this in many different areas of the world—England, Scotland, Wales, and the islands of the Pacific, as well as in North America, and some countries in Asia.

In the eighteenth century John and Charles Wesley were mightily used of God in reaching masses of people. Although he was ordained in The Church of England, John Wesley, following in the steps of George Whitfield, often ministered to large groups of people in fields and chapels. In his diary, published as *The Journal of John Wesley*, this itinerant preacher who logged thousands of miles on horseback, with a book in one hand and the reins of the horse in the other, records answers to prayers for healing in a matter-of-fact way. The following are some of his entries:

> FEBRUARY 4, 1739: I prayed for a lunatic boy today; he was instantly healed.

> MAY 19, 1739: My brother Charles was stricken with pleurisy. I prayed for him, bodily strength returned from that hour.

> APRIL 19, 1756: My disorder returned as violent as ever, but I regarded it not while I was performing the services at Snowfields in the morning, nor afterward at Spitalfields, til I went to the Lord's Table to administer [holy communion]. A thought came into my mind, "Why do I not apply to God in the beginning rather than the end of an illness?" I did so and found immediate relief.

SEPTEMBER 2, 1781: I believe it my duty to relate here what some will esteem a most notable case of enthusiasm, be it so or not, I aver the plain fact. In an hour after we left Taunton, one of the Chaise-horses was on a sudden so lame that he could hardly set his foot to the ground. It being impossible to procure human help, I knew no remedy but prayer. Immediately the lameness was gone, and he went just as he did before.[30]

John Wesley believed not only in prayer for healing but also in the efficacy of medicine. In 1746 "he opened the first free medical dispensary to be established in England for the treatment of the sick poor."[31] The following year he authored a book on practical medical advice that was so popular, it remained in print for more than a century. Wesley believed in integrative healing—medical treatment enforced by God's healing power.

Where Do We Go from Here?

The clear and compelling testimonies of godly men and women from the days of the apostles to the beginning of the twentieth century show irrefutably that the sovereign *Jehovah Rapha*, the God who heals, never ceased to touch suffering men and women at the point of their physical pain and need. The extended hand of God's compassion and mercy, however, touched the lives of people in relation to the way they honored God as men and women who humbly cried out to Him in faith for healing.

It is also evident that when the church went through seasons of disbelief and refused to abandon its own agendas, striving to fabricate miracles of healing as opposed to allowing God to work sovereignly His will in the lives of people, authentic works of healing became fewer. And God's hand of healing was seemingly withdrawn. Yet the nature of God did not change. But as Jesus could do no mighty works of miracles in Nazareth because of her people's unbelief, so the Father never forced Himself upon unbelieving men and women.

The twentieth century saw unprecedented changes in our world never before witnessed by any generation. Science and technology came into its own. Two world wars wrought devastation such as had never before even been conceptualized as the power of the atom was unleashed. And our world's population skyrocketed, bringing increased suffering and heartache. Man has walked on the moon, invented the Internet, grown more knowledgeable—yet in many ways, has grown weaker.

But where is God in relation to all of these changes, and does He will healing today just as He has for the previous twenty centuries? Read on. The best is yet to come.

What You Need to Know

• There is no biblical or historical evidence supporting the position that miraculous healings ceased upon the death of the last apostle or with the completion of the New Testament as we know it today.

• Miraculous healings, according to the writings of church fathers in different geographic locations, continued as a reflection of the supernatural character of the church until the days of Constantine and the emergence of the institutional church. Thereafter records are sparse until the times of the reformers; however, there is no reason to disbelieve that, on occasion, healings that could only be described as miraculous yet took place.

CHAPTER 6

Those Who Could Have . . . Should Have . . . Would Have Died!

Healings that Defy Human Rationale

M y wife and I had just come out of China to Hong Kong (before Hong Kong had become part of the People's Republic of China), and I received an urgent message from my father to pray for my mother. She had been treated for uterine cancer years before, and now it had returned. At that time radiation was relatively new, and subsequently the treatment she was given severely scarred her abdomen. "Pray that God will heal her," my father requested. "Daddy, I would love to see God heal her and He may, but I cannot pray for this. I will pray for God's will in this situation telling Him how I would rejoice in her healing."

I have always taken great heart in what Paul wrote to the Romans that applies to situations such as this. He wrote,

Likewise the Spirit helps us in our weaknesses
[the Greek word also means physical afflictions]. For

we do not know what to pray for as we ought, but
the Spirit himself intercedes for us with groaning too
deep for words. And he who searches hearts knows
what is the mind of the Spirit, because the Spirit
intercedes for the saints according to the will of God.
(Rom. 8:26–27)

While my father prayed, "God heal my wife!" I prayed earnestly believing that God would, indeed, answer His way.

What happened? Without radiation, chemo, or any other treatment, the tumor that was the size of a man's fist shrank to the size of a golf ball, then the size of a thumbnail, then disappeared entirely! I personally talked to her physician, who told me, "I have heard about things like this, but this is the first time in my career I have ever seen this happen!"

When my mother died almost a decade later, it was from heart failure—not cancer! Skeptics, of course, strive to disallow that God can and does, on occasion, intervene in an unexplainable manner. Giving God the freedom to be God and affirming that this Sovereign is a good God makes room for Him to work His will as He chooses—not as we dictate.

In this chapter I have written of healings that are about as "skeptic proof" as they come, having spoken personally with some of the physicians who were involved or having on file lab reports that document what I have described. A common thread weaving these stories together is that in the face of overwhelming odds, a compassionate, caring God did something miraculous that brought glory to Himself and often resulted in others embracing the faith of the one who was healed. Meet some of God's choicest works of grace.

John Margosian: The Man Who Lived Sixteen Years Beyond His Time

April 24, 1915 was a dark day in history because on that day Ottoman Turkish authorities arrested some 250 Armenian intellectuals and community leaders in Constantinople and forced them to march hundreds of miles to their deaths in what is now known as

Syria. It was the infamous beginning of what was to be known as one of the world's vilest genocides, recorded on that dark page of history along with the millions who died under Stalin's purge, the Holocaust, and the Killing Fields of Cambodia. Fear was struck in the hearts of thousands of Armenians who lived with the reality that they, too, were potential targets.

Among them was the Margosian family who had found Christ through the witness of missionaries. At the time John was a nineteen-year-old man living in the city of Smyrna (yes, the same place as is mentioned by the apostle John, writing to the seven churches of Asia). Little did John then realize that the word *Smyrna*, which means "suffering," would years later characterize his own personal life.

"When my grandparents settled in New York," reminisces John's daughter, Joanie Piper, "my father got involved with gangs and got into some trouble. All the while my grandfather prayed." When the depression of the 1930s created soup lines and desperation, John and his young wife decided to follow the family to the west coast, tantalized by the "California promise" of a better, more prosperous life. By this time John Margosian and his wife were expecting their first child when John's brother, Peter, for the sake of the forthcoming child, urged the couple to start going to church with him. When John rejected repeated invitations to go to church, Peter used straight talk. He told John that if he wanted to go to hell, it was his choice, but he should start thinking about the child that was near birth to give the baby a better life.

This time the message got through. The Margosians went to a little Baptist Church in Los Angeles where one Sunday Pastor Bill Britten preached about the thief on the cross. Joanie Piper explains: "He said that if there was anyone there who thought he was so bad God could not forgive him, he was wrong. My dad ran down that aisle and fell on his face and gave his life to the Lord. He never turned back."

Transformed, John became "a praying man." He would wake up at 5:00 a.m. to spend time on his knees and eventually joined a team of men who went into a local prison to minister.

But then in his early seventies, John's health declined. He began losing weight. His skin became jaundiced. An upper GI done by his health-care provider wasn't conclusive, and that's when Dr. Dennis Cope,[1] one of our day's most respected and celebrated endocrinologists, a humble physician who treats ordinary individuals with the same care as he treats celebrities of renown, examined John.[2]

Dr. Cope says, "John Margosian, along with his wife and daughter, came to see me as a patient in 1984 at the age of seventy-five. I was on the internal medicine faculty of the UCLA School of Medicine. He had been losing weight, his stools were pale, and his urine was the color of Coca-Cola. He clearly had an obstructive jaundice. A CT scan of his abdomen later day that revealed a pancreatic tumor involving the head of the pancreas."[3]

Then it was time for a surgeon to take over. Dr. Herbert Machleder, chief of Vascular Surgery at UCLA, opened the stomach of John Margosian to remove the life-strangling tumor. But what he found was beyond the skills of even one of the finest surgeons in the world. The tumor, which had wrapped itself around the abdominal aorta and inferior vena cava, was inoperable. While he was doing the surgery, Dr. Machleder biopsied the tumor, "demonstrating by surgical pathology that it was an adenocarcinoma of the pancreas," or, in layman's terms, cancer of the pancreas, one of the deadliest cancers known today.

Dr. Machleder, the surgeon, gave him three months to live at the longest. The sick man was given chemotherapy and radiation "just so that the tumor would not enlarge," explained Dr. Cope, adding that there was no cure for this type of cancer.

"But what we didn't know at the time," related Dr. Cope, "is that he had a bunch of brothers who were praying for him!" In addition, Joanie Piper explains, "The elders of the church came to the home and anointed him with oil and prayed. Also, the prisoners out at Chino Prison where my dad ministered for thirty years began to fast and pray."[4]

Following a bout with spinal meningitis, the patient was put in isolation for two weeks, and his family was told that if he did survive, "he would be a vegetable."

But the two long weeks passed, and the patient, whose funeral should have been scheduled, started eating and gaining weight. "It was amazing," says his daughter. "We took him back for follow-up, and they did all sorts of tests and could not find the tumor. He went back to ministering [in the prison] and back to his work at the church as custodian. Dad lived to the ripe old age of ninety-one."

In a conversation with Dr. Cope, I asked, "Do you consider this to have been a miraculous healing?" He responded, "Very definitely! There is no human explanation for what happened."

Brian Wills: The Man Who Had Only Ten More Hours to Live

Brian Wills graduated with honors from Drury University with a degree in business administration, but the great passion of his life was not business; it was tennis. As a collegian athlete, Brian had the most wins of any player in school history—121 of them. He was a nationally ranked player at the age of twenty-two, who had been invited to Europe where he would compete against some of Europe's finest athletes.

In January 1987, just days before he was scheduled to leave, a sudden pain that he described as "liquid fire" spread across his abdomen as he was practicing on the court. Concerned, he saw his family physician, who assured him it was nothing more than the results of training too hard.

Then the day before he was to leave, the pain struck again with vengeance. This time his family doctor told him that he was alarmed over his blood count and sent him to the hospital. Brian realized he wasn't going to be on that much awaited flight.

For the next nine days doctors tried to find out what was wrong with him. Then on February 6, the lead doctor delivered the equivalent of a death sentence: "I have some really bad news." He began telling the family that Brian had a mass in his abdomen the size of a golf ball that had been diagnosed as Burkitt's lymphoma—a quickly growing disease with no known cure.

At that time only three hospitals in the world dealt with this disease, and through the intervention of a doctor-friend, Brian was admitted to one of them, the National Institute of Health (known as the NIH) in Bethesda, Maryland. The doctor, however, was not optimistic and even told Brian's family that this disease often killed children in a single day.

After admission to the hospital, Brian was told that he was "too far gone" and that "nothing could be done for him." Remember, Brian was a muscular athlete in his physical prime, yet nothing could be done for him. The sentence of death hung over his head.

By then the cancer had spread to his lungs, liver, and most of the organs of his body. "Today is Tuesday," said Dr. Young, recognized as one of the world's leading authorities on Burkitt's lymphoma, "and your son won't be alive by Friday."

On Friday, however, Brian *was* still alive, but doctors had no hope for him. His right kidney hadn't worked for weeks, and doctors said the tumor was growing by the hour. "I don't know if you will make it until morning," he was told. Then turning to his parents, the physician said, "I give him ten hours or less to live."

In his book, *10 Hours to Live*, Brian describes how he felt: "Time stood still. The earth stopped spinning on its axis and skidded to a stop in its celestial tracks. Too stunned to speak I looked out my hospital room and thought, *I'll never step outside and feel the wind on my face again. I'll never play the European circuit. I'll never hit another tennis ball. What will my dog think when I don't come home?*"[5]

As doctors stood in the hall outside his hospital room talking with his parents, Brian began praying the most earnest, heartthrobbing prayer of his life, pleading with God to spare his life. Some call that kind of prayer "foxhole religion," but to Brian it was simply the earnest cry of a young man who knew God does heal and that He can be counted on.

Brian heard no audible voice, but deep within he heard the quiet voice of a loving God say, "Son, I am your Healer; and I will manifest healing to you as you take the steps I tell you to take. You will walk through the fire and not be burned." And the word *forgive* loomed before him. Immediately he visualized the face of a person with whom he had a disagreement a long while before. Brian had completely lost touch with this person, and then, strangely, he recalled his phone number.

Still able to speak, Brian called the individual and asked for forgiveness. While I don't know if Brian knew this passage from Scripture, he knew the concept. Long ago, David said, "If I regard iniquity in my heart, the Lord will not hear me" (Ps. 66:18 KJV).

If ever someone wanted God to hear his heart cry, it was Brian. Then in the early hours of the morning, the admitting nurse, the same one who less than twenty-four hours before asked him, "Have you made your funeral arrangements yet?" came to check on him. Turning on the light, she noted his vital signs, examined the readings of the monitors that were attached to his body, and suddenly exclaimed, "Oh, my gosh! Your kidney has started working."

Certain that he would die within hours—perhaps minutes— nurses as well as doctors stayed close by. Brian, however, did additional heart searching, asking God to reveal any remaining unforgiveness, sin, bitterness, or resentment in his life. Cramming for his finals before he met God? No! He was simply making sure he was *right with God.*

Brian, however, did not die as anticipated, although the medical staff who attended to him did not immediately recognize that the impossible was taking place. No one—not one single person diagnosed with Burkitt lymphoma in its advanced stage—had ever walked out of the NIH Hospital! The medical staff continued to prepare him for his death, something he refused to accept or believe. "Living in denial" was the actual phrase entered on his medical chart hanging on the wall over his bed.

Yet something inexplicable was happening. His kidneys both regained function; his distended, bloated abdomen began to shrink. The pain dissipated, and most important of all, HE WAS ALIVE!

Then on February 20, a CT scan was ordered after which he was told: "We don't understand what is happening to you. . . . There's no longer a tumor in your abdomen. No cancer in your liver, lungs, or muscles. No cancer in your kidneys or brain. There's no trace of Burkitt's lymphoma in your body! And we have no explanation!"[6]

The year Brian Wills made history, the only person ever to be so debilitated by this fatal disease and walk out of the hospital with no evidence of the lymphoma in his body, the National Institute of Health used his picture as their "poster boy." While physicians and medical personal, many of whom were openly skeptical, couldn't understand, Brian and his parents knew what had happened: *Jehovah Rapha*, the God who heals, the One whose Son raised the dead, set aside the sentence of death, and gave Brian a miracle.

Brian went on to play professional tennis for a period of time, then went to Bible school and has since gone all over the world spreading the good news that "there is a God who still performs miracles."[7]

"No Cancer Is Present" . . . But There Was Just a Few Days Ago!

Chuck Swindoll is one of the most trusted and respected evangelicals alive. Having served for many years as pastor of one of America's finest churches, his warm style, commitment to the Word, and gracious demeanor have endeared him to thousands of people. His award-winning radio program *Insight for Living* has reached hundreds of thousands. He is given neither to hyperbole nor exaggeration.

In his book *Flying Close to the Flame*, Swindoll has a chapter entitled, "A Biblical Case for Healing." In this he relates how he became friends with a fellow marine, and with the passing of years their friendship only deepened. One day, however, he received a phone call from his friend; and as soon as Chuck heard the man's voice, he knew something was wrong.[8]

The voice on the other end of the phone grimly said, "I need your prayers as I've never needed them before." The man's tone of voice immediately brought concern to Chuck as he replied, "What is it?"

The friend told him that he had been diagnosed with cancer of the tongue, and as he related his visits to the best medical specialists he could find, his voice quivered and broke. We live with the stereotype that "real men" don't cry; but for an ex-marine, you can take that one notch further, unless you happen to be the one who got one medical opinion, then another, then a third, *and they all were pessimistic.*

Hopeful that specialists at Mayo Clinic, one of the best medical facilities in the world, could operate and leave him with at least part of his tongue, the friend and his wife were packed and ready to go, X-rays in hand. "I'm asking you and about four other close friends to pray," he said. Chuck's friend was right with God and believed that God could bring healing and would—subject to His will.

In his basement was a "hiding place," where Chuck met God on a serious one-to-one basis, and there he prayed earnestly for almost an hour. Then, says Chuck: "I did not hear any voice. I did not see any vision. But I had an unusual feeling of confidence and a sense of peace about my friend's situation." He went upstairs with the assurance that God had heard his prayer, and he put the whole issue in His hands.

Several days later the phone rang. It was his friend who requested prayer for healing. His voice was different. The element of fear was gone. Calling from Minnesota where he had consulted with doctors in Mayo Clinic, he began, "I have great news!"

"Well, what is it?" Chuck asked.

"I have seen several specialists, and my wife and I have just met with our attending physician. He is baffled, Chuck. He tells us there is no cancer."

"Hey, this is great. Tell me what they said." Chuck responded.

"Well, actually they put me through all the tests again and took more X-rays. They don't believe I brought the correct X-rays with me."

But he had! In his possession were two sets of X-rays—one that showed the presence of cancer and one that showed his tongue to be completely clear—no evidence of cancer whatsoever!

In assessing the experience, Chuck wrote: "I can't explain what happened. He couldn't either. I have no powers within me that produce healing in anyone else. . . . I simply trusted Him and prayed for His will to be done. The Spirit of God healed my friend sovereignly and silently. And best of all, God got the glory."

The facts speak for themselves: Cancer was identified by three oncologists, specialists who diagnose and treat people daily. Earnest, fervent prayer was made for the man. Then within a few days, experts at one of the finest facilities in the world said, "No cancer is present!" And as Chuck Swindoll said, "Best of all, God got the glory."

The Healing that Allowed Guy Duffield to Trust God

Guy Payson Duffield was one of the most godly men I have ever known, a scholar and committed student of the Bible, whose passion was preaching and teaching the Word of God. In his ministry of more than seventy years, Dr. Duffield was a stabilizing influence in his denomination, conservative, not given to exaggeration, and certainly committed to absolute and forthright honesty. I preface sharing the story of how God met him by letting you know that this man held the medical profession in high esteem, having undergone several life-changing surgeries himself. While Dr. Duffield consulted a physician and followed the limited advice the doctor was able to give in that the incident took place in 1936, he completely sought God to do what only He can do. Had God not met him as He did that night, I am absolutely confident, he would have turned to the pediatrician for surgery in the morning. There was never the slightest blemish to his life of service; hence, the following testimony speaks for itself.

> Quite a few years ago now, when our daughter, Darlene, was about 1½ years of age, we were having special meetings in a church up north, and our daughter was not well. Mrs. Duffield told me she seemed to have a cold, so we prayed for her, but her illness continued.
>
> The next day or so my wife said, "Darlene has an earache." I asked, "What are you doing for it?" and she said, "Well, I'm putting a little warm olive oil on cotton in her ear, and that is about all I know to do." We continued to pray for her, as you do, of course.
>
> The next night when I came home from the church service, my wife said, "Darlene has an earache in the other ear." She wasn't improving. Her appetite was gone. She would just lie there listlessly in the carriage or in the crib, and we began to get concerned. I went downtown to the child specialist—Dr. McDonald, I think his name was—and I told him about the symptoms. I told him what we were

doing—just putting a little warm olive oil in her ear, and he said, "Well, that's about all you can do. I don't know anything else to suggest. Just keep her warm and continue doing that."

Almost as an afterthought, he asked, "Her ear doesn't stick out, does it?" I said, "Well, no, I don't think so." Then he said, "Of course, if it sticks out and fills in the back there, that's mastoid." I've always had an awful fear of mastoid. I almost had it one time myself, and the very thought of a doctor taking a chisel and a mallet and chipping away the bone behind my baby's little ear just sent chills up and down my spine. You may be sure that when I went home that evening I looked very carefully to see if her ears were flat against her head, and they were.

The next morning, however, one of her ears was sticking out absolutely at a right angle. There was no crease whatsoever behind that ear. You'd never know that there ever had been a crease; it was just absolutely solid. I knew immediately what it was.

My wife looked at me, and I looked at her. She said, "We're going to have to do something; either we're going to have to pray through on this thing, or we're going to have to get the doctor. Now which are we going to do?" I said, "I don't know. I'm going over to the church and pray."

I closed myself in the study, got down before God, and you know that sometimes you pray, and then other times you *really* pray. I want you to know that morning, I really prayed. As I talked to God there, it seemed to me that my whole ministry in regards to God's healing power was at stake. I either had to believe what I'd been preaching to others and apply it to myself and our own situation, or else I felt I could never preach it again. Now, I certainly would not say that that applies to everyone, but I know it applied to me that morning.

As I wept and cried before the Lord, it seemed that everything was at stake—my little girl's life, my ministry, what we had been preaching and telling others to do—it was all at stake that morning. Then, my friends, all of a sudden—I can't describe it to you any other way than this, but it just seemed to me that a great big chunk of faith dropped right down in my heart. I felt it there instantly, and I looked up and I said, "Lord, we're going to trust You."

I went home and told my wife my decision. She said, "All right, then let's fulfill the Word of God. Let's call the elders to come and pray." We hadn't done this yet, so we tried to get hold of the elders of the church, and we could only reach one of them, dear Brother Russell. He came over that evening. I knew that he was a man who knew how to pray. He had several children in his family, and I knew from personal contact that whenever they got sick, he laid them on the bed and looked to God for their healing, and I was encouraged that he was at our home to pray with us.

We went upstairs to the room where our little baby was in the crib, and we began to pray about 8:00 o'clock. We prayed there around the crib continuously until about 10:30 p.m., and by this time the other ear was in exactly the same condition, absolutely straight out at right angles with no crease in the back at all.

Finally Brother Russell had to leave. He encouraged us to keep on praying and keep on believing God, and we went back upstairs and began to pray some more. You know that kind of praying wearies you. I found that when Darlene was awake and tossing and crying I'd get busy praying. Then from sheer exhaustion she'd fall into a restless sleep and stop crying, and I'd sort of rest and we'd let up a little bit. Then I could see that that wasn't the right way. You had to keep praying and believing for her, whether she was crying or sleeping, whether she was resting or tossing.

So we prayed on through the night, hour after hour, holding on to God. By this time I was flat on my back on the floor crying to God. I remember telling the Lord, "Your Word says, 'I am the LORD, who heals you'" (Exod. 15:26 NIV). I said, "Lord, I don't know what it means except what it says. Some may think it means one thing, and some may think it means another; but Lord, all I know is what it says. It says, 'I am the Lord who heals you,' and I'm going to take it for what it says. Then I remember also realizing in that hour that everything was in Jesus. I remember lying there flat on my back looking up, and saying over and over and over again, "Lord, it's all in Jesus; it's all in Jesus."

I don't know how long this went on, but it must have been about 1:00 o'clock in the morning as I lay there with my eyes closed pleading the merits of the Lord Jesus Christ that suddenly a witness came to my heart—suddenly I knew! I didn't open my eyes; I didn't look at my baby; I knew in my heart that something had happened. I burst out weeping and my wife came over and asked, "What's the matter?" "My baby's healed," I said, "My baby's healed."

In just a moment I heard her stir, and the old devil said to me, "She's going to cry just like she has been." She had been doing this off and on for hours, sleeping about ten minutes, then crying, and then falling off into an exhausted sleep, then crying again. The old enemy said, when I heard her stir, "She's going to cry just like she did before." I said, "Lord,

it's all in Jesus. It's all in Jesus." You know, not a sound
came from her lips. She turned over and went to
sleep. I wasn't looking at her. I was just looking to the
Lord. In a few minutes more I heard her stir again,
and the old enemy said once more, "Now she's going
to cry just like she has been crying." I said, "Lord, it's
all in Jesus; it's all in Jesus."

That was the last sound I heard until about 7:30
in the morning, when we wakened to the sweetest
little song, the loveliest childhood cooing and singing
that you have ever heard. We got up from the bed and
went over to the crib. Those two little ears were just
as flat to her head as mine are, and the matter that
had poured out of both of those ears was all over that
pillow cover. My wife still has that as a remembrance
of what God did for us in that night. Blessed be His
holy name!

The postscript to the above testimony is that the baby girl who
was healed that night became my wife in 1959 and has served alongside
me since then. She is a women's conference speaker, author of almost a
million books in print, mother and grandmother of eight. Somewhere
in a trunk containing family heirlooms and old photo albums is a small
baby pillowcase, where the drainage from the infected mastoid stained
it—a visible testimony to the reality that *Jehovah Rapha*, the God who
heals, showed Himself strong, something for which I shall always be
grateful.

Fast Forward Three Generations

"He looked so very small the day he huddled up in his bed and
told me he 'just wanted to go to heaven,'" related his mother, Bonnie
Craddick. Here's the rest of the story:

My heart sank and I struggled to hold back the
tears. Andrew, our six-year-old, had been a happy,
healthy toddler.

And then the stomachaches began.

The stomachaches began and his appetite dwindled to nothing. The arrow on the bathroom scales froze in place, and struggles over eating began.

"He's fine," said the pediatrician.

But a year stretched into two, and Andrew wasn't fine. His tummy hurt, and he didn't eat, and he said his throat burned, and he lay down and sucked his thumb. We tested, we poked, we prodded, and Andrew never cried. "He must be used to being in a lot of pain," a specialist surmised.

First we found a bacterial infection. We bombed his thirty-eight-pound body relentlessly with three different drugs, three times a day, but he didn't get better.

"Lactose intolerance" another test found, so we went dairy-free and that helped . . . a little. An endoscopy showed ulcers and a hiatal hernia—acid reflux.

The pill parade intensified, *but he didn't get better.*

By summer Andrew practically couldn't function. He couldn't get in and out of the car without help; he would only eat a tiny bit in the morning and collapse onto the sofa by afternoon. He was cranky and said his "bones hurt."

"Maybe you should consider a child psychologist," one doctor ventured.

In desperation we called UCLA and booked an appointment—there was a six-week wait. That was the day Andrew talked about heaven. Distressed, we called again the next day. "Were there *any* cancellations?" "Why yes! Tomorrow at 1:00."

A family member had been praying specifically for a cancellation.

"Something is wrong," the new specialist said, "and I think it's celiac disease." It wasn't something that could be cured, but it could be managed. Another

look into his little body was needed to cinch the diagnosis. Upper and lower GIs were scheduled for August 4, 2000.

Family and friends at our church, and all over the world, had been praying for Andrew. In keeping with James 5, we asked the elders if they would also come and pray. They came the night before Andrew's procedure at UCLA, anointed Andrew with oil, and asked God to heal him.

August 4 was a strangely disappointing day. We were called into the procedure room where our small son lay, anesthetized. "There is no evidence of celiac disease," the UCLA specialist said quizzically. "In fact, there are no ulcers, no hernia, nothing that appeared in the previous tests. I find nothing abnormal." It somehow wasn't an answer. "Stop all medications, stop everything, and go home for a month," was the prescription.

We went home but something wasn't the same. A week went by and then two. "I'm hungry," said Andrew. "Let's play ball," he chirped to his brother." He ate, and he played, and he gained two pounds.

Weeks turned into a month, then nearly two, but *Andrew's stomach didn't hurt anymore.*

Back in the doctor's office, there was no human explanation for Andrew's improvement. "No explanation," said our UCLA man. "We can only tell you that we prayed," we explained to an incredulous physician. "Our friends, family, and church prayed to a God who is able to do 'exceedingly abundantly above all we ask or think!'"

Fall turned into spring. Andrew ate and grew. Within six months of that day in UCLA, Andrew was pitching his way onto the Little League All Star Team and earned the Presidential Physical Fitness Award, scoring among the top fifteenth percentile of children across the nation. *And his stomach didn't hurt anymore.*

Eleven years have come and gone now with no pain, no physical problems of any kind. *Andrew is well.* Inexplicably well.

He was touched by the God who healed his grandmother two generations before. You see, Andrew Craddick, is the grandson of the woman whose healing story as a baby preceded this one.

Andrew Murray: A Pastor Who Lost His Voice

William Lindner Jr. dedicated his biography of the life of Andrew Murray "to everyone who had hoped to one day meet the man behind the books." I include myself in that number. Murray was one of the most influential Christian leaders of the nineteenth century, touching three continents for God.

Born in South Africa into a pastor's home, young Andrew grew up where prayer was as common as having an evening meal. At the age of ten, he was sent to school in Scotland, and upon graduation from Aberdeen he went to the University of Utrecht in Holland where he received a theological education. In May 1848 Andrew, along with his brother, was ordained by the Dutch Reformed Church and sent back to South Africa, where he spent the rest of his life in ministry.

At the age of fifty-one, however, Murray's ministry was challenged. He lost his voice, and enforced rest didn't bring it back. Neither did a prescribed ten-day period when twice a day he inhaled a special mixture of medicine and steam. Forced to give up his responsibilities as a pastor as well as the moderator of the synod (an elected position of prestige), Murray grew frustrated and concerned that he might never preach again. He knew that God had called him to serve Him, but when he could not preach, something that he customarily did with volume and fervency, he wrote his first book, *Like Christ*. It became one of more than two hundred that eventually came from his pen, followed by *Abiding in Christ*.

During this time he focused almost relentlessly on what the Bible says about healing. He tried to figure out whether or not his sickness was caused by sin, which means sickness would be God's discipline, or sickness was simply the infirmity of living in a human body, abiding in a "tent" as Paul described the body to the Corinthians, which is weathered and worn.

While Andrew was away for a conference, he wrote the following to his wife:

> My thoughts have been a good deal on the ques-
> tion of God's purpose for this long silence enforced
> upon me. You know what I have previously said about
> the two views of affliction: One, that it is in chastise-
> ment for sin; the other that it is in the light of the
> kindness and love of God. I have felt that it was a very
> great kindness to have such a time for the renewal of
> my bodily strength and of mental quiet and refresh-
> ment for the work before me. . . . Let us pray earnest
> that our gracious God would search us and try us and
> see whether there be any evil way in us.[9]

About the time Murray's voice was growing somewhat stronger, he caught a cold that caused a serious relapse of his problem. This time, though, he was unable to speak publicly and had to give up all forms of public ministry. However, loved by so many in the Wellington, South Africa congregation he served, Murray and his wife were sent to England, where a "silent" Andrew Murray could only nod or shake his head in assent or dissent.

His biographer says of this period: "It was obviously a time of distress and great searching. One can see that in his letters during this time of silence, Andrew's love for God and his sense of being loved by God, seemed never to falter."[10]

During this time Murray wrote this now popular quote, some-thing I have had in the flyleaf of every Bible I have owned for the past forty years or more:

Andrew Murray:

In times of trouble, God's trusting child may say:

First: He brought me here; it is by His will I am in this strait place: in that will I rest.

Next: He will keep me here in His love, and give me grace in this trial to behave as His child.

Then: He will make the trial a blessing, teaching me the lessons He intends me to learn, and working in me the grace He means to bestow.

Last: In His good time He can bring me out again—how and when, He knows.

Say: I am here—1. By God's appointment, 2. In His keeping, 3. Under His training, 4. For His time.

Then underneath were the words of Psalm 50:15, "And call upon me in the day of trouble; I will deliver thee, and thou shalt glorify me" (KJV).

In the weeks that followed, two truths from James 5 became clear to him. There is a difference between "suffering" and "disease," and the pattern of James 5, where the elders of the church anoint the sick person with oil, praying the prayer of faith, would result in healing. Hearing of a newly opened retreat center in London that promoted prayer, Bible study, and small-group encouragement, Andrew and his wife, Emma, participated daily. And Andrew Murray's throat was healed! Whether it was instantaneous or gradual is unknown, but a new and different pastor Andrew returned to the church he had all but given up ever serving again in Wellington. He preached for more than thirty years, never again with a raspy or weakened voice. After he was healed, Murray preached at the Keswick deeper life conferences in Britain, teamed up in ministry with Dwight L. Moody, and four times served as moderator of the Dutch Reformed General Synod.

Two years later Murray's book *Divine Healing* was published, becoming one of his most widely read and beloved books, and it is still available today. For the rest of his life, Andrew Murray regularly prayed for the sick "and saw many though clearly not all healed."[11]

Healing In a Nepalese Village Where
a Westerner Had Never Set Foot

When Tom Hale applied for entrance to medical school, never did he think that, on the first day of school, the person assigned to work with him sharing a cadaver would eventually share his life experiences as his wife! Tom's specialty became surgery; Cynthia's became pediatric medicine. In 1970 they packed their bags, and with two sons in tow, journeyed to Nepal—a land of massive mountains, shamans, superstitions, and tremendous physical and spiritual needs. Their years in both the mountainous village of Amp Pipal and the capital city, Kathmandu, are chronicled in *Living Stones of the Himalayas* written by Dr. Tom Hale.[12]

To meet the medical needs of people in mountainous areas, both Drs. Tom and Cynthia would periodically trek for hours over mountainous trails, sometimes precipitously clinging to the side of a mountain. It was such a mission that Cynthia had embarked upon, going from Kathmandu to the medical station at Amp Pipal. Having heard about an isolated group of Christians where an outsider had never been, Dr. Cynthia went out of her way to find them, to let them know they were not alone, that others in Nepal shared their faith. She was also interested in finding out how they had heard the gospel and how this "Christian community" had been birthed.

As she plodded along hour after hour, she began thinking, *Perhaps this group doesn't exist, or if they do, I must have taken the wrong trail.* Yet about that time far in the distance she saw the roofs of a few houses. *This must be it,* she thought. As she approached the settlement, she noticed that the houses were sporadically placed here and there. She thought that the people did this so they might live as "secret Christians," avoiding attention from the authorities, who would have been hostile to their Christian faith.

As she approached the first house, a stocky tribesman with Tibetan features and a wrinkled face walked toward her with a warm and open expression. "Are you a Christian?" Dr. Cynthia boldly asked, and without hesitation the man replied, "Yes, I am. Who are you looking for?" Explaining that she had come to locate the Christian community, she inquired, "Is this it?" He acknowledged that it was, and then with a sweep of his hand, the man, whose name was Sukh Badadur, explained that most of the village was about an hour's trek away with houses on the crest of a ridge.

As the two of them climbed towards that ridge, Sukh Badadur stopped at every house, exchanging warm greetings and talking in their dialect. Cynthia later learned that at every stop, he was inviting people to a meeting that night.

Says Dr. Tom: "Before Cynthia's visit, no Western missionary had ever been to the village of Duradada. No one, it seemed, even knew of its existence. How then did this community of Christians come into being, springing up as it were out of nowhere?" Gradually Cynthia pieced the story together.

Some fifteen years earlier, Lok Bahadur, a Tamang tribesman from a district west of Kathmandu, had come to a village known as Pokhara carrying a load of goods to sell. While he was there, he learned about a hospital run by Christians who believed in a God who heals people in answer to prayer. These "Christians" didn't acknowledge Hindu deities; they didn't kill chickens or summon a shaman (an alleged healer who calls upon the spirits to heal). They simply prayed to their God, and people were healed.

When Bahadur returned to his village a few days later, he discovered that his ten-year-old daughter was sick—very sick. In his absence his wife had called in the leading shaman, and for three days the shaman had pronounced his incantations over the girl, whose condition grew progressively worse. Bahadur told his wife what he had just heard about Christians who simply prayed and the God of these Christians healed people. His wife and family scoffed at the thought. After all, for generations people there had used shamans and killed chickens as a sacrifice to evil spirits.

Nonplussed but determined, Bahadur called upon the God he had just heard about to heal his daughter. After he had prayed for several hours, he fell asleep; but when he awoke in the morning, the girl was completely well. His wife and neighbors were unconvinced. They credited the incantations of the shaman for her recovery. A week later, however, another girl became ill, and Badhur offered to pray for the child. "What do we have to lose?" reasoned the parents. Badhur prayed for the girl, whose parents had given up hope, realizing that death was near; and by the following morning the girl was completely well.

This time, though, a furor developed. Bahadur was accused of witchcraft and being in the same league with demons, but the parents of the healed girl thought otherwise. They believed it was God who healed their daughter. As time went on, Bahadur, with no theological background, no formal education, and no Bible, began praying with simple faith for people to be healed, and *repeatedly they were healed and then became followers of Jesus Christ.*

This, however, was not without a price to be paid in the currency of rejection and eventually persecution. Neighbors turned against the Christians, who had broken with tradition and customs. Acts of vandalism took place. Crops were destroyed. One believer's home was burned to the ground. Followers of the Christian's God were threatened physically. When Lok Bahadur left the village, the care and leadership of the believers fell upon a man whose wife had also been healed, Bir Bahadur.

Then one day the male believers were summoned to the center of the village. There they were angrily accosted by the shamans, who were being put out of business, and other critics. Their hands were tied behind their backs, and they were beaten with sticks and fined a large sum of money. If they should continue in their beliefs, they were told, they would be assessed more fines and receive further punishment.

Enough is enough, thought the determined little flock of fledgling believers. It was time to move. Having heard about a tract of land that the Nepalese government had set aside for homeless or destitute people, as thousands of other persecuted believers had done before them in far-flung places over centuries of time, four families left the village where they had been born and raised for a new home where they could pray without persecution. (At this point they had not yet encountered anyone who could fully explain the gospel, nor had they seen a Bible.)

After three days of walking while carrying their possessions, they came to the clay, waterless slopes of Duradada—uninhabited and very much uninviting. But they were free. Gradually other groups—mostly believers hearing about the new settlement—joined them. Then, in spite of the threat of persecution, Bir Bahadur began going back to his old village where he would be asked to pray for the sick, and more healings resulted. Gradually those who had been healed wanted to join the Christian group who prospered on the ridges of Duradada. Missionary medical doctor Tom Hale summarizes: "As Duradada grew, more and more new people began to join in the worship of the Christian God. Prayer for the sick became an integral part of the life of the entire settlement, and with each healing, the faith of the people grew."[13]

The night Cynthia spoke for the first time in the village, fifty Christians gathered to hear her. After she had spoken for thirty minutes, fearing that if she spoke much longer she would lose her audience, she stopped; but an uncomfortable silence followed. After prayer and a few songs, the leader asked for questions; and for the next ninety minutes, Cynthia explained what the gospel is about and answered their questions about the God who heals. Long before the last person left that gathering, Cynthia, exhausted from the rigorous trek as well as ministry, was asleep on a mat on the floor.

Dr. Tom concludes his story that unfolded in a Nepalese village where a missionary had never before gone by saying, "'A city set on a hill cannot be hidden.' Duradada is such a city."[14]

Healings Where the Word *Impossible* Is Not Spoken

Following the healing of a man who had been crippled from birth, Peter seized the opportunity to speak to a large crowd of people. This, of course, did not sit well with the religious authorities, who gave orders that they should be arrested and detained overnight. The following day when the religious authorities had gathered, they questioned them as to by what power or name they had healed the lame man. With the man who had been healed standing beside him, Peter, filled with a fresh infusion of the Holy Spirit, answered them. They were speechless. "What shall we do with these men?" they asked.

When the disciples were released, they met together and gave thanks to the Lord, ending their time of prayer with these words: "And now, Lord, look upon their threats and grant to your servants to continue to speak your word with all boldness, while you stretch out your hand to heal, and signs and wonders are performed through the name of your holy servant Jesus" (Acts 4:29–30).

Notice that supernatural healing was one of the attestations to the fact that God had empowered them, and the same miraculous healings that certified Jesus was the Son of God, authenticated their ministries as the continuation of what Christ did.

The hand of God often touches lives, bringing healing in order to certify His presence and power in dark areas of the world where unbelief and spiritual opposition are present. I have seen this in Africa, Latin America, and Asia. In 1979, after several years of being turned down for a visa, I was finally allowed to enter China, the land of millions of people who were raised under Communism and told, "There is no God!" When the Communists took over in China in 1949, the population of the entire country was about 450 million (today's estimate is about 1.39 billion).

As the Maoist government began systematically to purge the church, many people—fearful of reprisals, imprisonment, and death—renounced their faith and turned their back on Christ. David Aikman, a one-time bureau chief for *Time* magazine and author of the book *Jesus in Beijing*, has said that the number of Christians who stood fast was only about 500,000. Bibles were confiscated and destroyed. Churches were closed. Believers were given the choice of denying Christ or going to prison—a fate many chose.

As churches were closed and converted to warehouses or factories, tens of thousands of believers began to meet in secret. Gatherings of believers were often referred to as "the underground church." However, meeting in a tiny apartment behind closed doors, or in the forest to escape the prying eyes of "watchers" who were seeking out Christians much as Saul of Tarsus did prior to his conversion, did not really mean "they were underground." They were simply not meeting publicly. Neighbors knew. Relatives knew as well.

I have fond memories of the years following 1979, when my wife and I personally met with many such fellowships over a period of several decades. Never shall I forget the looks of inexpressible joy on the faces of people, meeting in unheated rooms in the dead of winter. The lyrics of the songs they sang reflected a simple faith, a determination to stay true to the Lord in times of persecution, a focus on heaven, and a love for Jesus. We also observed a childlike faith that God honored. This was especially true in rural areas where generally uneducated men and women, often having only one or two Bibles that were shared with a fellowship of fifty to a hundred people, would pray earnestly with tears mingled with faith, and God did the supernatural. Many of the stories of miracles they told were related to timing, circumstances, deliverances from prison, or the kind of events that could not have been happenstance but had to be orchestrated by God.

Along with these we heard firsthand accounts of healings, often expressed in a straight, matter-of-fact manner that was neither sensational nor drew attention to the pastor or whoever God was using to bring healing. The fabric of faith was this: "The Bible says that God will heal the sick. I believe what God said. Therefore, in simple faith I ask Him to do what He promised," and in a natural sort of way, God did the miraculous—something that has largely ceased to happen in Western churches.

In his Gold Medallion award-winning book *The Church in China*, Carl Lawrence, a man whom I have known personally for almost forty years, relates many accounts of miracles of healings, including the following testimony that has been corroborated by eyewitnesses.[15]

> Mr. Huang, a nominal Buddhist, began to see his health deteriorate. His stomach constantly hurt and he couldn't keep food from upsetting it. A doctor diagnosed his problem: "You have a cancer of the liver in the terminal stage." As Chinese will often do, Huang went to his ancestral home to die and eventually be buried. But to make sure, Huang saw another doctor, a Christian, who confirmed the original diagnosis but told him that Jesus was the Lord and had the power to heal any sickness, including the incurable cancer. The doctor also told him that whether or not Jesus healed him was not as important as having eternal life. He also explained that Jesus Christ healed many people when He ministered on earth and did the miraculous.

Huang said, "I want to believe in Jesus," so the doctor invited another brother to join them, and the three of them knelt in the clinic, and Huang became a believer in Jesus Christ. Returning to his home, he told his wife of his decision to follow Jesus and also removed all the idols from the house. Every night Huang and his wife prayed and he thanked God that he had eternal life, but every day his condition weakened. Seeing that her husband was about to die, Huang's wife had the grave dug on a hillside and purchased a casket.

Then Huang had a dream, something that Chinese put great faith in, and in the dream a man in white touched a knife to his body. In the morning Huang awoke with appetite, something that had not happened for a long time. He called for food and his wife prepared a bowl of steaming egg drop soup. Then he fell asleep. When he awakened two men in white apparel stood by his bed and one of them said, "You have been healed." Reaching down he felt his abdomen. The swelling had dissipated. He had truly been healed.

And as word spread throughout the village, people came to visit, and each one was told the same story. There is no human explanation for a testimony as this apart from the fact that in response to the prayers of a desperate man, a Christian doctor, and his friend, God wrought healing.[16]

The Doctor Who Should Have Died of Cancer

My wife and I were in Southern China ministering to a group of pastors, many of whom had come by train riding for many hours on a wooden seat in a third class coach. While we were there, a person in the group said, "Get xxx [she pointed to a particular woman] to tell you her story." With an interpreter translating, the woman told me that she had first been arrested because she was a Christian. Because she refused the order to tear up her Bible, she was locked up in prison for several years. Upon her release she was told that she could no longer work as a doctor. Instead she was publicly humiliated and assigned the duty of cleaning latrines.

Eventually a cancerous growth developed on her face and was surgically removed. Then after a period of several years, the cancer came back with a vengeance. This time the doctors said, "There is nothing more that we can do." At that point she summoned the elders of the home church group to anoint her with oil and to pray that the cancer would disappear. "It dried up and dropped off," she explained, showing us the noticeable depression in her face where the cancer had been. God used that healing to bring many to faith in Christ.

The Child Who was Used In a Satanic Ritual

Another notable healing took place in a village in a rural area of about six thousand people. Our team had driven through mountains and valleys where farmers' fields were waffled with rice paddies; then crossing a river and driving through a quarry, we came to the church that overlooked the village. Awaiting the start of the service, we enjoyed a cup of tea and got acquainted with the pastor, a man in his early forties. I had noticed the people coming to church, some on bicycles, many walking. I had been impressed by the size of his congregation in relation to the population of the village. In his little office I asked him the question I almost always ask a Chinese pastor when I am getting to know him: "How do you account for the growth of your church?"

According to him, the following explained the growth: A four-year-old girl had been used by the parents in a ritual sacrifice to Satan. He explained that an evil spirit had made her sick. The little girl was in the hospital at the point of death with a high fever. Doctors had tried to cure her but couldn't do anything to help, and it was merely a matter of hours until the sad wail of a funeral would be heard. "I went to the parents," he said, "and asked them if I could go to the hospital and pray for her." "Yes, yes," they exclaimed, grasping at any straw of hope.

The pastor went to the hospital and prayed for the little girl, and the fever dissipated. To their great joy she was completely restored.

Word of her healing spread like wildfire. This little girl, destined to die, was healed. He said, "Her mother and father, her grandparents, her aunts and uncles, neighbors and friends—half of the people in our church came to faith in Christ as the result of what happened."

And that was in a church pastored by a man who had never attended a church growth conference but one who had encountered the power of the Holy Spirit to heal the sick—the same thing the apostles prayed for long ago.

Are things such as I have just related still happening with frequency in China today? In all honesty, I would answer "yes," and "no." On occasion there are those situations that can be understood only by acknowledging that God sovereignly chose to heal someone, something that brings glory to His name and creates an awareness among many that there is a living God who has power not only to forgive but to heal as well. Yet it has been my observation that as China's standard of living has improved, along with better medical facilities and skilled medical practitioners, there are fewer accounts of God's miraculous intervention.

Assessing the Miraculous Today

The fact that thousands of people the world over flock to "healing crusades" is a reflection of the reality that suffering, pain, and sickness drive us to almost anything that offers hope and help. In this chapter I have demonstrated that God, on occasion, does intervene, bringing healing and health to some in such a manner that leaves no room for rational, human explanation. The doctor shakes his head, saying, "I cannot explain what has happened, but the cancer [or whatever malady that threatened the life of the one who is suffering] is gone." Of course, we rejoice when this happens.

God, however, loves His children far too much to heal everyone in a miraculous manner, thus denying them of some of life's greatest lessons—lessons that can be learned no other way than to walk through the valley of suffering. Only in this manner can they discover the presence of a compassionate Shepherd who walks with them teaching them truths about themselves and about God that can be learned no other way. In the next two chapters we will explore two alternative ways God brings healing, ways that produce the fragrance of a crushed rose and glorify God.

What You Need to Know

• While I could have written about many incidents, I have chosen those that are "skeptic proof." Because God is supernatural, He, on occasion, chooses to manifest Himself in ways that are beyond human comprehension. That's why these are called "miracles."

• In our twenty-first-century world miracles are yet taking place, often in countries where individuals exercise simple faith in the promises of God's Word, and as the result of the miraculous, Christ is glorified, and in many cases large groups of people embrace the faith.

• While sometimes God seems to display His mighty works and power for reasons unknown to us mortals, the miraculous usually takes place where people believe that God will do something, earnestly petition Him, and rest in the promises of Scripture.

CHAPTER 7

Integrative Healing
and Medical Science

You wake up one morning with severe pain in your abdomen. Sensing that something might be seriously wrong, you call your doctor, who tells you to head for the emergency room at the local hospital.

After the hospital signs you in, verifies your insurance or health card, and completes all your paperwork, an orderly finally seats you in a wheelchair and rolls you down to the emergency room. There you are placed on a gurney, and the privacy curtain is drawn around you. A nurse enters and takes your pulse, temperature, and blood pressure. Then the emergency room physician arrives and conducts his examination. As he pokes and prods your abdomen, he elicits tenderness around your belly button. As he slides his hand further to the right, you moan as the doctor's pressure sends excruciating pain radiating throughout the midsection of your body. "I think you have appendicitis," he tells you—not a pleasant thought under any circumstance but particularly disappointing since you were scheduled to leave for a vacation the following morning.

The doctor orders abdominal X-rays and calls a general surgeon for consultation. By now the lab results are back, and the high white blood cell count and low-grade fever indicate that you have an infection. The doctor orders that you be admitted overnight, and a nurse starts an IV containing antibiotics. In the morning you have an MRI (Magnetic Resonance Imaging).

By the following afternoon the MRI results are back, and your temperature and white blood cell count are getting back to normal. The surgeon confirms that your malady is not appendicitis after all but a problem with your colon. So he schedules your surgery for the following morning.

You have a restless sleep, and then "the day" arrives. The last thing you remember is the anesthesiologist telling you to count backwards from one hundred. By the time you reach ninety-eight, you've drifted into unconsciousness. The next thing you know, you're in the recovery room. When your eyes can finally focus, you glance at the clock on the wall and realize three hours have passed!

Whoa! Let's analyze for a moment what has happened.

- A well-trained emergency specialist, a professional with at least seven years of training, examined you and referred you to a surgeon.
- Laboratory tests and abdominal X-rays and your response to the IV antibiotics helped the surgeon rule out appendicitis.
- An MRI helped the surgeon define the problem.
- The antibiotic[1] eliminated infection in your body that would have otherwise complicated your post-op recovery.
- Anesthesia allowed you to drift into an induced sleep and numbness, blocking your nerve receptors from feeling the pain of a scalpel slicing through your abdomen; and a temporary amnesiac eliminated any frightening memories of what took place in the operating room.
- A surgeon's additional three or more years of specialty training gave him the expertise and skill to delicately remove the diseased part of your colon and to carefully reassemble your abdomen layer by layer as he exited your gut.
- Throughout the whole procedure, a constellation of the latest technological machinery monitored your condition. One special machine accurately infused you with the prescribed

IV fluids, providing your body with the support needed to keep you alive.

- The well-choreographed efforts of highly trained professionals working together in harmony saved your life.

But there is one more part to this scenario. Before you were admitted to the hospital for surgery, you had called your pastor; and he, along with several elders, had come to your home and anointed you with oil in the name of the Lord, praying fervently for your healing. So did God answer their prayer, dispensing both grace and the healing hands of doctors, nurses, technicians, laboratory analysts, and—yes, don't forget the brainy guys who figured out how X-rays[2] and MRIs work, and how anesthesia[3] makes you sleepy, and how the electronic box on the stand by your bed records your every heartbeat and sends information to a central computer? Did all of this simply happen, or was the God who told Moses His name was *Jehovah Rapha*, the God who heals, ultimately guiding the whole procedure which many of us take for granted today?

Let's Take a Look Back in History

Notice that God's Nature Is Reflective of Wholeness and Health—Not Disease and Death

Even a casual reading of Scripture leads a person to see that from the beginning of time two forces have warred against each other—God and Satan, light and darkness. Portrayed down through the centuries in art, literature, and Scripture, the contrast is vivid.

The God of the Bible cares about His children. He consistently sent His prophets to call back those who had strayed far from the narrow path. Under Moses, God gave stringent dietary laws (See Lev. 11 and Deut. 14) as to what food was considered to be healthy and what was to be avoided—regulations that are yet observed in the homes of Orthodox Jews as well as in hotels in Israel today.

Even a thousand years before Moses wrote The Torah, the first five books of the Old Testament, God already made a distinction between *clean* and *unclean* animals—something physicians today clearly see as being beneficial to the health of those who lived long before refrigeration.

I don't know anything except for what Jim's doctor said in his room after the surgery. He said that it must have been an infection or something because it is gone. Two weeks ago, he diagnosed it as cancer, after X-rays, and a blood test that came back positive. I told everyone that it was a miracle, and that I wanted to praise the Lord for His goodness to Jim in allowing him to stay a while in this life. I was careful to say, "If it is Your will to heal, I really want this to happen." —LuAnne Steinker

---

While God is viewed as a beneficent healer, Satan or the devil is pictured as a destroyer, the one who was cast from heaven after a failed rebellion and became the enemy of everything God wished for His people. Jesus described him as a "liar from the beginning," and "one in whom there is no truth" (John 8:44).

Consider the following:

- The first hospital established in the Western world was established about AD 399 by a dedicated Christian woman whose name was Fabiola. Never heard of her? Here's her bio in a few sentences. From a wealthy Roman family, this woman endured two difficult marriages followed by Roman-style divorces. Then she repented of her lifestyle and dressed in a penitent garb. Denouncing her sin, she embraced Christian faith. Seeing the suffering who had neither money nor anyone to care for them, she established the first hospital.

- The first leper colony in the history of medicine was established in about AD 379 by a fourth-century Christian leader, Basil of Caesarea (known as Cappadocia in Turkey today, an area known for its moonlike landscapes). One of nine children, Basil had intended to have a law career but instead felt pity for lepers who've been treated as the offscouring of humanity from time immemorial.

- The first asylum for the blind was established by Thalasius, a Christian monk.
- The first free clinic to dispense medicine to the poor was begun by a successful Christian businessman whose name was Appolonius.[4]

The story of modern missions has been one combining the good news of the gospel with the realization that God is concerned about the totality of your life—body, soul, and spirit. With that vision medical missionaries have gone the world over establishing Christian hospitals, clinics, and outstations. When they lacked the resources or personnel to set up a permanent medical facility, they packed their suitcases and traveled with everything from Band-Aids to antibiotics.

Notice that You Were Born with a Body That Is Equipped with a Built-in Healing Mechanism

Your body is not the result of evolutionary chance but the product of deliberate design as our first parents came from the drawing board of heaven with a body chemistry designed to fight infection. Let's suppose that you sustain a cut. Whether the trauma is accidental or purposeful in surgery, a sequence of events takes place, explains Dr. Tim James.[5]

- The first phase is known as "hemostasis," wherein the ends of the broken blood vessels constrict; and platelets, a vital component of blood, form a clot to secure the further escape of fluids.
- The second phase is the "inflammatory phase," when white blood cells kick into operation, cleansing the wound and carrying away debris and bacteria that would otherwise cause infection.
- The third is the "proliferation phase," when a network of collagen mesh forms at the base of the wound connecting the skin edges and forming the foundation upon which new skin cells fill in the defect. Tiny blood vessels extend into the wound, bringing fresh nutrients and further removing debris.

- The fourth and final phase is one of "remodeling," where the collagenous scar is remodeled and the surplus tissue is reabsorbed. This process can take several months to complete.

It was just before one o'clock and the surgeon and anesthesiologist had left for lunch. The patient had just had an operation and was in the recovery room when the nurse informed me that the patient had stopped breathing and there were no vital signs—no pulse and no respiration. I knelt beside his bed and asked God to spare the young man's life, then proceeded with mouth-to-mouth resuscitation. Within two minutes all was well.
—*Sister Freda, Kitale, Kenya*

And you thought that the cut just *healed itself!*

Ponder another scenario. You have a headache and take an aspirin that relieves your discomfort. Don't thank Bayer, the pharmaceutical company that manufactured the product; thank God, who supplied the natural ingredients found in aspirin. God, not Bayer, enables your body to respond in a positive manner to the medication. As C. Samuel Storms explains: "He is the one to thank for the successful surgical transplant of a kidney or for relief from depression or a head cold. It is God who deserves praise for the polio vaccine that enables children to walk, and for the corrective powers of eyeglasses that enable us to see, and for penicillin and other so-called 'miracle drugs' that enable us to live to his glory."[6]

One of my heroes is Dr. Paul Brand, whose story is told in *The Gift of Pain*, coauthored with Philip Yancey.[7] Brand, who without question was the greatest hand surgeon of the twentieth century, spent most of his life in India pioneering innovative surgical techniques that allowed lepers to regain partial use of their limbs, have a healthier self-esteem and a practical manner in which to earn a living.

Describing the awesome power of the human body to heal itself, Brand wrote:

An infected wound is red and swollen with pus:
the redness comes from an emergency blood supply
rushing white cells and agents of repair to the scene
and the pus, composed of lymph fluids and dead cells,
gives stark and dramatic evidence of cellular warfare
being fought. Similarly, a fever represents the body's
effort to circulate blood more quickly and also create
a hostile environment for some bacteria. Vomiting
coordinates scores of muscles in a dramatic reversal
of their normal process: designed to push food down
through the intestine, they now regroup in order to
violently expel the food along with toxins and unwel-
come invaders that had accumulated in the stomach.
All these irritations, which most of us view with alarm
and even disgust, reveal the orderly progress of the
healing body.[8]

When David, some three thousand years ago, described the
human body as "fearfully and wonderfully made" (Ps. 139:14), little did
he understand how deep a truth he had just articulated.

Paralleling the Revelation of God as Healer Was the Development of Medicine in Both Egypt and Greece

Between 1886 and 1906 two Oxford graduates, B. P. Grenfell and
A. S. Hunt, unearthed literally tons of papyri (writing material found
in abundance in Egypt) at Oxyrhynchus, a village in Al Minya, Egypt.
Among the many valuable manuscripts that were unearthed are several important documents that indicated that early in Egypt there had
already been physicians following the procedure of diagnosis, therapy,
and prognosis. In Egypt the priests were the healers, whereas in Israel
the priests only certified that God had healed someone. Also, during
the four-hundred-year sojourn of the Hebrews in Egypt, embalming
had been developing into a widely practiced art. Following Jacob's
death in Egypt, Joseph "commanded his servants the physicians to
embalm his father" (Gen. 50:2) before his body was taken to Canaan.

---

*On September 7, 2007, I got a miraculous healing after thirty-nine plus years of manic depression—and I hadn't even asked for the healing! Is God awesome or what? Freedom in Christ Ministry had started expanding our ministry to include healing. On this Friday evening I had an instant "knowing" in my spirit that I could stop taking the Prozac I had been on for almost fourteen years—because God had healed me totally of my manic depression. I had been prepared to take Prozac for the rest of my life and am thankful I no longer need it. I've had absolutely no side effects, nor has any hint of manic depression returned in the last three plus years. Hallelujah! —Beth Scanlan
(Author's note: If God heals you as He did Beth, go to your physician to confirm that it is safe to go off medication.)*

Frederick J. Gaisner, in his book *Healing and the Bible*, says that in Mesopotamia "medical documents (including parts of the Code of Hammurabi) are even far more numerous than those from Egypt."[9] We also know that during the fourth century BC healing temples arose in Greece, Rome, and Pergamos in Turkey.[10] According to Greek mythology, Asklepios, the son of Apollo, was raised by the centaur Chiron, who taught him healing arts. Over a period of time, Asklepios metamorphosed into a snake wrapped around a staff, which became the symbol for medicine and healing. At that time it was believed that the sick could find healing by sleeping in the courtyard of the healing temples. The snakes would supposedly cure them as they slithered freely. The origin of the symbol for medicine may have been based on myth, but truely hurting people searching for a cure gravitated to these healing temples that offered hope and the possibility of getting well.

Between Moses and Christ

How were physicians viewed, say, between Moses and the coming of Jesus Christ? While the Bible does not specifically deal with this subject, we are reminded that God instructed Moses to have a serpent, known as Nehushtan, put on a pole in the wilderness. Those who looked to it were healed, allowing God's healing power to trump what the medical science of that day could do. We also realize that Asa, the king of Judah, became diseased in his feet and, rather than seeking God for his healing, "sought help from physicians" (2 Chron. 16:12). Unfortunately, Asa died two years later. The sad inference that comes through clearly is that had he sought help from the Lord, he would have found healing.

Hippocrates (460–370 BC), known as the father of medicine, raised the profession to a new level with his oath, which is still taken in medical schools today, affirming that, according to his ability and his judgment, the physician would "never do harm to anyone."

Jesus Was Not in Competition with Physicians

While there were times when Jesus came down strongly on the unpopular sides of issues, He never expressed displeasure or censured individuals who went to physicians for relief from sickness. As I previously pointed out, Jesus' works of healing dealt with situations and issues that no physician on earth could cure. On several occasions Jesus alluded to physicians. In the house of Levi, a minor government official, Jesus was rebuked by the "scribes of the Pharisees" (like attorneys today), and He countered, "Those who are well have no need of a physician, but those who are sick" (Mark 2:16–17).

On another occasion Jesus told His detractors: "Doubtless you will quote to me this proverb, 'Physician, heal yourself'" (Luke 4:23). In Mark's Gospel we are told of a woman who "had suffered much under many physicians, and had spent all that she had, and was no better but rather grew worse" (Mark 5:26), yet Jesus neither condemned nor disparaged her for trying to find help. Mark, who includes her past medical history, only emphasizes the hopelessness and severity of her affliction.

It is also noteworthy that Luke, Paul's traveling companion, was a physician, probably from Antioch in Syria and the only Gentile who contributed to the New Testament, actually writing more in volume than even the apostle Paul.[11]

What Is Integrative Healing?

The word *integrative* means "combining and coordinating diverse elements into a whole." In the context of healing, it is the recognition that a sovereign God chooses to bring healing through a combination of medical science and God's grace in response to fervent prayer, with faith that God will honor the promises in His Word and the understanding that "in all things God works for the good of those who love him, who have been called according to his purpose" (Rom. 8:28 NIV). The phrase "in all things" encompasses many situations and circumstances, some of which are subject to human control but most of which are beyond our control.

Don Piper is a living example of integrative healing. He is the author of the best-selling book *90 Minutes in Heaven*, with more than a million copies in print. On a cold day in January 1989, Piper was driving home from a conference. He was crossing a bridge that spanned a lake when an eighteen-wheeler tractor-trailer truck, driven by a Texas State Prison inmate from the opposite direction, hit him head-on. The combined speed of the two vehicles in excess of one hundred miles per hour was devastating, crumbling the little Ford Escort Piper was driving. He was killed instantly.

Consistent with what Paul wrote to the Corinthians—"away from the body and at home with the Lord" (2 Cor. 5:8)—Piper found himself inside the gates of heaven. What happened following this, though, makes the story unique.[12]

A fellow pastor who had been at the same conference was stopped by the traffic that had backed up. Inquiring as to what had happened, he was told that a man had been killed in a head-on collision. Feeling a strange urging from the Lord, he explained that he was a pastor and wanted to pray for the person. "Didn't you hear what I said?" asked one of the police officers, adding bluntly, "He's dead!" Pressing his desire, the pastor asked again if he could pray for the victim.

Crawling into the wreckage—now almost ninety minutes after the accident—the minister began to pray that the man whose body lay tangled in the wreckage in a pool of blood would have no internal or head injuries. He then began to softly sing the words of an old hymn, "What a friend we have in Jesus, all our sins and griefs to bear."

Suddenly he realized he was hearing Piper softly mouthing the same words! Unbelievable, he thought. Dead men don't sing.

To be candid with you, when I first heard the account that I have just narrated, I was dubious; however, having gotten to know Don Piper personally, I believe him to be absolutely factual and credible in what he has related. His recovery following the accident was long and arduous, a tribute to the doctors and medical personnel who helped him regain his health. Piper now travels the world telling people that your life can change in an instant and that heaven is a reality for those who embrace Jesus Christ as Lord as well as the Great Physician.

Four years ago I was healed from cancer of the uterus. I thought of taking my life. I prepared poison ready for consumption, but the Lord saved me through Imani Radio when a servant of God was ministering to those who had given up and God wanted to deliver them. I felt the Lord touching me and healing me. I felt normal and at peace, completely healed. My uterus was healed. Surely God is a healer. —Catherine Wepkhulu, Kitale, Kenya

---

Today there is a large army of physicians, nurses, and related personnel who understand that medical science can go only so far, and that's where God can be trusted to do what medical science is incapable of doing. As Sister Freda, a nurse in Kitale, Kenya, whose compassion for the desperately poor and sick eventually birthed a thirty-two-bed hospital and the Nzoia College of Nursing, put it this way: "We give the medicine but God heals."

Representative of that same group and understanding is Dr. Diane Komp,[13] whom I first mentioned in chapter 2. She is a no-nonsense professional who sees her career as a physician and her faith in God as one entity—not separate elements. Her life and work have been featured in such publications as *The New York Times*, *The Washington Post*, and *Life*.

In her book *Images of Grace*, she writes, "These days if the word *healing* is used in conjunction with health, it is most often interpreted to reflect some activity other than medical practice."[14] Several years ago Dr. Di was invited to have lunch at a Trappist monastery with a former brother of that community. During a time of prayer with members of this order, one of the brothers asked prayer for Dr. Di's "ministry of healing."

Then as she was having lunch with the group, one of them inquired about her "ministry of healing." As she began to relate how she has a two-pronged approach as a physician—prayer and healing—her listeners were shocked. "They did not expect a 'healer' to be a medical doctor," she said. Explaining that she isn't really comfortable with the term "healer," she tells that a sign in a missionary hospital describes her mission in life: "We treat; Jesus heals."

The modality of her mission in life is summarized in these words: "As a physician, I will work as hard as I can in a profession with an honorable history. As a Christian, I will also pray as hard as I can in a religious tradition that I also hold to be honorable. Children need to be healed. So do the rest of us."[15]

Another outstanding physician who feels the same way is Dr. C. Everett Koop, who served as the U.S. Surgeon General under two American presidents. In an interview he acknowledged that he had performed more than twenty-four thousand surgeries, including ground-breaking procedures separating conjoined twins. Koop, who recognizes that all healing comes from God, said:

> Patients were coming to me from all over the world. And one of the things that endeared me to the parents of my patients was the way that my incisions healed. These "invisible" scars became my trademark. But was I a *healer?* I was the one who put the edges together, but it was God who coagulated the serum. It was God who sent the fibroblasts out across the skin edges. It was God who had the fibroblasts make collagen, and there were probably about fifty other complicated processes involved about which you and I will never know. . . . The question is not, "Does God heal?" Of course He heals! We are concerned with this question: "Granted that God heals, is it *normally*

*according to natural laws or an interruption of those laws
[that is, a miracle]?*[16]

A growing number of physicians integrate their faith and their medical expertise in treating people. Groups such as the Christian Medical and Dental Association, with a membership in excess of sixteen thousand physicians, World Vision, World Hope, Samaritan's Purse, Mercy Ships, Global Strategies for HIV Prevention, and others provide a platform for service allowing physicians to go into many corners of the world—some for a few days or weeks; others, full-time. Hats off to these medical warriors who, usually at their own expense, go where there are few if any medical services, lugging suitcases or tubs of medical supplies, punching holes in the darkness of suffering, doing what they can to make a difference in the lives of hurting people.

Dear Dr. Sala, I was with my doctor last Wednesday. Based on my tests, my doctor said that my illness [cirrhosis of the liver] is slowly reversing. Most of my tests are normal or have improved when compared with earlier results. I believe God has healed me. You have always pointed to the Author of my healing. My doctors are just instruments, and I rely more on Him as my healer. I have experienced God's grace in my life. He has given me a different attitude about how I should handle situations like mine. I have my ups and downs, but He has always been there to lift me up."
—Totick Arnaldo, Manila, Philippines

Another category of doctors who integrate their faith and medicine are those who choose to serve in Christian hospitals in countries such as India, Kenya, Tanzania, the Sudan, Hong Kong, Latin America, Sierra Leone, Ecuador, and elsewhere around the world. Others, however, never leaving the country of their birth, essentially reflect the same attitude. When I asked my personal physician if he had considered doing some missionary medicine, he replied, "Every morning I pray asking God to use me to make a difference in the lives of my patients."

Integrative Healing Is Healing

While I may be the first to use the descriptive term *integrative healing*, the concept was advocated by the apostle Paul himself when he told a young pastor whose name was Timothy to "no longer drink only water, but use a little wine for the sake of your stomach and your frequent ailments" (1 Tim. 5:23). What Paul wrote, however, invites closer scrutiny. Paul was saying, "Don't drink just water; use some wine because of your frequent stomach problems and your frequent illnesses" (my paraphrase). In his word studies, Marvin Vincent says that the word *wine* means the same thing here as it does throughout the New Testament: "fermented and capable of intoxicating, and not a sweet syrup made by boiling down grape-juice and styled by certain reformers 'unfermented wine.' Such a concoction," he contends, "would have tended rather to aggravate than to relieve Timothy's stomachache or other infirmities."[17] Paul is also kicking back at some of the ascetics who even in that day contended that abstaining from wine was a sign of moral purity. The word for wine was the same word Paul used when he told the Ephesians not to be drunk with wine but to be filled with the Spirit.

Though Timothy was a young man, he was not a novice. Paul had first encountered this potential leader on his second missionary journey, and he fully had Paul's full confidence. Had Timothy prayed for himself? In all probability. Had Paul also prayed for him? Most definitely. So are we to fault Timothy for his affliction? Could he not have been supernaturally healed? Of course! Paul had previously demonstrated that God's power, including His healing power, has no limit.

Stop for a moment and let's back up! Paul did not tell us whether or not drinking wine along with water was the solution to Timothy's condition. It is an indication, however, that some of God's choicest servants go through periods of illness and pain even when they are at the center of God's will and purpose.

In 2004, during a routine executive check-up here in Manila, the ultrasound showed a problem. A Doppler ultrasound was ordered, and its results confirmed ovarian cancer. My husband prayed for total healing. I prayed like Hezekiah (2 Kings 20 and Isa. 38:1–8), saying, "Lord, would You give me just five more years so I could have some closure and finish our missionary work? After all, I was fifty-seven years old and we'd only been on the mission field for three and a half years. When the pathology reports came back, NO CANCER! I had no problem figuring out that my miracle healing had nothing to do with my faith but rather with the purpose and plan of my GREAT God. —Joan L. Feuerstein

Meet Trophimus Who Almost Died

And who was Trophimus? Although we know little about him, we do know he was a traveling companion of the apostle Paul, having been with him on the third major missionary journey (Acts 20:4). Trophimus is one of the two Asians who joined Paul following the brouhaha in Ephesus. But what happened when Paul came to Jerusalem, being accompanied by Trophimus, made the Ephesian riots seem pale. The Jews thought that Paul had taken Trophimus (a non-Jew) into the temple with him. For his own protection Paul was seized by the temple guard. In Paul's second letter to Timothy, written from a prison cell in Rome, Trophimus is mentioned, almost as a postscript. Six words in Greek are these in English: "I left Trophimus, who was ill, at Miletus" (2 Tim. 4:20). Paul's mention of this sick companion is the last we hear about him. Did he die of the affliction? Did he recover and then follow Paul to Rome, where he was eventually taken? If it is God's intent to heal every affliction in a supernatural manner, why did God not see fit to heal him? It becomes readily apparent that supernatural healing is not the way God intends to answer all our prayers to be healed.

Epaphroditus, Paul's Brother in Christ and a Fellow Servant

Today in many parts of the world when people are sent either to prison or a hospital, unless there is someone who provides for their needs, they are faced with desperate circumstances; so was it in Paul's day. After the incident in Jerusalem, when the Jews thought Paul had taken Trophimus into the temple, the temple guard seized Paul. When Paul's nephew learned of a plot on his life, a contingent of two hundred soldiers took Paul to Caesarea by night.

A good friend of mine went into the hospital recently for a CT scan of her abdomen to determine the extent of obstructed bowels. As a cancer patient undergoing chemo, she has experienced this problem before, so she was prepared for the procedure. The doctors "accidentally" scanned her lungs also, and found a life-threatening clot of which she had no symptoms! The doctors told her this should have killed her, BUT GOD had other plans! He was glorified as He preserved her life, letting the doctors and nurses see Him at work in my friend's body. She gives Him all the glory.
—*Kim Gaines*

There he spent two long years doing battle with the Roman hierarchy. Felix, a corrupt governor, toyed with Paul, fishing for a bribe that would have freed him. Sarcastically he baited Paul by saying, "In a short time would you persuade me to be a Christian?" (Acts 26:28). Moving up the chain of command, Paul appeared before two other Roman officials, Festus and Agrippa. Sensing that this was going nowhere, Paul, as a Roman citizen, appealed directly to Caesar. Paul was then taken from Caesarea on the Mediterranean coast to Rome, where he spent the next two years of his life.

During his imprisonment, the church at Philippi heard of Paul's need and sent Epaphroditus, one of their best men, with a gift that would sustain him. But while in Rome, Epaphroditus, a man who is commended by Paul as a brother, a messenger, and a fellow soldier, became ill. He was not simply sick; he almost died. In Paul's letter to the church thanking them profusely for their gift, he tells them that

Epaphroditus was distressed because they did not know of his illness. In writing to them Paul says, "But God had mercy on him" (Phil. 2:27).

"But God"—Paul uses two powerful words, which can bring hope to those who live with the sentence of death whether it is from cancer, a rare disease, or any other condition that grows progressively worse day by day. He says, "*But God . . .*" Those two words deny God's indifference to Epaphroditus's need, or even to Paul's because Paul says that had God not demonstrated His mercy, he would have had sorrow upon sorrow. Paul asks the Philippians to honor Epaphroditus because "he nearly died for the work of Christ, risking his life to complete what was lacking in your service to me" (Phil. 2:30).

A final thought about Epaphroditus: Some afflictions can cripple you overnight, but generally speaking, serious illness is progressive, taking its victims a step closer to the grave day by day. Therefore, is it logical to assume that as Paul learned of Epaphroditus's weakness and realized that he was, in fact, dying, he prayed for healing more fervently?

Paul Had His Own Unique Health Issues and Discovered God's Solution

Some twelve years before the incident involving Trophimus, Paul wrote a letter to the Corinthians. (We call it "2 Corinthians," though this letter was Paul's fourth or even possibly fifth letter to the struggling church.[18]) In this letter, more than any other of Paul's letters, he opens his heart and bares his soul.

Here Paul is almost finished writing the letter when he tells of an experience of being "caught up to the third heaven" (2 Cor. 12:2), and explains that "to keep me from becoming conceited because of the surpassing greatness of the revelations, a thorn was given me in the flesh, a messenger of Satan to harass me, to keep me from becoming conceited" (v. 7). In this passage he makes three statements:

- A thorn was given to him (by God).
- The thorn was "a messenger of Satan" which constantly gave him grief or pain.
- The purpose was to prevent arrogance or pride.

What Was the "Thorn"?

For centuries people have speculated as to what Paul's thorn was. The Greek word for "thorn" that Paul chose to use, *skolops*, is found in secular literature but only in this one instance in the Bible. It is often rendered as an "impaling stake" and is also translated as a "crucifix" in secular documents, but the fact that the *skolops* here is "in the flesh" has prompted translators to uniformly use the word "thorn." With this we can identify. When you pluck a beautiful rose from a bush and in the process a thorn gets embedded in your thumb, what happens? It hurts when you touch it, and until you take a needle and dig it out, it is a constant source of discomfort and pain.

Since the apostle Paul did not expound on the challenge he faced, and the Word itself is not explicit, it has been assumed that his affliction could have been malaria, brucellosis, or epilepsy. It could also have been, perhaps more probably, an ophthalmic condition[19] that could have prompted Paul's statement to the Galatians about writing with such a large hand and commending their compassion and willingness: "If possible, you would have gouged out your eyes and given them to me" (Gal. 4:15).

There are times when what is *not said* is equally or more important than what is said! Why? Lacking precise identification, many people can relate to situations, afflictions, and—yes, people, who are a "thorn in the flesh." They know that Paul, too, was "there" and find hope in how he experienced God's grace in the process.

Where Did the Thorn Come From?

Paul identifies the source: Satan, in a scene that is reminiscent of how God granted Satan permission to afflict Job but drew the line at allowing him to take Job's life. Writing to the Corinthians, Paul told them that no temptation or trial would confront them that they could not withstand. God sovereignly allowed the trial of Paul's "thorn in the flesh" to enter his life. It was an experience Paul, obviously, would have preferred avoiding. But he accepted his condition, trusting God had permitted it to fulfill a purpose.

Is There a Purpose In Pain?

The next chapter deals with this issue at length; however, clearly in Paul's situation, the thorn that created distress, discomfort, and, in all probability, pain served to give Paul a sense of humility and revealed God's strength through his weakness. As John Bunyan, a man unjustly imprisoned, wrote, "He that is down need fear no fall. He that is low, no pride. He that is humble ever shall have God to be his guide."[20]

Three times Paul pleaded with God to remove the thorn, and three times his request was denied. Let me say a word about the intensity of Paul's prayer. Translated "pleaded," the word *parakalesa* means "to request, to ask, appeal to," or "strongly urge." "Aha," says the skeptic, "see, God didn't hear his prayer." On the contrary, God heard Paul's prayer but said, "No!" Just as a father loves his son so much that he will, on occasion, deny what the child wants, God sometimes says "No" when He has a better plan for us. John Calvin once wrote that God sometimes has to use "baby talk" to get through to us. Should Paul have received an immediate, affirmative answer, he would never have experienced the measure and sufficiency of God's grace.

God's Answer—Amazing, Abundant, All-Compassing Grace

Integrative healing involves God's compassionate, benevolent touch in your life, hereafter called grace, in combination with the skill of a physician and the blessing of medications that come from the earth that God created untold centuries ago.

"'My grace is sufficient for you, for my power is made perfect in weakness. Therefore I will boast all the more gladly of my weaknesses, so that the power of Christ may rest upon me" (2 Cor. 12:9), wrote Paul. Some have attempted to define *grace* by saying that it is "God's unmerited or undeserved favor"; but that definition never really satisfies me. In simple terms, I think of grace as God's reaching down to meet us at the point of our need, our pain, and our despair, giving us the strength to endure and the hope to survive. George Sweeting, who served as president of Moody Bible Institute for many years, says that some words were coined only for use in heaven. If so, surely the word *grace* is one of them.

Take a hymnbook, preferably an older one, and observe some of the words of the hymns that describe grace. In the eighteenth century Charles Wesley wrote of grace, saying, "O for a thousand tongues to sing / My great Redeemer's praise. / The glories of my God and King, / The triumphs of His grace."[21]

When Paul wrote to the Ephesians, he spoke of God's grace that brings salvation. He noted, "For it is by grace you have been saved, through faith" (Eph. 2:8), and based on that, thousands of hymns and songs have been written about the saving grace of God, such as John Newton's much-loved hymn which goes, "Amazing grace, how sweet the sound, / That saved a wretch like me! / I once was lost but now am found, / Was blind but now I see."[22]

The grace of God, though, is like a multifaceted diamond, and in addition to providing our salvation, another facet of grace is that His help allows us to endure when bad things happen. God's grace touches your life and lets you smile when the clouds are dark and gloomy and brings a measure of cheerfulness when you are in deep waters financially and wonder where your next meal is coming from. When things happen unexpectedly—often things that could well be described as "bad"—God's grace provides strength and help that you could otherwise never know.

Paul had a lot of experience when it comes to bad things happening. He began the letter that talks about the sufficiency of God's grace by telling the Corinthians that he felt he and Silas "had received the sentence of death." He explained, "But that was to make us rely not on ourselves but on God who raises the dead" (2 Cor. 1:9). Never forget that he raised a battle flag in that Roman prison, and emblazoned on the flag that has been carried for two thousand years are the words, "MY GRACE IS SUFFICIENT FOR YOU!" (2 Cor. 12:8). In Paul's second letter to the Corinthians, he wrote, "We are hard pressed on every side, but not crushed; perplexed, but not in despair; persecuted, but not abandoned; struck down, but not destroyed" (2 Cor. 4:8–9 NIV).

Today we would say Paul was down but not out; and what makes the difference? God's grace! The grace factor brings comfort and help. Paul then added, "Therefore, . . . we do not lose heart" (v. 1). The grace factor brings hope in the face of despair, allowing us to see beyond the darkness of circumstances. It brings strength in the face of weakness, the assurance of the presence of Him who said, "Never will I leave you; never will I forsake you" (Heb. 13:5 NIV), no matter how dark the night of suffering.

The grace factor allows you to take one more step, to endure one more chemo treatment, and to face one more new day. It is the strong hand of God touching your life at the point of need. Grace enabled Paul to say, "Praise be to the God and Father of our Lord Jesus Christ, the Father of compassion and the God of all comfort, who comforts us in all our troubles" (2 Cor. 1:3–4 NIV).

Our Weakness Gives Way to God's Strength

Linked to the assurance of God's grace is an acknowledgment of our weakness, as God says, "For my power is made perfect in weakness." The word Paul used for "power" is the Greek word *dunamis* from which we get the English word *dynamite*. What an encouraging word from heaven! Paul then adds his personal testimony: "For the sake of Christ, then, I am content with weaknesses, insults, hardships, persecutions, and calamities. For when I am weak, then I am strong" (2 Cor. 12:9–10).

This brings us to an important issue: If it is, indeed, God's will to provide miraculous healing for everyone, how do we explain what happened to people like Timothy, Epaphroditus, Trophimus, and the apostle Paul, who *were* in God's will, were doing God's work, and yet faced periods of illness? Either they were out of God's will when they were sick, or else sickness was part of God's will, allowed by a loving Father who continued to demonstrate His guidance and presence in their lives, accomplishing that which may have become evident only when they crossed the threshold of heaven.

Even today voices within the body of Christ strongly proclaim, *"God wants you miraculously healed!"*[23] Individuals who buy into that teaching often struggle with self-doubt, guilt, and disappointment when the Shepherd, instead of immediately healing them supernaturally, walks with them through the valley of suffering.

With that confidence Paul could boldly assert, "We know that for those who love God all things work together for good, for those who are called according to his purpose" (Rom. 8:28). In an equally powerful but not as widely known or quoted passage, Paul wrote to the Ephesians about "the purpose of him who works all things according to the counsel of his will" (Eph. 1:11).

Thus we see that we have an all-sovereign yet loving God who chooses the manner in which He brings healing, the situations and circumstances, and the occasions and methods of showing His might and power.

What You Need to Know

• Integrative healing is *healing* in that all healing comes from God whether it is miraculous, through the hands of a skilled physician, or through the ingredients of an antibiotic or medicine that were formed as part of creation.

• When human means are inadequate, God's power and ability to go beyond our means is never dwarfed by the enormity of our need. He, who breathed life into the dust of the earth, thus giving Adam existence, is also able to recreate that which is broken and needs fixing.

• Even in the days of the New Testament church, people who were serving God and living for Him faced times of illness when they were not supernaturally healed. In these situations, then, God has determined to meet the deep needs of our lives in a more redemptive way—the subject of the next chapter.

CHAPTER 8

Redemptive Healing—
Transforming Pain into
a Life Purpose

What is *redemptive healing*? How can not getting what you really want be redemptive in any sense? Let's begin by defining redemption:

Re·demp·tion noun

1. The act of redeeming or the condition of having been redeemed.
2. Recovery of something pawned or mortgaged.
3. Deliverance upon payment of ransom; rescue.
4. Salvation from sin through Jesus' sacrifice.

All of the above definitions are applicable to what I consider *redemptive healing* to be, which is what this chapter is about. Essentially it means turning pain into gain through the alchemy of faith and grace, to rescue the one suffering from his bewilderment and feelings of abandonment by God, and to endow suffering with purpose. Redemptive healing is what one can experience when God does not heal his body but chooses to bestow, instead, a measure of His grace in such a way that He is glorified. As a result the individual is used to bless the lives of others.

Ernest Hemingway said, "The world breaks everyone, and some get strong in the broken places." Though Hemingway really didn't see that happen in his personal life, in this he was right—some are broken by suffering, and others simply grow stronger in the broken places. In this chapter I'll introduce you to some of my heroes who, out of weakness and suffering, became "strong in the broken places." Then I'll focus on how their challenges became redemptive.

The Five Silent Years of Corrie Ten Boom

One of the women I have most admired was Corrie ten Boom, whom I met and talked with once. Whenever I take a group of people for a tour in Israel and we have a stopover in Amsterdam, we usually visit the centuries-old Dutch town of Haarlem. A ten-minute walk through the plaza and down a side street takes you to the house of the ten Boom family, where on the ground floor a watch shop used to be, with the family living on the second and third floors.

On occasions when the side door leading to the ten Boom apartment was not available to visitors, I have stood outside the watch shop and simply thanked God for Corrie ten Boom. Should you visit *Yad Vashem* (the Holocaust Museum) in Jerusalem and walk down the Avenue of Righteous Gentiles, where trees commemorate acts of supreme courage, you will see a plaque at the base of one tree celebrating the life of this woman and her family.

Who was Corrie ten Boom? Ask that question to a group today, and few people will raise their hands. Ask if they have read the book or seen the movie *The Hiding Place*, and a few more hands will be raised. Here briefly is her story:

Corrie, along with her aged father, Casper, a master watchmaker, her brother Willem and sisters Nollie and Betsie, lived a quiet and peaceful life. On Sundays the family worshiped in the old Saint Bavo Cathedral located just off the square, where her nephew played the organ. All of the ten Booms were known and respected in the community for their integrity and kindness. When Hitler's army invaded

Holland and it became known that Jews were being shipped to various concentration camps, the ten Booms decided they had to do what they could to save Jewish lives.

Casper ten Boom took weights from grandfather clocks and attached them to the back of an upstairs book case, allowing it to be raised quickly to give access to the attic—the "hiding place" for endangered Jews. The ten Booms saved the lives of hundreds of Jews by dyeing their hair a different color, giving them a change of clothes and warm meals, along with forged documents.

A neighbor turned them in to the Gestapo, and their world fell apart. The aged father died ten days after he was arrested. Corrie and Betsie were sent to the infamous Ravensbrück Concentration Camp, which Corrie described as "the deepest hell that man can create." Deprived of proper nutrition and medical care, Betsie grew weaker and eventually died. Corrie's trip to the gas chamber was scheduled, but God had another plan. Through a "clerical error of man and a miracle of God," she was released one week before her scheduled death, and she made her way home to Haarlem. After the war Corrie returned to Germany with the message of God's forgiveness and reconciliation. She became a celebrity, sharing about the terrible evils she endured.

Corrie's travels for the Gospel eventually took her all over the world. As the years went by and with advancing age, she was assisted by traveling companions who could help arrange her travel plans and schedules. Pamela Roswell Moore was one of them. In her book *The Five Silent Years of Corrie ten Boom*, Pamela tells of the beginning of the silent years, when for several days Corrie had been having a severe headache. One morning Pamela had prepared a cup of tea and quietly gone to Corrie's room, pulling back the drapes, when she froze upon seeing Corrie. She dropped to her knees and took Corrie's hand, which was cold and limp. Corrie didn't respond to her touch. "What's the matter, *Tante* Corrie?" Pamela asked.

When she was rushed to the hospital, medical personnel quickly assessed that she had had a stroke. Therapy helped a bit, but from that time on, doing public ministry was impossible. Whenever she was asked something, Corrie's answers were, at best, one or two words.

This was a new and frightening world, as confining and oppressive as Ravensbrück.

In her book *A Prisoner and Yet*, Corrie described her solitary confinement in 1944 at Ravensbrück in 1944 this way:

> It was oppressively quiet in the prison. The time dragged slowly by. So unlike former days! I always had been so very busy. There was never a moment in the day when I was not doing something. And now . . . ! However, my days of imprisonment would not be over until I had served my time; and my one purpose therefore had to be to pass away the time, somehow."[1]

But serving her time in the prison of disability lasted for five long years. During that time Corrie would get better, then again be felled by a stroke—not once, but twice.

How was Corrie's suffering redemptive? First, Corrie's life spoke when words failed her. When she could no longer travel and go to different parts to talk about God's grace and redemption, a steady stream of people from many different countries visited her. They wanted her to know what a blessing her life had been to them. Writes Pamela Rosswell Moore:

> The ministry that had touched millions continued as Corrie communicated through her eyes, through elaborate guessing games with those around her, through silent intercession for people God brought to mind. For those five silent years of imprisonment, Corrie's spiritual depth offered mute testimony to her ongoing trust in her heavenly Father.[2]

Another facet of how suffering for these years was redemptive occurred in her personal growth and understanding of God. Yes, Corrie had come face-to-face with the miraculous in her release from prison. There was never a question in her mind that God could completely heal her, a second miracle that would glorify Him. However, just as Paul determined to glorify God "whether it be by life or by death," Corrie reaffirmed God's sovereignty.

Immediately after the first stroke, Pamela and another friend had long conversations as to why God had allowed this. "We wondered, talked and prayed on the subject, but never came up with a complete answer to the mystery. . . . What came to us in increasing measure was an assurance of the absolute sovereignty of God. He allowed suffering, and in His sovereignty, this time in *Tante* Corrie's life had also been ordained."[3] Never once did Corrie raise the "Why?" question. She believed God was fully in control regardless of whether deliverance came by healing or homegoing. "God had shut her up with Himself in a kind of precious imprisonment, and, so far, what was going on in her spirit was a secret between the two of them."[4]

Corrie also gained personal intimacy with God, one that was observed by her caregivers but not fully understood. At times she would lift her hands toward heaven in a silent act of worship. At times her eyes would fill with tears as though she had looked through a window and seen heaven. On Easter Sunday, 1987, in response to prayer, it seemed that God healed Corrie's eyes, that had, indeed, been troubling her. But there were other times too, when she seemed confused and discouraged.

In the summer of 1979, Corrie was diagnosed with kidney failure. A burial plot was purchased, and it looked like death was imminent. Then, against all odds, Corrie improved dramatically. During this brief respite from the ravages of her second stroke, a policeman who desperately wanted to meet this saint came to see her. When the policeman told her he had seen the movie *The Hiding Place* twice, Corrie, notwithstanding her difficulty in speech, was able to ask him, "Did you understand the message of the movie that there is no pit so deep that the love of God is not deeper still?"

What a woman! Eighteen months later, in the autumn of 1980, after she had suffered a third and very severe stroke, friends gathered around her bedside and prayed for the Lord to take her home. "There were no heavenly revelations. The room was quiet and peaceful just before she left us. It was quiet and peaceful after she left us."[5] It was her birthday ninety-one years to the day of her birth on April 15, 1893. Corrie was "absent from the body" but at home with the Lord. Redemptive healing complete! Forever!

Amy Carmichael's Twenty Years as an Invalid

Raised in a strict Scottish Presbyterian family in Northern Ireland, Amy Carmichael enjoyed the benefits of affluence. At the age of eighteen, however, Amy took it upon herself to establish a Sunday morning class for poor mill girls. Her work prospered, and while she had never thought of ministry outside her beloved country, she came to the crossroads at a Deeper Life convention in 1887 where she heard missionary Hudson Taylor talk about missionary life. The words "Go, ye" found in Jesus' commandant to the disciples to go into all the world and proclaim the good news made an impact on Amy's life.

Eventually, she joined the Church Missionary Society and sailed to Japan. After fifteen months, however, the young Amy decided that Japan was not her calling. Without notifying the missionary society that provided most of her support, she sailed for Sri Lanka and found her niche in India where, with the exception of one brief visit to England, she stayed and served for the rest of her life.

Dyeing her skin with coffee to appear more "Indian" and donning the saris worn by Indian women, Amy tried to blend in. At first life was a challenge. She just didn't fit in. Yet when she saw a need, she wanted to do something about it. When she hit the wall of cultural respectability, she either went around it or knocked a hole in it and proceeded to do what she felt God wanted her to do. The casualness and even lethargy of the mission community vexed her. At one point there was a "Get Amy out of India Movement," which she ignored.

Seeing that young girls were often sold or given to Hindu temples where they were forced into temple prostitution, Amy decided that this practice must stop. When learning of a child who had been so coerced, she would enter the temple and snatch the child away—kidnapping was what the Hindu priests called it. During the course of her life, Amy saved the lives of more than a thousand girls, taking them to the Dohnavur Fellowship compound.

An often told story is that of Amy Carmichael's visit to an Indian village where the goldsmith would repeatedly put a small vessel containing gold in a clay tile over a fire, then remove it and take off the dross, and put it back over the fire. This he did not once but several times. "How do you know when it is finished?" a bystander asked the smith. "Ah," he said, "When I see the reflection of my face in the ore, then I know it is done."

At the zenith of her effectiveness, what has been described as "a tragic accident" left Amy crippled, and she was subsequently confined to either a bed or a chair for the next twenty years. With God, however, there are no "accidents," only "incidents." While I never met Amy Carmichael, I am convinced she would not have described this pivotal event in her life as either accidental or tragic.

The "accident" began a season that sidelined Amy for the rest of her life. During this time she learned that God's plan—not hers, would result in a legacy of grace and compassion touching the lives of thousands.

She once received a letter from a young woman who was considering becoming a missionary. In response to her question, "What is missionary life like?" Amy responded, "Missionary life is simply *a chance to die*" (the italicized phrase became the title of Elisabeth Elliot's biography of this remarkable woman).

What was redemptive about Amy's suffering?

The books and the thousands of letters she wrote to various people the world over became part of her enduring legacy. During the next twenty years, Amy would write thirteen books, numerous booklets and pamphlets, and edit and update previously written books.

Without question, with every anniversary of the incident that changed her life, Amy became a gentler, more caring, more sensitive person reflecting more and more the image of Christ, just as the gold in the refiner's fire reflected the image of the goldsmith. Did she ever ask, "How can I go on like this another year? another day? another minute?" Perhaps. Her answer, though, is found in what she wrote:

> We say, then, to anyone who is under trial, give
> Him time to steep the soul in His eternal truth. Go
> into the open air, look up into the depths of the
> sky, or out upon the wideness of the sea, or on the
> strength of the hills that is His also; or, if bound in
> the body, go forth in the spirit; spirit is not bound.
> Give Him time and, as surely as dawn follows night,

there will break upon the heart a sense of certainty
that cannot be shaken.[6]

Amy experienced God in a new dimension, one which her previously busy schedule would never have allowed. Her written words such as, ""Hold us in quiet through the age-long minute, While Thou art silent and the wind is shrill," speak of an intimacy that comes only by having been in the fellowship of Christ's suffering. This, of course, was possible only by an effusion of God's grace that, like His mercies, is new every morning.

In her little book entitled *If*, Amy describes the daily provision of God's grace:

> The picture before us is of a river. Stand on its banks, and contemplate the flow of waters. A minute passes, and another. Is it the same stream still? Yes, but is it the same water? No. The liquid mass that passed you a few seconds ago fills now another section of the channel; new water has displaced it, or if you please, replaced it; *water instead of water.* And so hour by hour, and year by year, and century by century, the process holds; one stream, other waters, living not stagnant, because always in the great identity there is perpetual exchange. Grace takes the place of grace; (Love takes the place of love) ever new, ever old, ever the same, ever fresh and young, for hour by hour, for year by year, through Christ.[7]

Instead of focusing on her pain, Amy focused on God and helping others connect with Him. She learned what Charles Haddon Spurgeon had written a generation before: "There is more in God to cheer you than in your circumstances to depress you."[8]

Shortly before her death in 1951, Amy asked that no stone be placed over her grave. Instead, the children she had loved and cared for affectionately and lovingly put a birdbath over her remains with the inscription *Amma*, which in Tamil simply means "Mother." Finally in God's time and way, the redemptive healing in this woman's life was complete!

Joni Eareckson Tada's More than Forty Years of Turning Pain into Gain

As I sit at my desk now in the early hours of the morning and ponder the urgency of addressing the issue of frustrated dreams and hope—that of supernatural healing that God has not seen fit to grant—I feel somewhat like an impostor. Why? In no way do I understand the subject as well as a woman for whom I have tremendous admiration—Joni Eareckson Tada. The closest I came to meeting her was when I was standing in the Denver airport awaiting the arrival of a friend and I saw Joni exit a plane, her wheelchair pushed by a faithful caregiver. As I saw the weariness in Joni's face, I did not have the heart to stop her and introduce myself.

For many years Joni has been painfully living out the life of Jesus in ways that in all probability I will never understand let alone embody. In the summer of 1967, Joni was a teenager who loved life, family, horses, and swimming. Diving into a lake that was shallow, Joni sustained an injury. Her neck was broken and that left her paralyzed. For the next two years she was in therapy and rehabilitation, and she struggled with her injury, with God, and with the value of life itself. But God met her. With no feeling in her body—apart from pain—from her neck down, and the added difficulty of wearing heavy braces to hold her body erect, Joni learned to write and draw with a pen in her mouth.

But instead of simply giving up, Joni allowed her pain to forge a relationship with Jesus Christ that has resulted in His love flowing through her to countless thousands of men and women around the world. Her story is unparalleled when it comes to the way God can turn pain into gain and suffering into purpose. Joni Eareckson Tada is the living embodiment of what I describe as redemptive healing.[9]

Have I personally ever known intense suffering? Yes, but what I have endured is akin to a splinter in the finger compared to the years of severe pain Joni has undergone. Between 2008 and 2010 Joni endured a period of great suffering when, seemingly, she could not find relief no matter how she sought help. Then, as if what she had endured wasn't enough, she was diagnosed with breast cancer. Upon hearing this news, I immediately thought, *Dear God, how much can that woman handle? Why her?*

In her book *A Place of Healing*, her final chapter is entitled, "Thank You, God, for This Wheelchair." Instead of withdrawing into a dark prison of self-pity, Joni has spent her life traveling the world over to speak to suffering and handicapped people and fighting for the rights of those who are often neglected and pushed aside because of disabilities. Far more meaningful is that her example and positive, upbeat message of faith and hope have changed the lives of thousands of people.

Her organizations, Joni and Friends, and Wheels for the World, have delivered thousands of wheelchairs to people around the world. While obtaining a wheelchair for the handicapped is a "given" in the industrial world, especially in the West, in many underdeveloped countries a crippled individual would have to drag himself or herself in the dirt or hobble with a crutch.

Shantamma, an eighteen-year-old young woman from a Hindu family in Ongole, India, was one of the many who became a beneficiary of Joni's ministry. Describing her plight, Joni wrote: "No one born in the poverty and despair of the teeming slums of this city has an easy life. But many have had it easier than Shantamma. Born with a disability, she has spent her life scooting around on the floor of the family's tiny home, dragging her legs behind her and rarely venturing outside her front door."[10]

The story behind the story of how she received a wheelchair through Joni's ministry is that about four years previously a pastor, knowing of how Joni challenged her disability, found a well-used book written by Joni and gave it to Shantamma. She read the book and then read it again. Eight times she read the book! Then with tears streaming down her face, "she made up her mind to trust in Jesus Christ . . . *just like Joni.*" No, not because she thought she would someday get a wheelchair, something that eventually was made possible by Joni and Friends, but because she wanted Christ to help her just as He had Joni.

Telling of the joy that came to the life of this young woman through both hope in God's grace and mercy and the gift of a wheelchair, Joni wrote:

> My friends, this is one of a million reasons why I
> am grateful God didn't heal me of my paralysis. What

if I had been healed at the Kathryn Kuhlman crusade
back in the early 1970s? What if God had answered
my prayers as a 17-year-old, released me from my
paralysis, and returned me to a life of a woman on her
feet? It might have been well for me, but what about
Shantamma?[11]

There would have been no *Joni* book for the pastor to give this
young woman with so little hope and so few prospects, and there
would have been no Joni and Friends or Wheels for the World to do
a wheelchair distribution for impoverished people in Ongole, India.[12]

> When someone goes to the doctor and asks, "Will I get well?"
> most of them really want to know:
>
> - If I do get well, will my life be worth living?
> - Will I ever be useful to anyone again?
> - Can I make a difference in our world?
>
> Why those questions? Because all together too often we
> equate the value of a person's life with their ability to relate to
> people and to accomplish certain things. Subsequently when one
> comes to grips with the fact that he or she is going to be either
> bedridden or in a wheelchair for the rest of his or her life, depen-
> dent on a team of helpers to bath, get dressed, handle phone calls
> and e-mail, and essentially take you where you want to go, the
> feeling of helplessness descends like a heavy fog gradually destroy-
> ing hopes and dreams, and that sense of helplessness and hopeless-
> ness can only dissipate by your becoming "strong in the broken
> places," as Hemingway described it.

What has Joni's suffering done for her?

My affliction has stretched my hope, made me
know Christ better, helped me long for truth, led me
to repentance of sin, goaded me to give thanks in
times of sorrow, increased my faith, and strengthened

my character. Being in this wheelchair has meant
knowing Him better, feeling His pleasure every
day."[13]

She followed this by asking, "If that doesn't qualify as a miracle
in your book, then—may I say it in all kindness?—I prefer my book
to yours."

No Suffering Is Ever Wasted

In his book *Why Us?* Warren Wiersbe tells of visiting a dear friend
whose world had come apart. Her husband had gone blind, and then
her own health failed. As she struggled with an incurable disease, followed by a stroke that ended her employment, she was forced to remain
at home to care for her husband when she actually needed care herself.

In a conversation with her, Wiersbe said what we often say to
people, at times without a great deal of thought, "I want you to know
that we're praying for you!"

"I appreciate that," she replied and then said, "What are you praying for God to do?" "As she waited for my reply," said Wiersbe, "I
found myself struggling for a mature answer. I had never really been
confronted with that question before!" He explained that he was praying for the Lord to restore her health and provide comfort and help.

Then she said, "Thank you, but please pray for one more request.
Pray that I won't waste all of this suffering." What a remarkable person—praying that her suffering won't be wasted.[14]

This dear woman understood that suffering is an investment God
makes in our lives because He trusts us enough to allow us to face the
dark hours of the soul.

Can suffering be wasted? Of course! Job's wife even suggested
that he curse God and die! What a waste that would have been! Some
people profit little from the investment of suffering, yet others capitalize on it and receive great gain. Here's what John Piper wrote about
cancer, which can apply as well to all other kinds suffering. It [cancer]
is wasted when . . .

    1.   You do not believe that it is designed for you by God.

2. You believe it is a curse and not a gift.
3. You seek comfort from your odds rather than from God.
4. You refuse to think about death.
5. You think that "beating" your illness means staying alive.
6. You spend too much time consumed with your illness rather with God.
7. You let your illness drive you into solitude or depression instead of letting it deepen your relationship with God.
8. You grieve as those who have no hope.
9. You treat sin as casually as before.
10. You fail to use it as a means of witness to the truth and glory of Christ.[15]

Over many years of radio broadcasting, I have received letters and e-mails from thousands of people around the world who describe the pain and suffering in their lives. Some become bitter; others become better. Some have written to tell how they have reaped rich dividends from suffering. Such was the woman who wrote, "Lately I've been going through some hard times. I heard your broadcast that said every bit of suffering will either draw you away from God or draw you closer. In my case, it has drawn me closer. I don't like it [suffering], but I still end up thanking God because the closeness [with Him] is what I've always wanted."

A woman, whose world collapsed to the point that she tried unsuccessfully to end her life five times, turned to the Lord and experienced the deep dividends from suffering. She wrote, "I've been telling all who would listen that my illness had been allowed to happen so I would be brought close to God, and even then I didn't fully realize that Christ, whom I had known and loved as a little girl, would be such a real and utterly fantastic part of my life."

A man who was injured in a sports accident that confined him to a sickbed, wrote, "Friends who come to visit ask why I am so cheerful." He explained, "I can't see any reason for being sad. I might not be happy that I have to be in bed, but I have a deep joy that even I marvel about. I know and love the God who loves and cares for me and shows it."

When we pray about needs, we usually pray to be delivered from the pain of suffering, from the loneliness of estrangement, from the vale of bereavement; yet when we pass through the valley, there is gain, and when we walk through the dark night, we sense the presence of Him who said, "I will never leave you nor forsake you" (Heb. 13:5).

When you face the hour of suffering, pray, "Dear God, grant that this will not be wasted in my life. Give me a teachable spirit and stay close to me that the investment of Your presence will not be lost."

The Fruits of Redemptive Healing

Redemptive Healing Brings Knowledge of Christ That Is Unsurpassed

Those who are to find purpose in pain sooner or later have to get beyond the "Why me?" question. The "Why not me?" question, on the other hand, is born out of accepting the reality that we are living in a broken world. The sun and rain fall alike on the just and the unjust, and while I believe God blesses His children, there are times when He blesses them with suffering so that their lives can be enriched in ways that would never happen apart from the lessons learned during difficult times. Joni Eareckson Tada describes pain as "a bruising of a blessing" but quickly adds, "but it *is* a blessing nevertheless."

What God has not revealed can never be explained satisfactorily. Some have, at times, conjectured whether or not there will be a "get your questions answered here" line in heaven. I, for one, believe that when we arrive at our eternal home in heaven, one of two things will be true: Either we will know . . . or it just won't matter, and I really believe that the latter carries more weight. Christopher Morley in his little book *Inward Ho!* writes of meeting God. He says, "I had a million questions to ask God: but when I met Him, they all fled my mind; and it didn't seem to matter."[16]

Generally, those who are mature in the faith handle the challenge of redemptive suffering better and profit more from it than those who are weak in the faith or have none. The former understand that God is our refuge, our hiding place, and the One to whom we can turn for strength. With David they cry out, "Lead me to the rock that is higher than I, for you have been my refuge, a strong tower against the enemy" (Ps. 61:2–3).

Take, for example, the popular talk-show host and former pastor, Rich Buhler, whose syndicated radio program *Talk from the Heart* has had a large audience of people who have responded to his warmth and understanding. Rich explained: "When I was diagnosed with inoperable and terminal pancreatic cancer . . . it was obviously a huge earthquake in all our lives as a family. My doctors were terrific but had nothing to offer. No surgery. No radiation. No chemotherapy. . . . I felt enveloped by God from the beginning. So if I was facing my final journey, I wasn't mad at God and didn't feel ripped off."

In response to my question, "Would you be comfortable in letting me know how your life has been affected?" Rich responded with the following:

1. I'm not afraid to die. I can't lose. I'll either live longer and do more work for God or I'll go home to be with Him. Either way is a win.

2. I'm more friendly with death now than I was before. I've realized that even if I survive this disease, I'm not going to survive forever. It's just a matter of timing. I don't feel in the company of the doomed. I feel in the large and nonexclusive company of those who will face death. That's all of us.

3. I want to live in faith and hope in God's power and make sure that nothing in me would block God's healing, but at the same time to let God be God and submit to His will.

4. Music has meant a lot [to me]. The "language" of my spiritual renewal in the 1970s was Southern Gospel music and the Gaithers so I've been soaking up those wonderful songs.

5. I'm grateful for what cancer victims call "the gift of time." I've had the privilege of preparing for my death. . . . I've been able to "get my house in order" and accomplish little tasks that needed to be done. . . . We have a close and loving family, but there has been resolution of things that would not have happened without this crisis.[17]

Finally, after expressing thanks for the thousands who made contact with him, expressing gratitude for his life and ministry, Rich concluded, "I would not have chosen this experience. . . . But I am deeply grateful for it and some of what it has accomplished in my heart that probably would not have happened otherwise. *We don't volunteer for the most intense experiences of our lives. God has been, is being, and will be faithful.*[18]

Those who experience Christ in the communion of suffering learn that

- He knows your pain.
- He understands your emotions and your feelings.
- He has suffered your pain, for He has been there and experienced death and resurrection.

Redemptive Healing Produces the Realization of Christ's Presence

After the resurrection of Jesus Christ, He made a promise to His followers that becomes especially meaningful in times of suffering and pain. He said boldly, "I am with you always, to the end of the age" (Matt. 28:20). Some thirty years later the writer of Hebrews affirmed that promise, quoting Jesus as saying, "'I will never leave you nor forsake you.' So we can confidently say, 'The Lord is my helper; I will not fear; what can man do to me?'" (Heb. 13:5–6). The force of the Greek text only strengthens what Christ promises. The thought can be paraphrased as, "Never will I leave you; never will I forsake you, *not even for a moment.*"

Oswaldo Magdangal, Wally to his friends, was an OFW (Overseas Filipino Worker), one out of some eleven million Filipinos working abroad. Taking a position in Saudi Arabia allowed Wally to send money home to his family every month. And it also afforded him the opportunity to serve as a pastor to a small group of Filipinos who met weekly for praise and worship. Wally did this knowing that there was risk attached—Christian worship was dangerous in this Muslim country where the Christian church had not been recognized for fourteen hundred years.

Then it happened. Wally, along with a coworker, was arrested after their meeting place had been raided by the Muttawa, the Saudi religious police force. For three-and-a-half hours he was tortured physically and mentally. Says Paul Estabrooks, "They slapped, boxed and kicked him on the face. Then using a long stick, they lashed his back and the palms of his hands. Then the soles of his feet. He could not stand without wincing and he described his bruised body as looking 'like an eggplant'."

When Wally was finally taken to a prison cell, he prayed for five hours, thanking God that he was counted worthy to suffer for the name of Jesus. He was reminded that Jesus said, "Blessed are you when others revile you and persecute you and utter all kinds of evil against you falsely on my account. Rejoice and be glad, for your reward is great in heaven, for so they persecuted the prophets who were before you" (Matt. 5:11–12).

Then something happened. In his own words Wally explained: "Suddenly there was light. The cell was filled with the *Shekinah* glory. God's presence was there. He knelt and started to touch my face. He told me, 'My son, I have seen all of it, that's why I'm here. I am assuring you that I will never leave you or forsake you'."

Eventually Wally drifted off into a restless sleep. Waking up a few hours later, to his great surprise, he saw that his bruises had faded and the cuts from the abuse had disappeared. He said, "God had completely restored me."

Following this ordeal, Wally and his coworker were condemned to death. Execution was scheduled for Christmas Day, but miraculously, at the last moment, he was deported to the Philippines instead.[19]

Few are ever allowed an encounter with Christ such as what Oswaldo Magdangal experienced, but every one of God's children is an heir of the promise He made long ago. While you may not always sense His presence or "feel it," remember that as the songwriter put it, "He was there all the time." Like the disciples on the road to Emmaus who did not know that Christ was walking with them, we are often unaware of His presence. In the dark quiet of the night, however, those who turn pain into gain can be confident of His presence and can be assured that He sees their tears and hears their pleas for help.

Redemptive Healing Brings a Sense of Peace in Times of Pain

When Jesus met with the disciples in the Upper Room for the last time, with the cross on the horizon, He was a picture of tranquility and complete peace. Jesus knew that driving the money changers from the temple area was akin to kicking a hornet's nest. He knew that the religious leaders were plotting His death, yet He gave the disciples a heritage of peace when He said, "Peace I leave with you; my peace I give to you" (John 14:27).

When Jesus, for emphasis, repeated the promise of peace, He used the possessive pronoun, "*My* peace I give to you—a sharp contrast to the peace of the world." Jesus knew what was on the other side of the last breath on earth—resurrection! And that assurance removes the fear of death that disturbs so many.

The greatest truth in the world is that death cannot keep those who are redeemed by His work of redemption. Upon the cross Jesus cried out, "*Tetelestai*"—one word in Greek, three in English, "*IT IS FINISHED*" (John 19:30).

Nothing can bring more peace than knowing that suffering and disease are not forever. There is an end. This assurance brings peace in pain and hope instead of despair. The noted surgeon, Dr. Paul Brand, wrote, "One of the most important gifts we in the health profession [and may I as the author add "the church"] can offer our patients is hope, thereby inspiring in the patient a deep conviction that inner strength can make a difference in the struggle against pain and suffering."[20]

Knowing that there is an eternal home in heaven awaiting those who have placed their faith in Christ provides a powerful motive to look beyond the pain. It brings purpose to our suffering by allowing us to view life as a redemptive process. As the Puritan preacher John Fuller put it, "If afflictions refine some, they consume others."

Redemptive Healing Brings Solidarity with Those Who Suffer

How many times have I attempted to console someone who had just lost a husband or a wife, and the person would respond, "You don't know how I feel; you haven't lost your wife," and in this they were correct. There are times when other people cannot understand our pain. But consider this: No individual will ever face a darker night than what Jesus faced. No person will ever suffer more intensely than He did on the cross. No one will ever feel more separated and estranged from the Father than He who cried out, "My God, why have you forsaken me?" (Mark 15:34). Jesus truly knows how we feel.

That's why we are told that Christ was "crowned with glory and honor because He suffered death for us. Yes, because of God's great kindness, Jesus tasted death for everyone in the world" (Heb. 2:19 TLB).

When someone says, "I know what you are going through because I've been there myself," you sense an understanding and a mutual bond that brings your hearts together.

David Jacobs, age seven, was fighting leukemia when he was sitting in a line of chairs, awaiting a certain medical procedure. Looking up at the man seated next to him, David asked, "Have you had this test before?" And when the man nodded, David asked again, "Does it hurt very much when they put the needle in?" Not wanting to mislead the little boy, the man said, "Yes, it hurts a bit." Then after a moment of silence, David said, "You know, Mister, Jesus knows what pain is about; they put a crown of thorns on His head and crucified Him."

He was right, and in this you know "the fellowship of his sufferings" (Phil. 3:10 KJV), as Paul described it. Writing to the Corinthians, Paul called God "the Father of mercies and God of all comfort, who comforts us in all our affliction, so that we may be able to comfort those who are in any affliction, with the comfort with which we ourselves are comforted by God. For as we share abundantly in Christ's sufferings, so through Christ we share abundantly in comfort too" (2 Cor. 1:3–5).

Redemptive Suffering Culminates in Eventual Resurrection— Ultimate Healing

You may say, "I'm more interested in talking about health, happiness, life, and pleasure *now*—isn't that what finding God's purpose for my life is about?" One of the things you don't learn in a classroom is that part of God's purpose for our lives is for us to be enriched, purified, and changed into His image through suffering, pain, hardship, and difficulty.

God's purpose in times of difficulty is to refine us until the world sees His reflection in our lives. He's always in control so that we never experience too much fire at too intense a temperature and never for too long. Suffering is something we can view with perspective only when we have crossed into His presence.

Paul's comments to the Corinthians aptly describe seeing beyond pain and suffering: "For now we see in a mirror dimly, but then face to face. Now I know in part; then I shall know fully, even as I have been fully known" (1 Cor. 13:12).

Alynne Mann Golding, the daughter of a pastor, understands redemptive suffering. During her high school years her mother became ill, a sickness that even prevented her from attending her graduation that took place a distance from their home. Alynne shares, "On a Saturday, in a roadside restaurant . . . my father told me that my mother had cancer. I had never been so scared in my life before that moment. Her surgery was planned."

Following surgery the doctor told them, "We got it all," yet the cancer returned. "I watched my mother go through those horrible treatments," Alynne says, adding, "I saw her lose her hair. I saw her lose her vitality . . . and eventually, I saw my mother turn into someone that at times I barely recognized."

There is one more part of this drama that you need to know. Alynne's father was the pastor of a church that believed in healing. A twenty-four-hour prayer chain had been formed. People had been fasting and praying. They knew that God loved her even more than they did and that He might, perhaps, call her home. And that was exactly what happened.

The church members became discouraged and left "wondering whether they had prayed enough, fasted enough, or been faithful enough." *Was a lack of faith on their part responsible for her death?*

Realizing that some of these issues had to be addressed, Pastor Mann went to the pulpit the Sunday after his wife's burial. Says Alynne, "My father spoke eloquently about my mother's final days. He spoke about her life and his confidence in the eternal reward she had entered into even at that moment. His voice broke as he expressed our eternal gratitude for how the people had walked with us. Then he heard the Lord whisper in his ear, "Don't forget to tell them that I've healed her.'"

"Don't forget to tell them that You've healed her? You've healed her? But she's gone. . . . why couldn't You have healed her here?"

Then wrote Alynne:

> We so often define healing narrowly . . . qualifying only what happens in this life. What happens here? Does God heal our illness here? Does He extend our time here? Because we want those we love to stay longer *here*, what happens *here* easily over-shadows the big story. But the big story tells us that those He heals *there* are healed forever. No more pain . . . no more death . . . no more sorrow . . . no more suffering.
>
> Then Alynne added a final thought: "Cancer eventually won the battle . . . but not the ultimate war. I'll see my mom again someday. And she'll be *healed.*[21]

At the end of redemptive healing, there is *ultimate healing—that which lasts forever.*

Turning Pain and Suffering into Redemptive Healing

Before we begin a new chapter, let me give you some guidelines that will assist you in tapping God's resources for your journey.

1. Focus on God—not on your pain. Remember, He is the "God of all comfort" (2 Cor. 1:3) who promises to walk with you through your challenge (see Isa. 43:1–3). When an angel sent from God appeared to Gideon (one of the Old Testament judges) with the message, "The LORD is with you" (Judg. 6:12), Gideon—a no-nonsense sort of person responded, "Please, sir, if the LORD is with us, why then has all this happened to us? And where are all his wonderful deeds that our fathers recounted to us?" (v. 13). A friend whose husband was struggling with the effects of chemotherapy wrote, "On occasion I want to run through the deep Hell's Canyon nearby and scream high, shrieky echoes." When you feel that way, remember God knows and understands. David wrote, "For he knows our frame; he remembers that we are dust" (P. 103:14). When you pray, vent your emotions and feelings.

Tell God exactly how you feel, but at the same time hold on to the promises of Scripture, that leads to the next suggestion.

2. **Tell your emotions where to get off.** Keep in mind that pain is a liar who attacks everything the Bible says about God and His compassion and care for you. While your head and heart are only some eighteen inches apart, there are times when they seem to be on different continents. How? Your emotions tell you that you have been abandoned by a God who is either disinterested, too weak to help you, or hard of hearing. But your intellect says: "I'm not the first who has walked through this valley, and neither will I be the last. I'm going to stand upon the promises of God's Word, trust Him, and focus on that which is positive. I will let the Word of God bring me comfort and hope." Don't believe all your doubts or doubt all your beliefs. Refuse to destroy by doubt what God by faith is bringing to pass in your life.

3. **Listen to the voices of God's servants** who have gone through difficult times such as you are facing. Read the biographies of individuals such as Corrie ten Boom, Joni Eareckson Tada, and Amy Carmichael, whom I wrote about in this chapter; Fanny Crosby, who was blinded in her childhood yet wrote eight thousand hymns touching the lives of millions; Hudson Taylor, missionary to China; Dr. Paul Brand, one of the twentieth century's greatest surgeons, known for his work with lepers, who combined faith and medicine; Lettie Cowman, a remarkable woman who cared for her husband during a long illness until his death and who wrote numerous classics such as *Streams in the Desert*; C. S. Lewis who lost his wife to cancer and who wrote, among many classics, *The Problem of Pain*; and Charles Spurgeon, one of the most influential pastors of the nineteenth century who struggled with bouts of depression so severe he was unable to even get out of bed. And, yes, read Philip Yancey, whose books *Where Is God When it Hurts* and *The Gift of Pain*, coauthored with Dr. Paul Brand, are unexcelled!

4. **Fill your life with music** that enriches, encourages, and helps you focus on God's healing power. Remember that all great music comes from God, regardless of how it is categorized. Do you recall how Rich Buhler affirmed that music allowed him to find solace when pain challenged him? When apologist Francis Schaeffer was struggling with cancer, he, too, found comfort and peace in listening to classical music.

5. *Ignore the well-intentioned but empty counsel of friends* who have all the answers to your illness but actually don't even understand the questions. Vance Havner, an evangelist of the past generation known for his pithy sayings, did that following the agonizing death of his wife. "I don't understand some of the things we went through," he wrote. "There were a lot of things I don't have any clever answers for. When I meet some brother who has smug and quick answers for some of these problems, I say, 'Brother, bless your heart; you're not for me; you know too much.'"[22]

6. *Realize that nothing but heaven is "forever."* When I had my first computer, which required an operating system known as DOS, it was necessary to write an operating batch file that would appear on the screen as I booted the computer. I wrote a line in mine that prompted me of this truth: *"Remember, this too shall pass."* Yes, I know that time almost stands still when you are battling pain, but don't forget what David wrote, "Weeping may endure for a night but joy comes in the morning" (Ps. 30:5 NKJV).

7. *Don't waste your suffering.* Listen to the quiet whispers of the Holy Spirit who will bring comfort, sometimes correct, and give you hope. Andrew Murray, the Scottish pastor whose writings have blessed hundreds of thousands over many decades, was felled by illness and during that time wrote to his wife, "I have felt that it was a very great kindness to have such a time for the renewal of my bodily strength and of mental quiet and refreshment for the work before me."[23]

It's time to turn the page.

What You Need to Know

• Individuals who have "all the answers" usually don't even understand the questions; therefore, you must never let anyone intimidate you with statements or even inferences that your sickness is the result of sin in your life (when your conscience is clear before God), or that if you only had faith to trust God for your healing, you would be made well. How are modern "Job's advisers" to know your heart?

• Praying according to God's will is not a "Well, Lord, I really don't expect You to do this even though it would be nice" sort of petition. When you earnestly and sincerely pray for God's will, you are praying at the highest level of faith. God always gives His best to those who leave the choice to Him.

• The Shepherd of your soul will never leave you alone. As Corrie ten Boom said, "There is no pit so deep that the love of God is not deeper still." Twice the New Testament records the fact that Jesus, who is a specialist in understanding how you feel when you suffer, said He would never leave you or forsake you (Matt. 28:20 and Heb. 13:5).

• When you have nothing left but God, you will discover that God is enough!

• Focus on heaven. There is an end to suffering and sorrow because death and resurrection are ultimate healing!

CHAPTER 9

What to Do When You Need Healing

W hy didn't you put this chapter at the front of the book?" you may be asking. Here's why! You need what has preceded this chapter as a foundation for the time when you find yourself facing the wall—a rerun of what Hezekiah did long ago—and crying out with scalding tears for God's help. Your sadness may be for yourself or for your spouse or child, but sooner or later we will all have to face the "wailing wall" of suffering.

At the risk of oversimplification, I'm going to outline eight steps that will help you find healing God's way. His way alone provides ultimate and lasting healing. Apart from God's answer to the need of your life, you will get lost or sidetracked on the journey and end up disillusioned and disappointed. Large fortunes have been spent by people desperately striving to find a cure in the wrong places, which is tantamount to looking for a light switch in a dark room where there is no lightbulb.

If you have known Jesus Christ only from a distance, please realize that God wills *wholeness* for you—spiritually, physically, and emotionally. When He touches your life, every aspect will be made anew. Many people today want a quick fix—a healing that means "no surgery, no more suffering, and no more dark nights of pain." God has far more than this in mind, and as you allow Him to invade your life, you will become a new person. That's the promise of God's Word that has your name on it.

We call the day Jesus was impaled on the old rugged cross "Good Friday." On that infamous day God's only Son paid the price of your redemption. And regardless of how skeptics strive to deny the power of that cross, the Bible affirms that "with his wounds we are healed" (Isa. 53:5; 1 Pet. 2:24).

There are steps to healing. The distance, though, between some of these steps may differ for you as you move progressively toward Him who invites, "Come to me, all who labor and are heavy laden, and I will give you rest. Take my yoke upon you, and learn from me, for I am gentle and lowly in heart, and you will find rest for your souls. For my yoke is easy, and my burden is light" (Matt. 11:28–30). These steps are like a staircase that allows you to transcend the shackles of your pain and suffering and kneel in front of Him who loves you and will heal you *His way*, which may not necessarily be your way.

Step 1: Stay Focused on the Great Physician

In the last section of the previous chapter, my first recommendation in turning pain and suffering into redemptive healing is to the degree that you can, stop being consumed with your sickness or pain and look to Jesus as your Healer. This, of course, is not easy when your body screams out in pain.

Do you remember the incident recorded in Matthew 14 that shows a story so improbable that we would certainly deny it had taken place apart from the fact that nature and the laws that govern it yielded to God's authority? On this occasion Jesus, weary from a long day of ministry, sought a place of solitude for prayer. Then between 3:00 a.m. and 6:00 a.m., He decided to cross the northern end of the Sea of Galilee, where the disciples were in a small boat battling a strong wind, going nowhere. Jesus came to them walking on the water. Here is the record. When the disciples saw Him coming toward them they were terrified, certain that it was a ghost. That's when Jesus assured them that it was He—not an apparition or a ghost—who was drawing near. And Peter, characteristic of his personality, said, "Lord, if it is you, command me to come to you on the water" (Matt. 14:28). And Jesus said, "Come" (v. 29). Then without thinking, Peter kicks one leg over the gunwale of the boat, then the other, and . . . yes, starts walking toward Jesus!

At this point Peter must have begun thinking, *This is not for real! I can't be walking on the water. Look at the waves with their frenzied whitecaps!* And that's when doubt destroyed what faith had just enabled. Peter cried out, "Lord, save me" (v. 30). And Jesus immediately reached out His hand, took hold of Peter, and said to him, "O you of little faith, why did you doubt?" (v. 31).

As long as your thoughts are on dying, don't expect God to do much for you. Turn your eyes instead upon the Great Physician and focus on living. Understand, as the writer of Hebrews affirmed, "Jesus Christ is the same yesterday and today and forever" (Heb. 13:8).

Henry Frost put it better when he wrote:

> If, therefore, He loved in the days of His flesh,
> He loves now; if He cared then, He cares now; if He
> healed then, He will undoubtedly heal now. It does
> not necessarily follow that He will do now all that He
> did then, or that He will do what He does now in the
> same way as He did then, for His purposes in some
> things are different at present from what they were in
> the past.[1]

Step 2: Accept that God's Nature and Desire Is to Heal the Brokenness of Your Life

The wife of Albert Einstein was once asked if she understood the theory of relativity that her husband had espoused. With a slight smile she replied, "No, but Albert does, and he is to be trusted." So it should be with us.

When Paul wrote to the Corinthians, who lived only a few miles from Athens and were highly influenced by Greek thought, he asked, "For who has understood the mind of the Lord so as to instruct him?"

Then Paul explained how we can know something of God's purpose: "But we have the mind of Christ" (1 Cor. 2:16). In the Upper Room, as Jesus met with the disciples for the last time, He told them that "whoever has seen me has seen the Father" (John 14:9).

Bringing your thinking into sync with God's purpose and will allows you to live as His child, intent on doing what He wants as opposed to what you want. Praying "Not my will but Yours be done" is scary until you learn that God is a loving, compassionate, and caring Father—not a bully who inflicts you with disease or pain just to see how you will react. No, He will meet you at the point of your need.

God sent His Son so that you could have a relationship with Him, and this means you can know God and converse with Him in prayer. If your attitude has been that of the comedian who, striving to be funny, prayed, "God, I won't bother You if You don't bother me," you don't know God. Only through getting to know Him will you understand His nature and character.

Step 3: Examine Your Heart and Make Sure You Are Right with God and Others

This means you need to take time for honest reflection, heart searching, and prayer. First, take inventory of your relationship with God and with other people. Whenever someone falls sick, it is very easy for that person to begin to reason that "my sickness is the result of something that I have done, something that God may well consider to be sin." But that is not necessarily true. Only honest examination of your heart can determine whether you have sin in your life that needs to be confessed.

Three Things to Ask Yourself in the Midst of Suffering

Am I the cause of my own suffering? Illness can be the result of a bad choice or human weakness, and a righteous God does not always spare us the consequences. It's like the teenage boy who borrowed his father's car without permission and inadvertently smashed the fender.

Looking at the damage, wondering how he was going to tell his father, he pled, "Dear God, I pray this thing didn't happen!"

More than a few have voiced this kind of prayer the morning after an evening they wish had not happened. Think of how an unwanted pregnancy or the exposure to someone with a sexually transmitted disease or HIV can bring unexpected guilt and eventual suffering.

There are situations that stand between us and God's mercy, things we can deal with. In Psalm 66 the writer says, "If I had cherished iniquity in my heart, the Lord would not have listened. But truly God has listened; he has attended to the voice of my prayer" (Ps. 66:18–19). He is saying that when we practice that which we know is wrong, it becomes a hindrance to answered prayer. Peter, in the first book that bears his name, also talks about prayers going unanswered because of the conflict between a husband and wife (see 1 Pet. 3:7).

If you are responsible for what confronts you, remember that if you confess your wrongdoing to God and ask His forgiveness, God will forgive you. As Isaiah 43:25 says, He blots out our sin and no longer remembers our shortcomings. The Bible is clear in asserting that "if we confess our sins, he is faithful and just to forgive us our sins and to cleanse us from all unrighteousness" (1 John 1:9). That means you must also forgive yourself and realize His grace and goodness begin afresh every morning.

A sidebar thought before we move on: Remember the story in chapter 6 about Brian Wills, the young man with Burkitt's lymphoma who should have died? As he cried out for healing, the image of the face of a person with whom he had had conflict years before strangely appeared in his mind's eye—someone he had neither seen in a long time nor had forgiven. Only when he forgave did God bring healing.

Does this mean, though, that you should simply "tough it out" when you face the consequences of your actions? No! This is where God's mercy and compassion come into the picture. David, a man who knew human failure, cried out, "But with you there is forgiveness, that you may be feared" (Ps. 130:4); and again, "The Lord is merciful and gracious. . . . He does not deal with us according to our sins, nor repay us according to our iniquities. . . . As a father shows compassion to his children, so the Lord shows compassion to those who fear him. For he knows our frame; he remembers that we are dust" (Ps. 103:8, 10, 13–14).

Can I expect the Father's presence and comfort as I go through my valley? A farmer's son would go to town and enjoy the company of his friends, often staying out later than his father had requested. Finally the dad said, "Son, if you are not home by midnight tonight, I'm locking the door, and you can't sleep in the house." Having a good time with his friends that evening, the son forgot to watch the clock and arrived home at 1:00 a.m. The door was locked, just as the father said would happen.

I can't believe Dad is doing this to me, the son thought as he turned toward their barn, opening the old barn door and slowly climbing into the hayloft, where he lay down. A few minutes later, he suddenly heard the creaking sound of the barn door being opened. At first fearful that an intruder might have entered, he lay still and listened. There was the sound of footsteps. Then the silence was penetrated by the strong voice of his dad saying, "Son, I told you that if you got home after midnight, you couldn't sleep in the house, but I've come to spend the rest of the night with you."

As a father who grieves over what a wayward son has done but who refuses to turn his back on him, a compassionate, loving God will allow His Son, the Great Physician, to be your companion through the dark night of your soul.

If, however, your illness—whatever it may be—is not the result of *anything* you have done, don't live under an assumed burden of guilt. We live in a broken world and have no choice when it comes to the DNA we receive from our parents or what happens to us in life. The many illnesses that fill the pages of medical textbooks are not electives; they are challenges that confront us, but they are never greater than the grace of God and His compassion and care.

If you drive from Jerusalem to Jericho, you will see, near the Inn of the Good Samaritan and located on the right side of the old highway, an actual valley which for centuries has been known as the Valley of the Shadow of Death. During the winter months a shepherd taking sheep from Bethlehem (now a suburb of Jerusalem) at an altitude of twenty-five hundred feet must go down through that valley to reach a lower altitude where there are green pastures. Much of the land leading to the valley is desolate, and cloudbursts occasionally fill it with water, imperiling the lives of anyone who might be there. "I have seen this valley with water as high as the roof of a car," says veteran Israeli guide David Kidron. It was through this valley that the psalmist David undoubtedly led his father's sheep, yet he said, "Even though I walk through the valley of the shadow of death, I will fear no evil, for you are with me" (Ps. 23:4).

On April 27, 2011, David Wilkerson, founder of Teen Challenge and author of *The Cross and the Switchblade*, was killed in a head-on collision with a tractor trailer as he drove east on U.S. 175 in Texas. The morning of the accident, Wilkerson had blogged, "To those going through the valley of the shadow of death, hear this word: Weeping will last through some dark, awful nights, and in that darkness you will soon hear the Father whisper, 'I am with you.'"[2]

None is exempt from passing through that valley in life; neither is any exempt from the promise of the Father to be with us and the assurance of the Son never to leave or forsake us. This gives us heart and courage to face the valleys of life.

Is the devil responsible? Or is my pain simply the result of living in a broken world?[3] Is your affliction the result of the devil's attack on your life? While it is possible, it is improbable. Frankly, the devil gets credit for a whole lot more than he deserves. I'm thinking of a dented fender I saw on one occasion where someone had painted the words: "The devil made me do it!" But sometimes suffering is an attack of Satan. Scripture tells us Paul's thorn in the flesh was a messenger of Satan. He hindered Paul and Silas from going east into Bithynia on their second missionary journey, according to Luke who wrote the account. The source of your illness or pain, however, is in all likelihood the result of living in a broken world.

Take a flight on an airplane and you breath recirculated air—germs, bacteria, and whatever. While wearing a mask would be more hygienic, you don't want to appear paranoid so you brave it, and you catch a cold. And the doorknob you turned this morning had been held by a hundred people before you touched it, right? So when your hand touched your face, you transferred a virus that soon caused a sinus infection.

Frederick Gaiser puts the dilemma so well:

> And what of us—finite humans, beset by the
> random ills brought through the complex rules of the
> game of creation, the ills we bring upon ourselves by
> our own most grievous faults, and the ills perpetrated
> by others, of which we are sometimes victims? And
> maybe the ills and illnesses that are the mask of death
> itself, the demons stalking us before our time. In all
> these ways we are like other humans. But for the
> people of God, the rules are the same, only different.
> We are exempt neither from the laws of nature nor
> from the consequences of evil, our own or that of
> others. But God is with us, God who chose to enter
> the game under the same rules as we. If that is true,
> what will it look like to be well?[4]

In the seventh century before the birth of Christ, Isaiah recorded the words of the Almighty to Israel, and while they were directed to a specific group of individuals, they apply equally to all of God's children, whom Paul refers to as "the Israel of God." Isaiah says, "When you pass through the waters, I will be with you; and through the rivers, they shall not overwhelm you; when you walk through the fire you shall not be burned, and the flame shall not consume you. For I am the LORD your God" (Isa. 43:2–3). Isaiah then adds that we are precious in His sight and that He loves us—truths that are fleshed out in the New Testament.

Note, however, that all of the above is prefaced by a powerful adverb, "*When* . . ." This means that *everybody*, sooner or later, will pass through that dark valley. But this reality is tempered by the promise that the Shepherd of our soul, the Lord Jesus Christ who brought healing and help to troubled people during His ministry, will "never leave you nor forsake you" (Heb. 13:5).

While most of us prefer not to think about it, "Everybody is terminal!" Everybody! No exceptions. When a certain man was fighting a losing battle with cancer, he was asked, "How does it feel to know that you are going to die?" He immediately responded by asking, "How does it feel for you to pretend that you are not?"

Dr. Diane Komp tells of visits to her favorite vegetarian restaurant, where the walls are decorated with signs proclaiming the virtue of fiber and the evils of nuclear waste. At this restaurant, which specializes in healthy food, servers write the patron's first name on the checks. When asked her name, Dr. Komp would reply, "Dr. Di." Somewhat amused, she noted that on at least five occasions one waiter had written, "Dr. Die." When she asked the young man why he spelled her name in that manner (rather than thinking of Princess Diana's nickname), he said: "I am absolutely terrified by death. I can't even tolerate saying the word."[5] Little did he realize he was talking with a world-renowned pediatric oncologist who had battled the grim reaper of children all her adult life. So healing, while it is wonderful, is temporary! Ultimate healing is death and resurrection.

A relationship with God helps you see beyond the fear of death. The writer of Hebrews says that through His death, Christ has delivered us "who through fear of death were subject to lifelong slavery" (Heb. 2:15). That's why Paul could defiantly say, "O death, where is your victory? O death, where is your sting?" (1 Cor. 15:55).

Step 4: Pray and Believe God for Your Healing

"Who? Me pray?" you may be asking, thinking that you are not good enough, not spiritual enough, or not on good enough terms with God to reach heaven with your request for healing. First, you have to understand that God won't answer your prayer because *you* are good enough! The fact is that *no one* is "good enough" to merit special favor with God. God answers my heart cry for one reason—I am His child and He is my Father. Remember that when the disciples heard Jesus pray, they came to Him with a simple request: "Lord, teach us to pray" (Luke 11:1).

Jesus began by telling them, "Your Father knows what you need before you ask him" (Matt. 6:8). Then He said, "Pray, then, like this: Our Father in heaven" (v. 9). Forget about using the right terminology (as if such a thing exists). Prayer is conversation. If you are not accustomed to praying, it may seem awkward, like riding a bicycle for the first time. But God gives you the freedom to tell Him exactly what's on your mind.

Pray with humility. To say, "God, I'm at the end of myself, and I have nowhere else to turn," is humiliating. It's like being absolutely broke and having to go to a friend and say, "Hey, could you give me a loan? I don't have enough money to buy bread and milk for the children."

If you can fix something by yourself, you can sit back and say: "Hey, look at what I did! I pulled strings. I fixed my problem. I made the right connections. I'm pretty good." But when we pray, we're asking from a position of weakness. Our resources are bankrupt, and in poverty of spirit we beseech the Lord for His help. Something about the old nature does not like to be put in that position—something called pride.

Stubborn, fierce independence always militates against prayer, yet the stark reality is there are a lot of things we cannot fix—the sorrow and pain of broken relationships, the devastating reality that we are mortal. In spite of what medical technology can achieve, there is a limit to what anyone can do to bring healing. But "man's extremity is God's opportunity," as someone has said, so our poverty of spirit combined with our great need drives us to knock on the door of the King of kings.

How do you overcome a position of weakness? You don't. But it helps to understand that God is not expecting you to come to Him as an equal, to drive a deal with Him by agreeing that if He bails you out of your problems, you'll do something equally helpful for Him in return. This is where grace comes in. Grace comes from the hand of a loving, compassionate Father who delights in meeting you at the point of your need and pain. As the songwriter of "Rock of Ages" put it, "Nothing in my hand I bring, simply to the cross I cling." Prayer is not overcoming God's reluctance but yours.

Pray specifically. When the thief on the cross believed that Christ could make a difference, he got right to the point: "Jesus, remember me when you enter your kingdom" (Luke 23: 42 *The Message*). Peter, attempting to go toward Christ by walking on the water, took his eyes off Christ and, realizing he was sinking, also got to the point and cried out, "Lord, save me" (Matt. 14:30). On another occasion Jesus had fallen asleep in a boat with the disciples while crossing the Sea of Galilee when a severe storm arose. His disciples wakened him and said, "Teacher, don't you even care that we are about to drown?" (Mark 4:38 TLB).

Many promises in Scripture relate to asking specifically for what we need. "Ask, and you will receive, that your joy may be full" (John 16:24), Jesus told the disciples. Again, Scripture says so plainly that we have not because we ask not (see James 4:3).

"Ah," you may say, "but perhaps I can't say it right." Think of how a baby communicates with his mother long before he can express himself verbally, and think of how the mother understands what her child needs.

When some people pray for their own healing, they literally place their hand on the part of their body that needs healing, asking that the Great Physician put His hand where their hand is. If others pray with you and it's appropriate, ask them to place their hands on you, affirming the prayers of the entire group.

Pray earnestly. When the prophet Isaiah delivered a death sentence to King Hezekiah, the king turned his face to the wall, and with scalding tears he made his plea to God. He didn't beat around the bush nor attempt to snow God with "You should do this because I'm a good king!" (see 2 Kings 20). When you are confronted with an appointment with your Creator, no matter who you are or what you have done, you are a pauper standing at heaven's gate, ready to ask for the smallest crumb from the table.

James, the brother of Jesus, describes the prophet Elijah as "a man with a nature like ours" (James 5:17 NKJV)—fully human, fully flawed, fully seeking God for what he could not do himself. James observes, "The effective, fervent prayer of a righteous man avails much" (v. 16 NKJV) He tells how Elijah "prayed fervently that it might not rain, and for three years and six months it did not rain on the earth. Then he prayed again, and heaven gave rain, and the earth bore its fruit" (vv. 17–18).

In a previous passage I said that this verse can be translated as, "The down-to-business prayer of a man who has been justified brings great gain." Simply put, every child of God has been justified in the sight of God on the basis of what Christ did—not what we do or have done; therefore, "Let us therefore come boldly to the throne of grace, that we may obtain mercy and find grace to help in time of need" (Heb. 4:16 NKJV).

The word translated "boldly" is an action word that can also be translated, "to speak freely, openly, fearlessly, express oneself without restraint."[6] This is not license to demand from God or to blame Him for your distress, but it does give you the freedom to express your deep emotions, feelings, and thoughts without fear of condemnation.

Pray in faith. The writer of the book of Hebrews says, "And without faith it is impossible to please him, for whoever would draw near to God must believe that he exists and that he rewards those who seek him" (Heb. 11:6).

What is faith? The American humorist Mark Twain once said that faith is believing what you know is not true. Yet vast numbers of men and women have found it to be the opposite. St. Augustine (c. AD 354–530), one of the most revered Christian leaders of all time, contended that "faith is not believing what we see, and the result of faith is seeing what we believe." Martin Luther, the one-time village priest turned reformer, said, "Faith is a lively, reckless confidence in God." And George Müller, the man who set up orphanages in Bristol, England, and lived by faith in caring for hundreds of orphans, wrote that "faith is the assurance that the thing which God has said in His word is true, and that God will act according to what He has said in His word. This assurance, this reliance on God's Word, this confidence is faith." A final definition, one that I very much like, was given by Quaker scholar Elton Trueblood, "Faith is not belief without proof, but trust without reservation."

When Jesus was stopped by two blind men in Jericho as He made His way toward Jerusalem, He had a conversation with them that went like this: "Have mercy on us, Son of David!" they cried out to Him, a cry that was a self-evident request for him to heal them. In reply He asked them, "Do you believe that I am able to do this?" And they answered, "Yes!" Matthew recorded, "Then he touched their eyes, saying, 'According to your faith be it done to you.' *And their eyes were opened"* (see Matt. 9:27–30).

When Paul was on his first missionary journey, he and Barnabas encountered a man who had been crippled from birth and had never walked. The man listened intently to Paul, and as he heard Paul's teaching, faith was born in his heart. Luke recorded, "And Paul, looking intently at him and seeing that he had faith to be made well, said in a loud voice, 'Stand upright on your feet.' And he sprang up and began walking" (Acts 14:9–10). God honored his simple faith just as He will honor yours. In a previous chapter we observed that one of the motivating factors that results in healing is someone's faith that God will heal—whether it is the sufferer's faith or someone else's. This is not to imply that if you are not supernaturally healed, it is because you don't have enough faith. God will honor your faith and heal you His way—whether supernaturally, integratively (through medical science and the touch of His grace and goodness), or redemptively, turning your suffering into an experience that will glorify Him and touch lives in the process.

Faith consists of two elements: belief and trust. Belief is mental or intellectual assent. It is the attitude: "God can, that is, He is capable of doing what I've asked." Trust is believing something so strongly that you act upon what you believe to be true. For example, you believe that a bridge across a raging river is strong enough to hold you; trust, however, is walking across that bridge step-by-step. Put God to the test! As the psalmist challenged, "Oh, taste and see that the Lord is good! Blessed is the man who takes refuge in him!" (Ps. 34:8). Both elements—belief and trust—are vitally necessary.

In 1899, the Boxer Rebellion in China, fueled by hatred for foreigners, took the lives of hundreds of missionaries and foreigners. The China Inland Mission, founded by Hudson Taylor, lost fifty-eight missionaries and their twenty-one children—the greatest loss of any single mission. Taylor was devastated and never fully recovered from the loss of his friends, colleagues, and partners in ministry. The shocking news of suffering and death affected his weakening body, and his strength failed him. Looking up from his bed one day, he spoke to his wife, saying, "I cannot read; I cannot pray; I can scarcely think," and then with a smile he said, *"But I can trust!"* That is faith in action! Great faith is not necessary. Small faith in a great and powerful God is far more potent than great faith in that which is subject to human failure. Remember the old adage, "Weak faith in a strong plank is more powerful than strong faith in a weak plank." Jesus talked about the simplicity of a child's faith, and having that kind of faith often requires humility born of the overwhelming conviction that you have nowhere else to go.

Pray with expectancy, asking God to honor what you read in His Word, the Bible. "Faith comes by hearing," wrote Paul to the church at Rome, "and hearing by the word of God" (Rom. 10:17 NKJV). The greater your knowledge of the Word of God, the Bible, the greater your faith will be that God will meet your need. You can pray with confidence when you know what God has said He will do, and you can gently remind God that you are believing He will do what He has promised.

One of the men who greatly influenced my life was Armin Gesswein. When he was a young Lutheran pastor, age twenty-four, striving to plant a church in Long Island, New York, things were not going well. In his church fellowship was a retired blacksmith, Ambrose Whaley, about fifty years his senior. Armin had noticed that when this man prayed, things happened. He said, "The prayer and the answer were not far apart—in fact, they were moving along together." Armin went on to explain, "His 'prayer muscles' were extremely strong because of much exercise." Wanting to learn Ambrose's spiritual secrets, Armin asked if he might join him in prayer.

At the old blacksmith's home, the two men crossed the driveway and went to the barn where they climbed up into the hayloft. Armin prayed. Then the blacksmith prayed. Finally Armin turned to Ambrose and said, "You have some kind of a secret in praying. Would you mind sharing it with me?"

"Young man," said the blacksmith, "learn to plead the promises of God." The old man had knelt between two bales of hay, and on each bale was an open Bible. His two large hands, gnarled and toughened by years of hard labor, were open, covering the pages of each Bible.

"I learned more about prayer in that haymow," said Armin, "than in all my years of schooling for the ministry. Understanding the relationship between the promises of God's Word and what we ask our heavenly Father to do has helped me immensely in my personal life. God honors His Word, and when you pray it back to the Father, He takes notice."

Pray with confidence that God's will shall be done. Many people believe God *can* heal if only God *will* heal. When I was a student studying for ministry, each evening at 10:00 p.m. about a dozen of us collegians would meet together for prayer. Whenever someone prayed "If this is Your will," there would be uncertainty bordering on doubt. James, in the third paragraph of his letter to the Jewish Christians scattered by persecution, says that when we pray, we should "ask in faith, with no doubting, for the one who doubts is like a wave of the sea that is driven and tossed by the wind" (James 1:6).

Jesus gave us an example in the Garden of Gethsemane, right? He prayed, "Not my will, but yours, be done" (Luke 22:42), thereby giving us a pattern to follow; however, don't think for a fleeting moment that prayer changes God's mind (so you can have whatever you want) as much as it changes *our minds*, bringing our wills into conformity with His. So have no concern thinking that your knocking on heaven's door in prayer is going to result in God's giving you what He really doesn't want you to have. That's not going to happen.

Having been in radio since 1963, I have received thousands of prayer requests from listeners. Rather "out of bounds requests" have included petitions such as that which came from a woman who was a florist, asking us to pray that "more people would die" so that her business could sell more funeral wreaths. There was also the lady requesting prayer for a certain man (happily married as far as we knew) to divorce his wife so that she could marry him.

After we have prayed, God often surprises us with answers we had not even considered. Remember that on two occasions Jesus chided the disciples, using the analogy of a human father who gives good things to his children, reminding them that, likewise, our Father in heaven gives good things to those who ask. John, who is described in the Gospel that bears his name as "the disciple Jesus loved," wrote, "And this is the confidence that we have toward him, that if we ask anything according to his will he hears us. And if we know that he hears us in whatever we ask, we know that we have the requests that we have asked of him" (1 John 5:14–15).

Step 5: Form a Support Group of People Who Will Stand with You in Spiritual Encouragement

Some fifty-eight times in the Bible you will find the expression "one another" in relation to our responsibilities toward fellow Christians. It was in the context of physical healing that James 5 was written—to instruct us to "pray for one another, that you may be healed" (v. 16). I told you about John Margosian who had essentially been given up to die. The surgeon had given him three months at the longest to live, "but what we didn't know," said Dr. Dennis Cope, who himself is a committed Christian, "is that he had a bunch of brothers who were praying for him." Surrounding yourself with friends who stand with you, who encourage you, who pray for and with you, allows them to become part of the healing process God uses.

Why is James urging us to pray for one another? There are times when the person who is battling for his life is so flattened by the illness emotionally, spiritually, and certainly physically, that it is difficult for that person to even whisper a prayer. That's where you who love the suffering person can stand with him or her, encouraging, praying, and focusing on what God wants to do.

Step 6: Follow the Pattern of James 5 to Find Healing

Here's what James said about how we should pray:

> Is anyone among you suffering? Let him pray.
> Is anyone cheerful? Let him sing praise. Is anyone
> among you sick? Let him call for the elders of the
> church, and let them pray over him, anointing him
> with oil in the name of the Lord. And the prayer of
> faith will save the one who is sick, and the Lord will

raise him up. And if he has committed sins, he will be forgiven. Therefore, confess your sins to one another and pray for one another, that you may be healed. The prayer of a righteous person has great power as it is working. (James 5:13–16)

For those in need of healing, the steps are simple:

Call for the elders of your church. Some of you who are reading this have no church connection. I encourage you to find a church where the pastor believes God heals people. Usually, browsing a church's Web site can give you a feel for where the church is theologically. However, if you do not have access to pastors who believe God for healing but know individuals who believe God's Word and know how to pray, ask them to join you and follow the procedure James outlined. While healing should be part of the life of the church, God is not limited by the failures of churches when it comes to actually healing someone He chooses to heal.

The elders are to anoint you with oil. Why is this step important? First, it is an act of simple obedience. Is there anything curative about oil? While oil had medicinal usage in Jesus' day, it has, more importantly, been a centuries-old symbol of the Spirit of God, He who is the agent of healing. When the prophets of old anointed kings with oil, it was to certify that they were the choice of a sovereign God who would empower them to lead His people. When Jesus sent out the Twelve, He gave them authority over demons and they "anointed with oil many who were sick and healed them" (Mark 6:13). Is oil essential to healing? No, many people have been healed in all kinds of situations where there was no anointing; however, God honors the simplicity of the ceremony.

The elders are to pray for healing. Notice that the word "elders" is in plural form. When this word is used in the New Testament, it is, with only one exception, always plural. Why include all the elders? Jesus taught that there is power in united prayer. He said, "If two of you agree on earth about anything they ask, it will be done for them by my Father in heaven. For where two or three are gathered in my name, there am I among them" (Matt. 18:19–20). When elders pray jointly, they are not only being obedient to Scripture, but they are also standing with the sick brother or sister in trusting God for healing.

The Lord will raise up the one who suffers. Note that it is not the responsibility of the elders to raise the sick person from his bed. How and when God does this is His choice; elders are simply responsible for being faithful in complying with what Scripture asks them to do. This, of course, reminds us that healing involves not only your physical body but your spiritual and emotional natures as well.

Step 7: Thank God for Hearing Your Cry and Answering Your Prayer His Way

God "works all things according to the counsel of his will, so that we who were the first to hope in Christ might be to the praise of his glory," wrote Paul to the church at Ephesus (Eph. 1:11–12). This, of course, parallels what Paul wrote to the Romans long ago (Rom. 8). Reflect on these thoughts:

- "I consider that the sufferings of this present time are not worth comparing with the glory that is to be revealed to us" (v. 18).
- "We know that the whole creation has been groaning together in the pains of childbirth until now" (v. 22).
- "The Spirit helps us in our weakness. For we do not know what to pray for as we ought, but the Spirit himself intercedes for us with groanings too deep for words" (v. 26).
- "And we know that for those who love God all things work together for good, for those who are called according to his purpose" (v. 28).
- "I am sure that neither death nor life, nor angels nor rulers, nor things present nor things to come, nor powers, nor height nor depth, nor anything else in all creation, will be able to separate us from the love of God in Christ Jesus" (vv. 38–39).

Should God choose to heal you miraculously, *praise the Lord!*

Should God choose to heal you by integrating medical science, including the vast array of medicines (the ingredients of which have been grown or mined from the earth), with His grace through the remarkable way your body heals itself, *praise the Lord!*

Should God choose to heal you redemptively, using your sickness to bless the lives of many and showing them the reflection of the Father's presence in your life, *praise the Lord!*

Step 8: Walk in Simple Obedience, Thanking Him for the Gift of Life for Another Day

Does this mean you pronounce yourself "healed" even if you feel no different and the symptoms of illness persist? My answer is that word games are never necessary, but what is vital is that you walk by faith and strive to glorify God no matter what type of healing God brings to your life. As Paul put it, writing from a prison in Rome, "I know that through your prayers and the help of the Spirit of Jesus Christ this will turn out for my [put your name here] deliverance, as it is my eager expectation and hope that I will not be at all ashamed, but that with full courage now as always Christ will be honored in my body, whether by life or by death" (Phil. 1:19–20). The word "honor" that Paul uses means that Christ may be "magnified," "praised," or "exalted" no matter what happens.

Is it possible to find "healing" in the broader sense of the word while the symptoms of your affliction persist? Indeed, it is. The individuals of whom I wrote in the previous chapter would certainly have rejoiced had God given them physical deliverance from years of pain and suffering, but in a real sense their healing has gone far beyond the bed or wheelchair in such a manner that God has been exalted! Praise Him and thank Him that He has touched your life, and give Him the glory for the great things He has done!

Don't give up! Paul prayed three times for the same thing, his own thorn; and while God hears your prayer the first time you pray, I encourage you to pray until you feel a witness or a peace in your heart that God has heard you, and from that point on begin to thank Him that He has heard you and will answer in His time. The confidence that He has heard you comes when the truth of 1 John 5:14–15 sinks into your heart and becomes personal: "And this is the confidence that we have toward him, that if we ask anything according to his will he hears us. And if we know that he hears us in whatever we ask, we know that we have the requests that we have asked of him." Whatever you do, don't give up!

A final word of encouragement comes from a man who inspired Britain to fight on during the dark days of World War II. At the onset of the war, Sir Winston Churchill was invited to return to Harrow School, where he was once a student.

There Churchill gave one of the shortest speeches in history yet one of the most important. He said, "Never give in—never, never, never, never, in nothing great or small, large or petty, never give in except to convictions of honor and good sense. Never yield to force; never yield to the apparently overwhelming might of the enemy."[7] Unbelief—not your sickness—is your greatest enemy. Walk in Jesus' footsteps and never give in!

How better to end this chapter than with the words of Paul to the church at Ephesus? "Now to him who is able to do far more abundantly than all that we ask or think, according to the power at work within us, to him be glory in the church and in Christ Jesus throughout all generations, forever and ever. Amen!" (Eph. 3:20–21).

What You Need to Know

• Prayer—earnest, sincere prayer—moves the heart of God. The Bible is replete with stories of how God responded to the tears of individuals such as King Jehoshaphat, whose deep sorrow was marked with anguish and tears; and Hannah, who wept because she could not conceive a child. God knows and understands the agony in your heart.

• Your relationship with God is important. While healing is not to be understood as a reward for some and not for others, God honors those who honor Him. It would be far better to have a relationship with God and spend eternity in His presence than to find healing in this life and be forever separated from Him. You can enjoy God's presence both now and through eternity as you allow Him to have His work and His way in your life.

• God will never give up on you, so don't you give up on Him!

Encouragement for Pastors and Church Leaders

This book would be incomplete if I did not address you who are pastors and Christian leaders. Yours is not an easy task. God's calling and commissioning, however, comes with an empowering to do and to be all that He requires.

A solemn reminder that we are simply representatives of Jesus Christ comes from Luke's account of Paul's meeting with the Ephesian elders who had come to Miletus to meet with Paul, who was about to depart for Jerusalem. It was an emotional encounter sealed with embraces and tears. They knew they would never see him again this side of heaven.

Paul exhorted them saying, "Pay careful attention to yourselves and to all the flock, in which the Holy Spirit has made you overseers, to care for the church of God, which he obtained with his own blood" (Acts 20:28). Some things never change. The responsibility of caring for a body of believers, likened to the responsibility of a shepherd who must care for a flock of sheep, who are defenseless against their enemies and who will follow almost anything or anybody, is much the same today as it was when Paul wrote the words just quoted.

- The shepherd leads the flock to green pastures and cool water.
- He defends the flock from the enemies that would destroy them.

- He ensures that their wounds are bound and cleansed.
- His task is a 24/7 responsibility.

In both of Paul's letters to the young man Timothy, he tells him to "guard the deposit entrusted to you" (1 Tim. 6:20; 2 Tim. 1:14). When you were ordained to the ministry, other men probably gathered around you, laid their hands on you, and prayed over you; and you were given an admonition that went something like this: "I charge you before God and men that you will faithfully proclaim the good news of the gospel." It was a solemn moment, filled with emotion. You had probably spent years preparing for this, and then reality gradually began to sink in.

You are expected to walk on water like Peter, teach like James, be as motivational as Peter Drucker or Zig Ziglar, and become as saintly as Paul himself. You have also learned that no matter what you do someone in the congregation isn't going to like it.

"Preach the word" was Paul's exhortation to Timothy as Paul, from a prison in Rome, awaited execution. And what exactly are the implications of what he said? Writing to the Corinthians, Paul gave what many believe constitutes the first doctrinal statement that defines the essentials of the faith: "For I delivered to you as of first importance what I also received: that Christ died for our sins in accordance with the Scriptures, that he was buried, that he was raised on the third day in accordance with the Scriptures" (1 Cor. 15:3–4).

Like me, if you went to an evangelical seminary or Bible college, undoubtedly you were confronted with the reality that men and women are lost without a relationship with God's Son, and, therefore, you felt your first and major responsibility would be dealing with the issue of salvation.

Never shall I forget the refrain that "preacher boys" sang every week in our ministerial class, "Souls for Jesus is our battle cry / Souls for Jesus we'll fight until we die / We never will give in while souls are lost in sin / Souls for Jesus is our battle cry." While these words are true, have we fulfilled our calling and mandate once a person has come to faith in Jesus Christ? Is there more?

The Great Commission:
The Marching Orders of the Church

For two thousand years the church has quoted the words of Jesus to the disciples found in all four Gospels as well as the book of Acts. Matthew, writing from a Jewish perspective (and don't forget—at that point his audience was exclusively Jewish), made the most comprehensive statement of our task. He said, "All authority in heaven and on earth has been given to me. Go therefore and make disciples of all nations, baptizing them in the name of the Father and of the Son and of the Holy Spirit, teaching them to observe all that I have commanded you. And behold, I am with you always, to the end of the age" (Matt. 28:18–20).

Notice the components of this charge:

- Go into all the world.
- Make disciples.
- Baptize in the name of the Father and of the Son and of the Holy Spirit.
- Teach them to observe everything that Christ taught the disciples.

Focus on the phrase "teaching them to observe all that I have commanded you." What are the implications of this? Answering this question should define what the life of the church is all about.

Certainly we know that Jesus' ministry embraced the intertwined proclamation of the Good News of the Kingdom of God as well as the healing of many people—no doubt more than we know about—who were delivered from physical illness, emotional and mental disorders, and demon-related sickness. Can this be distilled into a thirty-minute message on Sunday morning, timed almost to the minute so that your people can race to the parking lot thinking, "Start your engines, brothers; let's get this show on the road"?

The Implications of "Teaching Them to Observe All That I Have Commanded"

A casual reading of the Gospels should convince even the most hard-core skeptic that Jesus' interest in those who sat under His ministry went far beyond ensuring that they would have a home in heaven when they died. He was also concerned about the quality of their lives here on earth. The early church understood this. Luke recounts, "And they devoted themselves to the apostles' teaching and the fellowship, to the breaking of bread and the prayers. And awe came upon every soul, and many wonders and signs were being done through the apostles" (Acts 2:42–43).

These fledgling churches had no programs, no buildings, no organized staff, no four-color publications, no internet or promotional mailings; but they were Spirit driven and the church was very much alive.

A study of the early church—from the days of the book of Acts to the emergence of the institutional church under Constantine—indicates that churches prayed for the sick. They ministered to widows and orphans. They embraced a holistic gospel that involved the spiritual, the emotional, and the physical.

A friend of mine recently vented, telling how his mother had financially supported her church for decades. Even when she became an invalid and could no longer attend worship services, she would faithfully mail her tithe to the church. "Never one time," my friend said, "did anyone from the church either call to see how she was or visit her. Never!"

Think Outside the Box

What I've just suggested is fraught with peril. Why? Daring to think outside the box, to break with tradition, and to do something different is not always appreciated. But you must realize that if you seek to please men, you would not be the servant of Christ (see Gal. 1:10). Two words are enemies of doing what God wants—"always" and "never." "We've always done it this way in our church," which usually means, "We have done nothing!" or "We've never done this before," which really means, "I'm afraid people will think I've become a fanatic (a fanatic, as you may know, is simply 'someone who loves Jesus more than you do')."

If you are convinced, having read this far in the book, that "all things that I have commanded you" includes addressing the issue of healing—both physically and emotionally, as well as spiritually—dare to follow your convictions and be led by the Holy Spirit.

Martyn Lloyd-Jones, the Welsh pastor of Westminster Chapel in London for almost thirty years, was both a medical doctor and a pastor-theologian. He strongly believed that the church has abdicated its responsibility to address more than spiritual needs. He believed that we have consigned emotional needs to psychology and psychiatry and physical needs to the medical profession. In some cases we "shoot our wounded," condemning them for their failures—broken marriages, lives troubled by emotional illness or distress; or, embarrassed by their failures, we shuttle them out the back door of the church, not wanting to attempt to meet these issues head-on.

Nothing will change in your church until you begin to see people as Jesus saw them and develop a God-given conviction that you have an obligation to address needs in addition to those that are spiritual in nature. Your attitude should reflect the mind-set of Christ, and the result will be that suffering men and women realize you care deeply and compassionately about their needs, just as Jesus did for those to whom He ministered.

The Longest Journey in the World Begins with the First Step

James, the half brother of Jesus, had an encounter with the risen Christ that convinced him that his brother, whom he had never fully understood, was indeed the Christ, the Messiah, "the anointed One." He became the leader of the early church, and the book that bears his name has a distinctly Jewish flavor. He begins by writing, "James, a servant of God and of the Lord Jesus Christ, to the twelve tribes in the Dispersion" (James 1:1). Simply put, he is writing to all Jewish believers throughout the entire world.

His letter, written in about AD 45, preceded Paul's second and third missionary journeys. Paul, following his conversion on the road to Damascus, fled to Arabia where he lived for three years, rethinking his vast knowledge of Old Testament Scripture in relation to what he had learned about the risen Lord Jesus Christ, the fulfillment of the law. After that he went to Jerusalem, where for fifteen days he met with James (Gal. 1:18–19). During that period of time, Paul and James had intimate fellowship and much theological discussion. Matthew's birth order suggests that James was the second child of Mary (Jesus having been the firstborn). Surely James must have told Paul of incidents never recorded for posterity about his older brother and their years growing up together—stories I would like to hear.

What James wrote about healing became foundational not only for Jewish believers, but also for churches everywhere. There is reason to believe based on the writings of the church fathers in the pre-Constantine churches, that Paul not only knew of James' approach to physical healing but also taught the same thing, which became the practice of churches everywhere.

James instructed that the ministry of healing was and should be an integral part of the life of the church. It is not an optional adjunct to it, and it is certainly not something that would only be addressed by "faith healers."

Although I grew up in a church that theoretically believed in healing, I cannot recall that subject ever being addressed from the pulpit or in a Bible study. Preparing for ministry included graduate work in four different evangelical seminaries, where I also cannot remember the issue of healing ever being specifically addressed apart from the stories told by Dr. Timothy Lin, who described healings in his homeland, China—well outside the comfort zone of traditional American churches.

When I became a pastor, people learned that I believed in the instruction of James 5, that we are to call for the elders of the church and they, in turn, are to anoint with oil, in the name of the Lord, the one who is sick. Never have I prayed for the sick publicly. Following the example of Jesus, who at times took one or two of the disciples apart with Him and prayed for someone, I would choose several elders who likewise believed that God is our Healer and that His Son Jesus is the same yesterday, today, and forever. We would meet in a small chapel and pray according to James's pattern.

What happened? Some individuals were healed; some were not—at least outwardly and visibly. Never shall I forget the lad who was on his way home from school when another boy threw a rock, hitting him in the eye and damaging his cornea. Doctors said he would have no sight in this eye because it would be too scarred for him to use. As the result of prayer, however, the boy regained full sight in the injured eye. There were also several other notable healings involving people who had been diagnosed with cancer, as well as sicknesses confirmed by biopsies, X-rays, or MRIs.

But what about those whose conditions were unchanged? One of the challenges you must overcome in praying the James 5 prayer is that God—not you—is the one who heals! When God chooses to heal integratively or redemptively, you have not failed; neither has God ignored your plea. He has simply chosen to answer *His way*.

When people in our fellowship were healed, I would encourage them to share their testimony, give glory to God, and give thanks to Him not only for what they had received from the Lord physically but also for what He had taught them through the process.

Breaking Out of the Mold

In our day many churches have established biblical counseling programs. Many have trained laypeople to be counselors who are qualified to assess a person's needs, lead him into God's solutions, and then walk with him through the healing process. Other churches have begun recovery programs to assist those who have experienced the trauma of an addiction or a broken marriage. This is pleasing to God, but more needs to be done.

Few churches are working on programs in response to the needs of the elderly, and of those living with physical illness—whether it is individuals who need healing or seniors who are no longer able to attend church and participate in the life of the body of Christ. Nothing can be more hurtful than to support a church for years, attend faithfully, and then be forgotten in the sunset years of life.

Take, for example, Evelyn Johnson, now age ninety-five. In the late 1930s a home fellowship was born in the Johnson home. Eventually the fellowship grew and became a denominational church in a major city. The Johnsons supported the church their entire lifetime. Evelyn, who outlived her husband by many decades, served as Sunday school teacher, deaconess, a provider of care for the elderly, and, yes, a consistent financial donor. The Johnson home was always open to church family and strangers. Then with the passing of years, Evelyn could no longer drive and could not be as involved as she used to be—though she continued to support the church as best she could.

Venting his disappointment over the fact that she has been neglected, her son, who himself has served as both a missionary and denominational pastor, wrote, "Now at age ninety-five she is confined to her own home, not able to get a ride to 'her' home church and is a forgotten person. No pastoral visits, no people to reach out to her with love and encouragement."

When Evelyn's daughter, who had been involved in ministry most of her adult life, became bedridden and finally succumbed to cancer, the family's request to use the church for a memorial service was met with indifference. A secretary told them that "they could hold the memorial service there, but since they were no longer a visible part of the church family and hadn't attended for years, the deaconesses would serve only cake and coffee instead of a full meal as they usually did following a memorial service."

The needs of widows and orphans were addressed by both James and Paul (see James 1:27 and 1 Tim. 5:16). When did God release us from our responsibility to them?

How Is Your Church Helping Those In Need?

Find out how medical personnel in your church (doctors, nurses, dentists, psychologists and counselors, physical therapists, and related personnel) can extend the ministry of your church to assist the physical needs of the homeless or train hospice workers to walk with dying men and women through their last days on earth. Start a healing fellowship. Challenge professionals to not only support the church with their finances but also to give some of their time to assist those in need.

Ministering to homeless or indigent individuals where you live may not be as exciting as flying to Kenya or somewhere far to minister to needy people, but for those near you who are in pain, who have no money, or who are lonely, your help is just as needed and important.

In the churches addressed by James, the following groups were involved in healing ministries:

1. Elders in the church whose authority comes with faithful compliance with what God expects of them in relation to their personal lives and obedience to the Word. (Remember that with one exception in Scripture, the word is always plural—elders).

2. Individual members of the body of Christ who, by confession to one another and prayer for one another, found healing.

3. Those who had received gifts of healing—perhaps individuals like Peter who healed the lame man at the entrance to the temple, or Ananias who laid hands on Paul, who was immediately healed. The gift of healing was and is an individual gift or unction given by God for the specific need of another, not the ability of an individual to walk through a hospital ward and heal everyone he or she touches or prays for.

Why Are We Not Seeing More Today That Was Part of the Life of the Early Church?

The following story may answer this question. A small boat was traveling along the mouth of the Amazon River when its sailors found themselves in a serious predicament. Their supply of fresh water had run out. Seeing a ship nearby, they sent a distress signal, and soon the ship drew near to see what was wrong. "Have you any fresh water?" pleaded one sailor. "We've been without water for days and are desperate." Hearing their plea, the captain of the ship called out, "Just put your bucket over the side, and you'll have the answer to your question!" The thirsty, deprived sailors didn't know that fresh water—not salt water—flowed in the delta of one of the greatest rivers in the world.

The moral is obvious: Many churches could satisfy the thirst that people have for healing and help by lowering their buckets into the wide ocean of grace. Churches that encourage prayer and become involved in the healing process see God do things that can be accounted for only by recognizing a sovereign God who responds to the needs of one of His children and does what only He can do.

Any serious student of Scripture can recognize that at different periods of church history God worked in different ways and capacities. Although this has led to differences among godly men in relation to what spiritual gifts are extant in the body of Christ today, those who believe that God's Word is true have no problem with acknowledging that God answers prayer and sovereignly does what only He can do.

Such was the case with one of today's most respected and esteemed pastors, author and Bible teacher Dr. John MacArthur. Walking in the footsteps of his father, in 1969 John became pastor of Grace Community Church in Sun Valley, California. His radio broadcast *Grace to You* is heard around the world, and the Master's College and Seminary, founded by Dr. MacArthur, has produced hundreds of well-equipped men and women who have taken their place in the church today.

In July 1991, John's wife Patricia and their daughter Melinda were involved in a terrible automobile accident. While Melinda was not seriously injured, Patricia sustained life-threatening head injuries after their car turned over and crushed her. Thousands of people the world over prayed for Patricia's recovery. In his book *The Healing Promise*, Richard Mayhue, an associate of John, tells about an interview he had with the MacArthurs seventeen months after the accident.

Both John and Patricia talked about the recovery John attributed not to medical science but to the power of the body to heal itself as God did what only He could do. "It seemed like something was going on here that was really remarkable—God was restoring everything as the healing process was sovereignly controlled by His power," John explained.[1]

Then Mayhue asked, "Has the severity of the accident and the completeness of the recovery changed your view of how God deals with our physical lives? For example, how He heals, whether He heals, when He heals, and to what extent He heals?"

John's response succinctly conveys the message of this book:

> I've always believed that God heals. I've never
> questioned the power of God to heal. I've never
> questioned the power of God to do anything consis-
> tent with His nature because when Jesus was here,
> He healed. God has healed in the past and there is
> no reason to assume that God doesn't choose to heal
> in the present. So the accident never really changed

anything, but it sure personalized the reality of God's healing.[2]

One of my favorite movies is based on Lew Wallace's book *Ben Hur, a Tale of the Christ*. In this moving story Judah Ben Hur becomes the adopted son of Arius, the Roman tribunal. Fast-forwarding to the end of the story, Judah is a spectator on the day Jesus is crucified at the hands of Roman soldiers. Graphically, the blood from the wounded side of the crucified Christ mingles with the driving rain which pelts Golgotha and runs down to the cave of the lepers below the escarpment where three crosses are silhouetted against a dark, angry sky. Judah Ben Hur's mother and sister are among the sordid group of lepers dressed in tattered rags, forlorn and rejected; however, when they dip their hands in the water mingled with blood, they are healed. Yes, of course, this is a fictional account, but it brings to mind the impact of Peter's statement, "By his wounds you have been healed."

OK, you believe that *Jehovah Rapha*, the God who heals, is still compassionate, caring, and a present help in time of trouble. What do you do? Where do you start (besides on your knees in prayer)? Consider the following steps.

1. Talk with your fellow elders, pastors, or deacons about needs you see and how you can address them. Come to grips with what is the context of the church's relationship to society. Begin by using this book and working through it progressively as a group, a chapter at a time. Acknowledge your blind spots and the needs you have ignored or felt incapable of meeting. Then talk about how you as a fellowship of believers can meet some of these needs. Assess the resources you have involving both personnel and finances. And when God has burdened your heart for something, don't let a lack of resources stop you from doing His will. Remember the dictum of Hudson Taylor, the renowned nineteenth-century missionary to China, who said, "God's work done in God's way will never lack God's supply." Then develop an action plan. Prioritize. While you cannot do *everything*, you can do *something*. When you stumble across a need that you can address, consider that to be what God wants you to do.

While your church should be a lighthouse driving back the darkness of the world, it should also be known as a place for healing, a hospital for hurting people, where the Great Physician applies the balm of Gilead[3] to the sick and suffering, a refuge for the distressed, and a "safe place" for those who feel rejected by society and our culture.

2. Teach about healing. Stress that God is sovereign, that He is full of surprises, and that He heals His way—whether it is in a supernatural manner, or through the skilled hands of a physician supported by the prayers of His people, or through redemptive suffering as the Shepherd of our souls walks with us through the valley to heaven's gate. Help your people to realize that while everyone wants immediate deliverance, God often has other plans. Remind your people that doctors give medicine, but it is God who gives healing!

3. Emphasize the power of united prayer. "I believe in God" begins the affirmation of the Apostles' Creed. But does what you believe make much difference in how long you live, or, even more pointedly, in the quality of the life you live? It does, contends a growing body of scientific evidence. The relationship between your belief system and your health is better documented every year. Dr. Harold G. Koenig, director of Duke University's Center for the Study of Religion/Spirituality and Health, says scientists and doctors "have to confront it. They can't just say religion is irrelevant to health. It is relevant." And may I add that a vital part of that relevance is united, corporal prayer.

In the 1990s the subject of prayer and healing gained impetus when a medical doctor began praying with his patients and noticed improvement immediately. Then wanting to make his study more scientific, he formed control groups where the individuals themselves did not know people were praying specifically for them. He then documented and published his findings to the great disdain of the skeptics who were convinced that prayer and faith are religious hocus-pocus.

More than two hundred studies later, the evidence is overwhelming, proving there is a correlation between your belief in God and your health. And what are the conclusions of Dr. Koenig's research?

- People who attend church regularly are hospitalized less often than those who never or rarely participate in church services.
- People who pray and read the Bible have lower blood pressure.

- People who attend religious services have stronger immune systems than their less religious counterparts.
- There is a correlation between religious involvement and health.
- People who are deeply committed to the Lord have fewer heart attacks, recover more quickly if they do have heart problems, and live longer than those with no profession of faith.[4]

Research has done it again! Science has certified what has been obvious to pastors, hospital chaplains, and even morticians who have been witnesses to the fact that people who live by the Bible have less worry, cope with stress better, and come through the storms that maim or kill individuals of lesser faith.

Does that mean Christians have fewer problems? Not necessarily, but they are able to better cope with them. Their problems make them better, not bitter, and they outlive them.

4. Give people an opportunity to share their testimonies. When I was a lad, a now-defunct company which manufactured Packard automobiles used the slogan, "Ask the man who owns one!" No testimony is more powerful than that of the one who says, "I just know this—I was blind but now I see," or, "The doctors told me I had cancer, but after the pastors anointed me with oil and prayed for me, I went back to the doctor and he shook his head, saying, 'I can't explain it; I've heard of "these things" happening but I've never seen it before. The cancer is gone. I guess you'd call it a miracle!'"

5. Take action where you see needs. Victor Hugo, the French novelist, is credited with saying, "Nothing in all the world is as powerful as an idea whose time has come!" When Jesus was here and saw needs, He didn't depend on a government agency for solutions. He chose imperfect men and women and endowed them with the power of the Holy Spirit. Then He gave them a mandate to go, sending them forth to pray for the sick, to anoint them with oil, to do battle with spiritual darkness, and to make a difference. You can do the same thing with God's enabling and help. When you understand that you are a servant sent by the Great Physician, a strengthening and an empowering brings purpose to your ministry.

6. Get started. Jesus never advertised, and neither will you need to! You will be amazed as to how quickly word will spread that "pastor and the elders will pray for you, if you only ask them!" James, of course, instructed that those who are sick are the ones who should initiate the process. Your part is to be prepared, which may require focused time in prayer alone with God, perhaps even fasting, before you meet with the person in need of healing. Ask God to show you what should be done, step-by-step, and give you the courage and resources to do His will.

Realize that God will empower you and use you to make a difference in the lives of people, helping them look beyond their illness to the Lord, who gave His life for the redemption of the world. May you be a tool in the hands of *Jehovah Rapha*, the God who heals, and be the one who leads the flock, protects them, and brings healing to those who need it—spiritually, emotionally, and physically!

8.17.13
ms

Notes

Preface

1. Ian MacPherson, "If I But Knew Thee," public domain.

Chapter 1: Is the Great Physician Still Practicing?

1. John J. O'Connor, *The New York Times*, May 19, 1988, www.nytimes.com/1988/05/19/arts/review-television-when-prayer-is-fatal.html, accessed January 2, 2011.

2. Joni Eareckson Tada, *A Place of Healing* (Colorado Springs: David C. Cook, 2010), 15–18.

3. Harold J. Sala, *Why You Can Have Confidence in the Bible* (Eugene: Harvest House, 2008).

4. Lewis Smedes, ed., *Ministry and the Miraculous: A Case Study at Fuller Theological Seminary* (Pasadena: Fuller Theological Seminary, 1987), 44. Used by permission.

5. The term "Sovereign Lord" is found more than three hundred times in the New International Version of the Bible. The English Standard Version, however, uses the expression "Sovereign Lord" only eight times, expressing the combination of words translated as "Sovereign Lord," the expression used so frequently in the NIV, as "Lord God." The NIV translators strive to express what they consider to be the dynamic equivalency of the words rather than a strictly literal rendering.

6. Henry Frost, *Miraculous Healing* (Scotland, UK: OMF Publishing, 1931), 115.

7. M. R. De Haan, "Small Beginnings," *Our Daily Bread* (Grand Rapids, MI: RBC Ministries), October 27, 1962.

8. See Revelation 9:11.

9. Frost, *Miraculous Healing*, 99–107.

Chapter 2: Beneficiaries and Victims

1. Duane Miller, *Out of the Silence* (Nashville: Thomas Nelson Publishers, 1996), 125. Used by permission.

2. Ibid.

3. Ibid., 144.

4. Timothy Keller, *The Reason for God* (New York: Riverhead Books, 2008), 88.

5. John Macquarrie, as quoted by Keller in *The Reason for God*, Ibid.

6. Francis Collins, *The Language of God* (New York: Free Press, 2006), 4. Details of the survey are amplified in Keller's book, *The Reason of God*, 92.

7. Richard Dawkins, as quoted by Collins in *The Language of God*.

8. Adam Gabbat, "Stephen Hawkins Says Universe Not Created by God," (London: *The Guardian*, September 2, 2010, http://www.guardian.co.uk/science/2010/sep/02/stephen-hawking-big-bang-creator.

9. Benjamin B. Warfield, *Miracles: Yesterday and Today, Real and Counterfeit* (Grand Rapids: Eerdmans, 1954), 23–24.

10. Among Bible schools and Christian colleges that generally hold to dispensational teaching are leading institutions such as Moody Bible Institute, Bob Jones University, Biola University, and Talbot Seminary, Baptist Bible Seminary, Cedarville University, Dallas Bible University, and Dallas Seminary.

11. Benjamin Warfield as quoted by C. Peter Wagner in *How to Have a Healing Ministry in Any Church* (Ventura: Regal Books, 1998), 148.

12. The respected D. Martyn Lloyd-Jones, who left a medical practice to eventually become pastor of Westminster Chapel in London, where he served for thirty years, said, "I personally have always found myself unable to accept the well known teaching that everything belonging to the realm of the miraculous and the supernatural as manifested in New Testament times came to an end with the apostolic age. There is no statement in the Scripture which says that—none at all. There is no specific or even indirect statement to that effect. Likewise, I am not satisfied by B. B. Warfield's answer to those who have claimed that miracles did continue after the apostolic age. It is well known that Tertullian and Augustine both made use of the argument that miracles were happening in their time and age in defense of, and as a part of their apologetic for, the Christian faith; and I have never been satisfied with Warfield's answer to that." D. Martyn Lloyd-Jones, *Healing in the Scriptures* (Nashville: Oliver Nelson, 1988), 27.

13. J. I. Packer, as quoted by Jack Deere in *Surprised by the Power of the Spirit* (Grand Rapids: Zondervan Publishing House, 1993), 53.

14. Deere, *Surprised*, 126.

15. In his book *Miraculous Healing* (pp. 49–50), Henry Frost, a contemporary of both Simpson and Gordon, points out the fact that both wrote a book on healing, and both held to the same theological position which asserts that it is God's will to heal everyone; and reliance upon God—not medicine—is sufficient, though both men in the latter years of their lives sought medical help.

16. In her book *A Place of Healing* (p. 48), Joni Eareckson Tada tells of visiting a Kathryn Kuhlman crusade with the anticipation that she might be healed. She says, "Never did they aim the light [spotlight] at the wheelchair section where all the 'hard cases' were: quadriplegics like me, stroke survivors, children with muscular dystrophy, and men and women sitting stiff and rigid from multiple sclerosis."

17. Warren Wiersbe, *Why Us? When Bad Things Happen to God's People* (Old Tappan, NJ: Fleming H. Revell, 1984), 25.

18. Epicurus, quoted by Wiersbe, *Why Us?*

19. Henry Frost, *Miraculous Healing* (London: OMF Publishing, 1931), 4.

20. Ibid., 110.

Chapter 3: Jehovah Rapha (the God who Heals) in the Old Testament

1. John Wilkinson, *The Bible and Healing* (Exeter, England: British Printing Company, 1998), 13. Used by permission.

2. The term *canon* refers to the books of the Bible which were recognized as having been inspired by the Holy Spirit and, therefore, were included in the sixty-six books of the Bible.

3. Ezekiel 14:20 mentions Noah, Daniel, and Job. James 5:11 refers to the "patience of Job."

4. Job 12:21, 24 seems to allude to Psalm 107:40 and Isaiah 41:20.

5. F. F. Bruce as quoted by David J. A. Clines in *International Bible Commentary*.

6. Sarah was actually a half sister since Abraham and Sarah's father were the same, but they had different mothers. This was the second time Abraham used this deception to protect himself (Gen. 12:13); nonetheless, God acknowledged Abraham's position as a prophet (Gen. 20:7), something which greatly impressed Abimelech in that he gave him a gift of one thousand pieces of silver when only thirty pieces was, at that time, the price of a slave.

7. See http://www.quotedb.com/quotes/3681, accessed February 19, 2011.

8. Other examples of this are as follows: *Jehovah-Jireh* translated "The Lord, our provider" (Gen. 22:14); *Jehovah-Nissi*, "The Lord our Banner" (Exodus 17:8–15); *Jehovah-Shalom*, "The Lord our Peace" (Judg. 6:24); *Jehovah-Raah*, "The Lord our Shepherd" (Ps. 23:1); *Jehovah-Tsidkenu*, "The Lord our Righteousness" (Jer. 23:6); *Jehovah-Shammah*, "The Lord is Present" (Ezek. 48:35).

9. Frederick J. Gaiser, *Healing in the Bible* (Grand Rapids: Baker Academic, 2010), 25. Used by permission.

10. Karl Barth, *Church Dogmatics* (Edinburgh: T&T Clark, 1961, vol. 3, part 4), 369.

11. Kenneth Laing Harris, *English Standard Version Study Bible* (Wheaton: Crossway Bibles, 2008), 170.

12. See 2 Kings 20, 2 Chronicles 32:24–26, and Isaiah 38:1–22.

13. Wilkinson, *The Bible and Healing*, 49. A footnote to 2 Kings 20:7 in the ESV states, "Figs had long been cultivated in Palestine. They could be eaten fresh or dried, made into cakes, or fermented and made into wine. Here a cake of figs, serving as a compress, is applied to what may have been an abscess. The belief that figs had medical qualities is also attested earlier at Ugarit and later in Rome. But the healing of such a serious illness probably included a supernatural work of God as well."

14. Charles Ryrie, ed., *The Ryrie Study Bible* (Chicago: Moody Press, 1978), 1067.

15. See http://www.bartleby.com/105/72.html, accessed February 9, 2011.

16. The weights of precious metals in today's equivalent are as follows: Ten talents of silver represented about 750 pounds (341 kgs), and the six thousand shekels of gold equaled 150 pounds (68 kgs).

17. See Matthew 8:16–17, 1 Peter 2:24, and Romans 4:25.

18. Donald Fairbairn, *Life in the Trinity* (Downer Grove, IL: IVP Academic, 2009), 98–99.

19. Acts 13:22 says that God raised up David "to be their king, of whom he testified and said, 'I have found in David the son of Jesse a man after my heart, who will do all my will.'"

20. Pamela Rosewell Moore, *The Five Silent Years of Corrie ten Boom* (Grand Rapids: Zondervan Publishing House, 1986), 163.

21. See 1 Kings 14:17 and 1 Kings 15:29.

22. See 2 Kings 1:2 and 16, which explain that King Ahaziah received the pronouncement of death because he worshiped the god of Ekron and sought help from that god instead of *Jehovah*, the God of Israel.

23. See 2 Kings 5:27. As punishment for his greed, Elisha told Gehazi that he would be a leper to his death.

24. See 2 Chronicles 26:19–29 describes how King Uzziah, a proud and arrogant monarch, decided that he should be able to offer incense on the altar in the temple, something reserved only for the priests, and God's punishment was leprosy.

Chapter 4: The Great Physician and His Work in the Early Church

1. Says David Hocking, "The Greek language of the New Testament uses two words, *therapeuo* and *iaomai*. The first emphasizes the care of the sick and is not quite as strong as the second word. The word *iaomai* seemed to center on the results—a person restored to physical health. The words sometimes are used in the context and often seem interchangeable." David Hocking, *What the Bible Says about Healing* (Portland: Multnomah Press, 1982), 6.

2. Ignatius, Ephesians 7.2, *The Loeb Classical Library edition*, Vol. 1 (Cambridge, MS: Harvard University Press), 181.

3. John Wilkinson, *The Bible and Healing* (Grand Rapids: Eerdmans, 1998), 63.

4. Ibid., 65.

5. Ibid., 67.

6. Among those who were healed by Jesus' touch were Peter's mother-in-law (see Matt. 8:15); the blind man (Mark 20:34), and the woman who had been crippled for over eighteen years who was healed when Jesus "laid his hands on her" (Luke 13:13). Additionally, see Luke 14:4; Luke 22:51; Mark 6:5; etc.

7. Matthew records Jesus' ministry at Gennessaret where they brought to Him all who were sick and implored Him that they might only touch the fringe of His garment. "And as many as touched it were made well" (Matt. 14:35–36).

8. Peter's mother-in-law received both (see Matt. 8:14). Additionally, Matthew 8:3; Mark 5:41; Matthew 9:29; Luke 13:12–13; etc.

9. The nobleman's son, John 4:50; the centurion's servant, Matthew 8:13; the Syrophoenician girl, Mark 7:29. At other times Jesus could have healed from a distance but chose rather to go considerable distances, such as in the case with the daughter of Jairus, Luke 8:41–42.

10. The deaf mute, Mark 7:33–34; the man who was blind in Bethsaida, John 9:6–7, and the man who was born blind, John 9:6–7.

11. The healing of the man who had been born blind, which John 9 relates, demonstrates that as God's Son, Jesus could extend forgiveness, demonstrating His power and authority.

12. In Capernaum many had been oppressed by demons, and they were brought to Jesus, "and he cast out the spirit with a word and healed all who were sick. This was to fulfill what was spoken by the prophet Isaiah: 'He took our illnesses and bore our diseases'" (Matt. 8:16–17).

13. A. J. Gordon, *Quiet Talks about the Healing Christ* (New York: Fleming H. Revell, 1924), 21.

14. Ibid., 150.

15. Suppose that same criteria had been used when Paul was at Ephesus; and handkerchiefs, aprons, and anything that had touched his flesh brought healing. Skeptics would then have disallowed the reality of what happened, saying, "This didn't happen in Jesus' day!" When itinerant Jewish exorcists attempted to get into the healing business, they failed miserably (see Acts 19:13–17).

16. Older versions of the Bible such as the King James use the figure of seventy whereas the New International Version and the English Standard Version use the figure of seventy-two who were sent forth. Our oldest and most reliable Greek texts are evenly divided, using both numbers. Newer translations go with the larger number; however, no doctrinal issue is involved.

17. The explosion of mass communication is in direct relationship to the population explosion, further indicating that God intends all people everywhere to hear the good news of redemption and healing.

18. Two of the best Greek manuscripts known as Sinaiticus and Vaticanus, both dated about 350 AD, have the shorter rendering of Mark's Gospel, yet some other early manuscripts (identified as A, D, and D) have the

longer version which is quoted by numerous church fathers such as Irenaeus. Many resolve the issue contending that while it was not included in the earliest manuscripts, there is substantial evidence to support the belief that Jesus spoke these words. To make this a doctrinal issue of importance is unwarranted. *English Standard Version* (Wheaton: Crossway Bibles, 2009), footnote 1933.

19. J. A. T. Robinson, *The Body: A Study in Pauline Theology* (London: SCM Press, 1952), 9.

20. Wilkinson, *The Bible and Healing*, 189.

21. R. J. S. Barrett-Lennard, *Christian Healing after the New Testament* (Lanham, NY: University Press of America, 1994), 184.

22. The woman with an issue of blood, Matthew 8:5–13; Bartimaeus at Jericho who was told, "Your faith has made you well," Luke 18:42; a leper, Matthew 8:24; and ten lepers, Luke 17:11–19.

23. The four who lowered the paralytic through the roof of a house in Capernaum, Mark 2:1–12; the centurion previously mentioned, Matthew 8:5–13; the Syrophoenician woman who pled for her daughter, Matthew 15:21–28); among others.

Chapter 5: Healing after the Close of the New Testament

1. John Bouvier, *A Law Dictionary, Adapted to the Constitution and Laws of the United States* (place unknown: 1856).

2. Dates quoted in this chapter are from *The Oxford Dictionary of the Christian Church*, ed. by F. L. Cross and E. A. Livingstone (Oxford: Oxford University Press, 2005).

3. Justin Martyr, *Apologies for the Christians*, vol. 2, ch. 6 as quoted by A. J. Gordon, *The Ministry of Healing* (Brooklyn: Christian Alliance Publishing Company, 1882), 60.

4. Irenaeus, *Apologia versus Heretics*, book 1, ch. 34, as quoted by Gordon, *The Ministry of Healing*.

5. R. J. S. Barrett-Lennard, *Christian Healing after the New Testament* (Lanham, NY: University Press of America, 1994), 120.

6. Ibid., 125.

7. There is no hard and fast evidence that Tertullian was either a lawyer or a priest. His analogies lend to identification with law; however, it is noted that as the son of an educated Roman, he would have a working knowledge of jurisprudence.

8. Tertullian, *Apologia*, xviii.

9. Tertullian, *Ad. Scap*, IV, 4. as quoted by Gordon, *The Ministry of Healing*, 60–61.

10. Clement, *Epistles*, ch. 12.

11. Origen, *Contra Celsum*, book 3, ch. 24.

12. While Origen combated Greek philosophy, his contribution to the Christian faith was diminished by the fact that three hundred years following his death, he was condemned as a heretic.

13. A. J. Gordon, *The Ministry of Healing*, 58.

14. "Origen in the third century, Basil the Great and his brother Gregory of Nyssa in the fourth century and Chrysostom in the fifth century, all believed that the Church still had the power to heal," says John Wilkinson in *The Bible and Healing* (Grand Rapids: William B. Eerdmans, 1998), 275.

15. Evelyn Frost, *Christian Healing* (London: A. R. Mowbry, 1949), 50.

16. Clement Peterson, "Constantine and His Sons," Philip Schaff, ed., *A Religious Encyclopaedia or Dictionary of Biblical, Historical, Doctrinal and Practical Theology, 3rd ed.*, vol 1 (Toronto: Funk & Wagnalls, 1894), 545–47. After his alleged conversion, Constantine had no compunction about having his son and second wife, along with several other relatives and some of his closest friends, executed because he felt that his position was threatened politically.

17. Peter Leithert, *Defending Constantine* (Downer Grove, IL: IVP Academic, 2010), 22.

18. Eusibius as quoted by Leither, *Defending Constantine*, 22–23.

19. In a personal e-mail to the author, Donald Fairbairn, a recognized authority on the early church fathers, writes, "Persecution was really very sporadic except during the years 249–51, 257–58, and 303–13. During those years and only during those years was there severe persecution throughout the Roman Empire."

20. Says Wikipedia, "In 314, the cross appeared on Constantine's coins, but so did the figures of *Sol Invictus and Mars Convervator*. He raised his children as Christians and secured Christian clergy as personal advisors, but retained the title *pontifex maximus*, the chief priest of the state cult, until his death," http://www.religionfacts.com/christianity/history/constantine.htm.

21. Church history Clemens Petersen writes: "For political reasons, however, unity and harmony were necessary; and in 325 the Emperor convened the first great ecumenical council at Nicæa to settle the Arian controversy. It was the first time the Christian Church and the Roman State met each other face to face; and the impression was very deep on both sides. When the emperor stood there, among the three hundred and eighteen bishops, tall, clad in purple and jewels, with his peculiarly haughty and sombre mien, he felt disgusted at those coarse and cringing creatures who one moment scrambled sportively around him to snatch up a bit of his munificence, and the next flew madly into each other's faces for some incomprehensible mystery. Nevertheless, he learnt something from those people. He saw that with Christianity was born a new sentiment in the human heart hitherto unknown to mankind, and that on this sentiment the throne could be rested more safely than on the success of a court-intrigue, or the victory of a hired army. The only rational legitimation which the antique world had known of the kingship was descent from the gods; but this authority had now become a barefaced lie, and was difficult to use even in the form of a flattery. At Nicæa, however, the idea of a kingship of God's grace began to dawn upon mankind. Constantine also met there with men who must have charmed and awed him by their grand

simplicity, burdened, and almost curbed, as he was by the enormous complexity of Roman life. After the Council of Nicæa, he conversed more and more frequently and intimately with the bishops. His interest in Christianity grew with the years; but, as was to have been foreseen, he was sure to be led astray, for the needle lacked in the compass. He was more and more drawn over to the side of the Arians, and it was an Arian bishop who baptized him. (Clemens Peterson, "Constantine the Great and His Sons," Philip Schaff, ed., *A Religious Encyclopaedia or Dictionary of Biblical, Doctrinal, and Practical Theology*, 3rd ed., vol. 1 (New York: Funk & Wagnalls, 1894), 547).

22. While Emperor Constantine was converted in 313, the complete recognition of Christianity was not accomplished until the year 380, when Emperor Theodosius established the Christian faith as the official state religion.

23. Theodore of Mopsuete, *Chris Tlieb: Modern Doubt*, 321, as quoted by Gordon, *The Ministry of Healing*, 61.

24. See http://www.newadvent.org/cathen/04463a.htm.

25. Johannis Lukawitz Waldensis Confession 1431, as quoted by Gordon, *The Ministry of Healing*, 65.

26. Deere, *Surprised*, 101.

27. Gordon, *The Ministry of Healing*, 92.

28. Ibid.

29. Ibid., 93–94.

30. John Wesley, The Journal of John Wesley, II, 437; VI, 334 as quoted by Duffield and Van Cleave, *Pentecostal Theology*, 387.

31. Wilkinson, *The Bible and Healing*, 276.

Chapter 6: Those Who Could Have . . . Should Have . . . Would Have Died! Healing that Defy Human Rationale

1. Dennis W. Cope, MD, FACP is professor and chair of internal medicine at Olive View / UCLA Medical Center. Early in his career he was voted the most outstanding professor in UCLA's School of Medicine. He is currently governor of California in the American College of Physicians. He serves as vice president of the American Academy on Communication in Healthcare.

2. Dr. Cope is noted not only for his professional excellence but also for his care and compassion. He has personally diagnosed and treated Muhammad Ali, whom he diagnosed in the early 1980s at UCLA. Subsequently, Dr. Cope shared some of that story on the CBS production *60 Minutes*. Other celebrity patients have included Richard Pryor, Rock Hudson, Charlton and Lydia Heston, Tony Curtis, and members of the UCLA faculty. One of his patients, Paul Monette, wrote a book about the diagnosis and death of his partner, Roger Horwitz, *Borrowed Time: An Aids Memoir*, and dedicated it to Dr. Cope. Dr. Cope was heavily involved in diagnosis and treatment in the early years of the AIDS epidemic.

3. Dr. Dennis Cope in a personal e-mail to the author, dated February 14, 2011.

4. Joanie Piper, e-mails to the author dated January 14 and 16, 2011, used by permission.

5. Brian Wills, *10 Hours to Live* (New Kensington, PA: Whittaker House, 2006), 27–28.

6. Ibid., 33–34.

7. Ibid., 66.

8. Charles Swindoll, *Flying Closer to the Flame* (Dallas: Word Publishing, 1993), 198–200. Used by permission.

9. William Lindner Jr., *Andrew Murray* (Minneapolis: Bethany House, 1996), 108.

10. Ibid., 109.

11. Ibid., 113.

12. Thomas Hale, *Living Stones of the Himalayas* (Crowborough: East Sussex, England); chapter 13, "A City on a Hill" tells the story in detail that I have summarized.

13. Ibid., 142–43.

14. Ibid., 149.

15. Carl Lawrence, *The Church in China* (Minneapolis: Bethany House, 1985), see pages 72–88.

16. Ibid., 74–75.

Chapter 7: Integrative Healing and Medical Science

1. Antibiotics are descendants of the work of Sir Andrew Fleming. As the result of working in battlefield hospitals in World War I, Fleming observed that most deaths were the result of infection involving bacterial growth. By 1928, Fleming was pursuing an investigation on the properties of staphylococci. That summer before going on vacation, Fleming stacked dishes of staphylococci on a bench in the corner of his laboratory. On his return he noticed that one culture was contaminated with a fungus, and the colonies of staphylococci that surrounded it had been destroyed whereas other colonies further away were OK. He immediately understood the process, and the name *penicillin* came from the substance he was working with. He later said, "When I woke up just after dawn on September 28, 1928, I certainly didn't plan to revolutionize all medicine by discovering the world's first antibiotic, or bacteria killer, but I suppose that was exactly what I did." Upon his death his body was cremated, and his remains were interred in St. Paul's Cathedral, honoring him as a pioneer of modern medicine.

2. Wilhelm Rontgen is credited with discovering X-rays. His first print was that of his wife's hand, taken on December 22, 1895, one of a series he produced to show academic colleagues.

3. The use of anesthesia was the result of investigation by two men: Horace Wells and William Morton, a dentist who began using anesthesia for dental treatment and oral surgery. After a tragic death Wells was honored by the Medical Society of Paris as "the discoverer of anesthesia." Later the American Medical Association granted him the same recognition.

4. Henry Frost, *Miraculous Healing*, 237.

5. Dr. Timothy James, personal e-mail to the author, January 28, 2011.

6. C. Samuel Storms, *Healing & Holiness* (Philadelphia: Presbyterian and Reformed, 1990), 43.

7. Philip Yancey coauthored three books with Paul Brand: Fearfully and Wonderfully Made, In His Image, and The Gift of Pain. Yancey eulogized Brand by saying: "I see the world largely through his eyes. My father died just after my first birthday, and in so many ways Dr. Brand became a father figure to me in the best way. I have never known anyone more brilliant, nor anyone more humble," http://www.christianitytoday.com/ct/2003/julyweb-only/7-7-41.0.htm.

8. Paul Brand with Philip Yancey, "A Surgeon's View of Divine Healing," *Christianity Today*, November 25, 1983, 16.

9. Frederick J. Gaiser, *Healing in the Bible* (Grand Rapids: Baker Book House, 2010), 28.

10. Kenneth Carlson explains the procedure of exposing patients to therapy. Upon arrival "the patient was given a summary of people who had been healed from disease similar to his, thus pumping some hopeful air into his mind. Then came a guided tour of the facilities with special attention focused on the stops and corners where miraculous cures had occurred. Next, the afflicted one was dressed in a fresh white robe, placed on a couch and told that the god would come while he slept. Prayers were offered, the lamps turned out, and in the morning, as the sun came up, yellow snakes were permitted to glide over the patient. If he had never had a nightmare, that should have done it! But it was said that the spirit of the god dwelt in those harmless snakes. Then came the anointing with oil. There were *cures* recorded, to be sure." *Religion and Healing*, booklet published by First Methodist Church, Glendale, CA, nd.

11. Considering the fact that Luke wrote both the Gospel bearing his name and the book of Acts, the total content is greater than the thirteen letters of Paul.

12. The context of the Greek text of Paul's quote in 2 Corinthians 5:8 indicates that being absent from the body takes place at the precise time being present with the Lord occurs. There is no time lapse between the two events.

13. Dr. Diane Komp served as chief of Pediatric Oncology at the Yale University School of Medicine until her retirement. She is the author of *Why Me? A Doctor Looks at the Book of Job, A Window to Heaven*, and *The Anatomy of a Lie*, among others. She has brought hope and healing to hundreds of children in both the US and Sierra Leone.

14. Diane Komp, *Images of Grace* (Grand Rapids: Zondervan, 1996), 156.

15. Ibid., 159.

16. C. Everett Koop, "Faith Healing and the Sovereignty of God," in *The Agony of Deceit*, ed. Michael Horton (Chicago: Moody Press, 1990), 169–70.

17. Marvin Vincent, *Word Studies in the New Testament* (Grand Rapids: Eerdmans, 1946), IV, 270.

18. See Acts 20:4.

19. In 1 Corinthians 5:9 Paul refers to a previous letter in which he told them not to fellowship with immoral individuals. In 2 Corinthians 2:3 Paul refers to a letter which may have been carried by Titus which has been lost to posterity.

20. An exhaustive discussion of what Paul's "thorn" may have been is found in *The Bible and Healing* by John Wilkinson, M.D., senior fellow of the Royal College of Physicians of Edinburgh, who has spent most his life as a missionary doctor or public health consultant in his native Scotland. (See chapter 11, "The Thorn in the Flesh: Its Identity," 211–26.

21. Charles Wesley (1707–1788), "O for a Thousand Tongues to Sing," public domain.

22. See www.royaltyfreemusic.com/public-domain-music-voh.html.

23. In an article entitled, "Faith for Healing is based on Knowledge," healing evangelist Andrew Wommach, writes, "Here's another indispensable basic truth you must know and understand about healing: *It's never God's will for us to be sick; He wants every person healed every time.* That's nearly-too-good-to-be-true news, but that's the Gospel. Most Christians don't know or believe that. They think the Lord makes them sick, or at the very least, He allows Satan to make them sick to either punish or correct them. That kind of thinking will get you killed; it's not what the Bible teaches," http://www.awmi.net/extra/article/healing knowledge, accessed December 28, 2010.

Chapter 8: Redemptive Healing—Transforming Pain into a Life Purpose

1. Corrie ten Boom, *A Prisoner and Yet,* as quoted by Pamela Rosewell Moore, *The Five Silent Years of Corrie ten Boom* (Grand Rapids: Zondervan), 131.

2. Moore, *The Five Silent Years of Corrie ten Boom*, 131.

3. Ibid., 138.

4. Ibid.

5. Ibid., 186.

6. Amy Carmichael, as quoted by Joni Eareckson Tada, *A Place of Healing*, 95.

7. Amy Carmichael, *If* (Grand Rapids: Zondervan, 1980), part 3, 3.

8. Charles Spurgeon, "A Prayer for Revival," No. 2426, 14; www.spurgeongems.org/vols40-42/chs2426.pdg, accessed September 2, 2012.

9. Joni has authored seventeen books. As of this writing her most recent struggle and victory over circumstances is told in her book *A Place of Healing*, which I quote several times in this chapter. It's excellent! I recommend it wholeheartedly.

10. Tada, *A Place of Healing*, 191.

11. Kathryn Kuhlman was a woman whose healing ministry attracted thousands of people in the 1960s and 1970s. *Her book God Can Do It Again* contains testimonies of miraculous healings and conclusive supporting documentation; however, others walked away from the healing crusades disappointed because their afflictions remained the same. In 1975 she was diagnosed with a

heart condition. As the result she had open heart surgery but never recovered from it.

12. Tada, *A Place of Healing*, 193.

13. Ibid., 57.

14. Warren Wiersbe, *Why Us? When Bad Things Happen to God's People*, 101.

15. John Piper, "Don't Waste Your Cancer," http://www.crosswalk.com/1383847.

16. Christopher Morley as quoted by Warren Wiersbe, ibid., 51.

17. Rich Buhler, February 11, 2011. Used by permission.

18. Ibid.

19. Paul Estabrooks, "Standing Strong through the Storm," a booklet produced by Open Doors, Canada. Used by permission.

20. Paul Brand, as quoted by Ardy Roberto, *The Heart of Healing* (Manila: OMF Literature, 2008), 64.

21. Alynne Mann Golding, personal e-mail to the author. Used by permission.

22. Vance Havner, "Things I've Learned in the Night," *Moody Monthly*, June 1974, 28.

23. William Lindner Jr, *Andrew Murray* (Minneapolis: Bethany House, 1996), 108.

Chapter 9: What to Do When You Need Healing

1. Henry Frost, *Miraculous Healing*, 111.

2. Dan Wooding, *Assist News Service*, April 27, 2011, www.assistnews.net/images2/banners/Breaking News.gif.

3. The Bible uses several different terms for the devil including "Lucifer" (from the Latin "light bearer), *Abbadon* (meaning destroying angel), *Apollyon* (meaning destroyer), Satan, and "the god of this world."

4. Gaiser, *Healing In the Bible*, 224.

5. Diane Komp, *A Window to Heaven* (Grand Rapids: Zondervan, 1992), 52.

6. F. Wilbur Gingrich, *Shorter Lexicon of the Greek New Testament* (Chicago: University of Chicago Press, 1965), 165.

7. See http://www.quotationspage.com/quote/27170.html.

Addendum: Encouragement for Pastors and Church Leaders

1. Richard Mayhue, *The Healing Promise* (Britain: Mentor in the Christian Focus Publications, Fearn, Ross-shire, 1997), 247.

2. Ibid., 248.

3. Jeremiah challenged Israel saying, "Go up to Gilead, and take balm, O virgin daughter of Egypt! In vain you have used many medicines; there is no healing for you" (Jer. 46:11).

4. Eric Gorski, "Health and Spirit," *Orange County Register*, Health and Fitness, January 26, 2000, 1, 4. Also see Philip Yancey's *Prayer: Does it make any difference?* (Grand Rapids: Zondervan, 2000), 255–56.

About the Author

Dr. Harold J. Sala is an internationally known radio personality, author, Bible teacher, lecturer, husband, and grandfather. His radio program, *Guidelines—A Five-Minute Commentary on Living*, is heard on more than 1,000 stations. The program has been the recipient of the Catholic Mass Media Award for Moral Excellence in Broadcasting. Dr. Sala holds a Ph.D. in English Bible from Bob Jones University with proficiencies in Hebrew and Greek. His further graduate studies have been at the University of Southern California, California Baptist Seminary, Fuller Theological Seminary, and Denver Seminary.

In 1963, Harold and Darlene Sala began the ministry of Guidelines. Since then mail and e-mail messages have come to them from 112 countries, more than half of all the countries in the world. For fifteen years, Guidelines produced a weekly television program featuring Sala as the speaker that was seen on more than two hundred stations in the United States, and a network of stations through out Asia.

Fifty-one books and hundreds of publications have been authored by Dr. Sala, focusing on marriage, parenting, singles, counseling, and daily devotionals. His book *Heroes—People Who Have Changed the World* received the prestigious Angel Award for moral excellence in the media in the United States. Dr. Sala has also been honored by CASA with the Heritage of Faithfulness Award. He serves on the board of the Far East Broadcasting Company and he is chairman of the board of Joy Partners, a ministry to China.

His warm, personal style of sharing wisdom and insight from God's Word has brought hope to many. Dr. Sala is a frequent guest lecturer and teacher at many churches, schools, and international conferences. His hobbies include playing golf, dabbling in photography, and reaching out to people—the driving focus of his life and ministry. Residing in California, Dr. Sala and his wife, Darlene, have three adult children and eight well-loved grandchildren.

Dr. Sala welcomes your response, thoughts, or testimonies as to how this book has helped you. E-mail will reach him at healing@guidelines.org, or you can contact him at the following address:

Dr. Harold Sala
Guidelines International
Box G
Laguna Hills, CA 92654
www.guidelines.org
Phone: 949-582-5001

P923
36
42-43

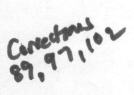

P 58-59
92

164

Corrections
89, 97, 102

172
180
189